T0305444

Civilizing Money

Also available:

Clipped Coins, Abused Words, and Civil Government:
John Locke's Philosophy of Money
George Caffentzis

"Caffentzis has been the philosopher of the anti-capitalist movement from the American civil rights movement of the 1960s. A historian of our own times, he carries the political wisdom of the twentieth century into the twenty-first. Here is capitalist critique and proletarian reasoning fit for our time."

—Peter Linebaugh, author of *The Magna Carta Manifesto*

Civilizing Money

Hume, his Monetary Project,
and the Scottish Enlightenment

George Caffentzis

Foreword by Peter Linebaugh

First published 2021 by Pluto Press
345 Archway Road, London N6 5AA

www.plutobooks.com

British Library Cataloguing in Publication Data
A catalogue record for this book is available from the British Library

ISBN   978 0 7453 4151 4   Hardback
ISBN   978 0 7453 4152 1   Paperback
ISBN   978 1 78680 680 2   PDF
ISBN   978 1 78680 681 9   EPUB
ISBN   978 1 78680 682 6   Kindle

Typeset by Stanford DTP Services, Northampton, England
Printed and bound by CPI Group (UK) Ltd, Croydon, CR0 4YY

Contents

Figures and Tables

TABLES

Acknowledgments

First, I must acknowledge my Midnight Notes collective friends and comrades who would not let me abandon the project of completing the trilogy on the Philosophy of Money when I was tempted to do so. Every time we got together, some one would ask, "How is the Hume book going?" Thanks for asking!

I thank the members of the Kress Seminar on the History of Economics, especially Paul Wendt, for their useful comments on an earlier version of the chapter on "Why Was Hume a Metallist?"

The project of completing *Civilizing Money* and the trilogy of books on the philosophy of money needed new energy, but my meeting with Arlen Austin changed all that. He brought passion, humor and technological capacity to the project that got me over the moat of authorial inertia. A thousand thanks, Arlen, for your generosity with your energy and knowledge!

Finally and inevitably, I thank Silvia Federici for her thoughtful advice throughout the Philosophy of Money project. She is a philosopher who is a walking and talking counter-example to Marx's Thesis 11 on Feuerbach.

The following essays have been previously published and are reproduced by permission:

Chapter 1 "On the Scottish Origins of 'Civilization'" was originally published in Silvia Federici (Ed.), *Enduring Western Civilization: The Construction of the Concept of Western Civilization and its "Others"* (Westport, CT: Praeger Publishers, 1995).

Chapter 2 "Civilizing the Highlands: Hume, Money and the Annexing Act" was originally published in *Historical Reflections* 37 (2005): 51–60.

An earlier version of Chapter 4 "Why Was Hume a Metallist?" was originally published as "Hume, Money, and Civilization; Or, Why Was Hume a Metallist?" *Hume Studies* 27(2) (2001): 301–335.

Chapter 5 "Did Hume Read Berkeley's *The Querist*?" was originally published in Timo Airaksinen and Bertil Belfrage (Eds.), *Berkeley's Lasting Legacy:*

300 Years Later (Newcastle Upon Tyne: Cambridge Scholars Publishing, 2011)

An earlier version of Chapter 6 "Fiction or Counterfeit? Specie or Paper?" was originally published as "Fiction or Counterfeit? David Hume's Interpretations of Paper and Metallic Money," in Carl Wennerlind and Margaret Schabus (Eds.), *David Hume's Political Economy* (London: Routledge, 2008).

Foreword

1.

Caffentzis writes that his project of the philosophy of money began in August 1971, when President Nixon severed the link between the dollar and gold. He further developed the project through SDS (Students for a Democratic Society) and URPE (Union of Radical Political Economics). It began to take form in his writing with *Zerowork* (when our paths crossed). Did the end of gold mean the end of work and did the end of work mean the end of capitalism? It achieved a major breakthrough with the Wages for Housework campaign. Owing to the crisis of the oil market and then the dangers of nuclear energy, he formulated an approach to the philosophy of money in which class analysis was combined with philosophical epistemology and the specifics of historical conjuncture. The first volume of what was to become a trilogy was completed in Calabar, Nigeria, at the time of structural adjustment under the IMF (International Monetary Fund).[1] Political presentism and autobiographical reflection enliven the philosophic pages. He has venerable examples of such combination from Clarendon's *The History of the Rebellion and Civil Wars in England* (1702–1704) to Gibbon's *The History of the Decline and Fall of the Roman Empire* (1776–1789).

The approach in all three studies—Locke, Berkeley and Hume—could not be more different than what we were taught in school. Traditional teaching had it that these three formed in the eighteenth century a coherence of empiricism, which could take its prideful place alongside Newton's *Principia* or Bacon's *Essays* of the seventeenth century. Known as British empiricism in contrast to the rationalist philosophers of the continent (Leibniz, Spinoza), it found its place in the Anglo-American curriculum, and became one of the means through which new members of the ruling class were introduced to their philosophical heritage. The method of study was to go from one philosopher to another without any difference in time between them, except the meanest chronology. The nationalism was implied rather than proclaimed. So, for instance, the fact that one was Irish, and another Scottish, and only Locke was English was not of significance to an understanding of their philosophical ideas. Instead, we were to infer from their dates (Locke 1632–1704, Berkeley 1685–1753, Hume 1711–1776) that there was a steady progression to ever greater and greater truth.

Caffentzis puts history back into chronology. The British empiricists— Locke, Berkeley and Hume—appeared at the consolidation of finance capitalism stretching from the foundation of the Bank of England and the recoinage of 1695–1696 to the American War of Independence and the consolidation of the settler-colonial project. Caffentzis understands these philosophers as human beings living at a time when particular monetary issues arose within specific historical setting. Yet, this is not cultural history which relates philosophical ideas to other cultural expressions such as music, art, architecture or literature. Nor is it quite economic history as one might find, for example, in Schumpeter, which discerns phases in the economic -isms (mercantilism, capitalism).

Caffentzis abruptly breaks with these expectations. Class struggle is first. Thus, Locke is seen in relationship to crimes of coining, clipping and counterfeiting. Berkeley is studied in relationship to the tarantella and monetary hysteria, in relationship to the experience of slavery from Rhode Island, and to the Irish controversies over Wood's halfpence and over agistments. Hume is studied in his relationship to a Bristol accounting house of sugar and slaving to his arguments about the Annexing Act following the defeat of the Scottish 'Forty-Five. These might appear to be singular episodes until they are brought up against the thinking of the philosophers.

2.

David Hume (1711–1776) was a Scottish philosopher, moralist and historian, occasional diplomat, and long-time librarian in Edinburgh. In the immediate aftermath of the Jacobite Rebellion of 1745, he was secretary to General James St. Clair. In 1763–1765, he served as secretary to the British embassy in Paris ("le bon David"). He was the central figure of the Scottish Enlightenment, whose students included Adam Ferguson and John Millar. He was a close friend to Adam Smith. His major works include two philosophical books, *A Treatise of Human Nature* (1738) and *An Enquiry Concerning Human Understanding* (1748); a collection of essays on moral and political subjects; and a six-volume *The History of England* (1754–1762).

Caffentzis provides a methodology which helps us see these diverse literary genres of thought—philosophy, morals and history—as a whole. His methodology is ampliative: he amplifies the philosopher's themes of semantics and language to the socio-historical fears and possibilities of their time.

Has philosophy ceased to love wisdom? Has it abandoned its namesake, the goddess Sophia? Has it sold itself to that craven, greedy demon, the wretched Mammon? Caffentzis leaves us with no doubt. He does not elevate philosophy to a perch above the fray. Locke, Berkeley and Hume were in service of capitalism, yes; Locke, Berkeley and Hume were in service to imperialism, yes. They were instructors to the ruling class, and often directly to their persons. Theirs was the philosophy of the Anglo-Atlantic capitalist class. Caffentzis reminds us that philosophy acted like Perseus' mirror. Perseus was able to slay Medusa whose gaze would turn you to stone by reflecting her in a mirror. The philosophers did not "reflect" those class interests as if on a superstructure high above the materialist base directing advanced tools of surveillance or composing elaborate models of futurity. (Of course, capitalism requires its visionaries and futurologists, its statisticians and gatherers of data.)

They were thinkers and apart from their epistemology and their experimental method, which gives them the name empiricist, they were thinking about the most mystified of capitalist ideas, money. It was the concentrated abstract of the commodity form with all its "metaphysical subtleties and theological niceties." Money is their god; it is money that they worship—coins, bullion, specie, notes. Thanks to Hume's philosophy, Caffentzis is able to show that the niceties and subtleties of the money form imbue self, causality and society.

Hume detested "enthusiasm," a term which at the time had not lost that meaning found today only in its etymology, possessed by *theos* or a god. There were two kinds of false religion according to Hume, namely, superstition and enthusiasm. Weakness and fear are the sources of superstition; the sources of enthusiasm are a "warm imagination" and pride. Enthusiasm led to "the menace of egalitarian republicanism." He wrote that in the English Civil War "the levellers insisted on an equal distribution of power and property, and disclaimed all dependence and subordination."[2] "Enthusiasm" as well as this "menace" was still felt more than a century later as the hymns of Charles Wesley rang in the vales of the Calder Valley among other places in the Methodist revival. The evangelical emotionalism of these preachers contrasted with the latitudinarianism of the Church of England which was the structurally sadistic partner to the hangman, which was dogmatically opposed to the commons ("the riches and Goods of Christians are not common, as touching the right, title, and possession of the same," Article 38 of its 39 Articles), and the Church of England was serviceable to the whips and chains of the global slavocracy. The Church of England was the exclusive and *established* religion of state.

Both the "secular outlook" with science and the "economy" with money become achievements of the Enlightenment, which will become essential to future statecraft. The construction of "economics" as well as of the "economy" have their beginnings here. This philosophy must be treated as ideology because that is a way that it can be contrasted with what Tacky thought in Jamaica, or the Whiteboys thought in Ireland, or what Neolin and Pontiac thought amid the Great Lakes. These were three powerful rebellions of the 1760s. A moment which considers the fetish of West Africa or notions of the soul, a moment which finds among the fairies of the Irish rath a philosophy with guerrilla powers, a moment which appreciates the abundance of Turtle Island as expressed in the gratitude of the Haudenosaunee. These alternative world-views allow us to see the ideological particularity of the "nation of shop-keepers" (Adam Smith).

3.

The Highlanders twice invaded England, once in 1715 and again in 1745. Their defeat at the Battle of Culloden in 1746 was the last pitched battle on British soil.[3] Thousands of near-naked, shouting Highlanders were slaughtered by disciplined ranks and files of English soldiery, by their relentless musket fusillade, and the blast and roar of cannon. The Duke of Cumberland, the King's brother, led the slaughter and was known ever after as the "Butcher Cumberland." Two modes of war, two cultures, two forms of rule, in short, two modes of production, faced off with hideous and grievous result. The way was paved for the clearances.

History ceased to be an unfolding of providence or divine will. Neither was it that cynical tale told by an idiot, nor was it Voltaire's pack of tricks the dead play on the living. The human story was in four acts or modes of production as Marx said or "modes of subsistence" as Hume's friend, the royal historiographer, William Robertson put it. Foraging, herding, farming and trading were the characteristic activities of the four stages of mankind in the inevitable progression from the rude to the refined: savage, barbarian, feudal and commercial. It was a magnificent formula both for capitalism and the history of property and for imperialism and the history of war. The violence done upon the rest of the world was tragic rather than cruel. In this perspective, history is the result of inevitable social determinations rather than the result of the deliberate volition of individuals. In this perspective, the violence done upon human activity (work) was necessary rather than mean or murderous. All this because, like it or not, so claims the theory, technological imperatives propelled human history through these inevitable stages. This was economic determinism or "vulgar" (i.e., bourgeois) determinism. This theory of history proved a great excuse for conquest abroad or exploitation at home.

Civilization required: a) rationalization of intra-capitalist relations; b) disenfranchisement of the English working-class notion of its "rights"; and c) the destruction of the communal relations of the Scottish Highlands. Civilization was not a timeless ideal but a specific historical process. The Highlanders of Scotland had refused English rule; the English monarchy was illegitimate (Hanoverian rather than Stuart). More was at stake than royal dynasty. All the king Georges (George I, George II, George III, George IV) represented a regime dedicated to real estate, world conquest, strict hierarchy and money. The Highlanders represented autonomy, common land and a personal economy of gift and tribute. The law of the commons had to be assimilated to civil law: hence, civilization.[4]

The path forward was not automatic. The transition from rude to refined requires roads, bridges, inns. It requires the plough; it requires the commodity. But how to excite a desire for gold if not through the instillation of widespread pleasure and vanity? The transition from the clan to the city requires money. It becomes "the language of strangers." Money must be diffused, laws of property instituted, and the arts and manners refined. Money is a means of social engineering as well as of estrangement.

As a money theorist, what was important to David Hume was convention; he was relatively indifferent whether money was fictional, fake or fallacious. Money made history possible, and hence a path out of the impoverished conditions of the Highlands by commercial development.

A theory of the wage becomes necessary. The wage links money and labor power. Labor power, or the capacity to labor, is an abstraction, a potentiality and immaterial. The covariance of self and money necessitated the autonomy of the ego. Bourgeois individualism and the modern self have their necessary connection to the money form. Here is Hume's "pathos of identity," his "mechanics of the soul," his "melancholy and delirium." The self, like money, is a fiction. Hume has a philosophy of the self ("human nature"); he has a philosophy of "natural religion"; he has a philosophy of causality; he has a philosophy of civilization. These are linked through the philosophy of money. Caffentzis considers them systematically, that is, historically, semantically, ontologically, practically and epistemologically. All this against a background of aggressive world conquest in which London replaced Amsterdam as the center of world finance. To service the formation of the home market, private banks increase in number and issue paper money.

Throughout the period, good coinage was scarce. In 1727, Defoe wrote *The Complete English Tradesman* in which he observed that in former days "fellows went about the streets crying 'Brass money, broken or whole.'" Counterfeiting copper was not criminalized until 1771 (11 George III c. 40). The problem of counterfeiting and "uttering" (putting base coin into circulation) is the subject of the first chapter in Patrick Colquhoun's *Treatise on Police of the Metropolis* (1795).

Locke argued that silver was best suited as the universal measure of value. The face value of silver was less than its international value as bullion. Hence, tons of it was exported. British silver currency deteriorated dramatically in Hume's lifetime. Silver lost 48 percent of its face value in 1777. Owing to the flight of silver, gold became the national standard. The gold guinea (21s. nominal value) and half guinea lost 4 percent over 100 years of normal wear. The shortage of gold coins was mitigated by an imported Portuguese coin known in England as the "moidore" (corruption from the Portuguese *moeda ouro* or "gold money") whose value fluctuated between 27s. and 29s.

Between 1760 and 1765, an Irishman, Charles Johnston, published *Chrysal; Or, the Adventures of a Guinea*. In it, money talks. This coin was composed of "the universal monarch GOLD." Chrysal (from the Greek word for gold) was "the general minister of the divine commands." It was the first person narrator of the novel. Its spirit was the spirit of self and consciousness. It began in Peru as an object of theft 200 fathoms underground, and then became the voice of adventure (and venture capital) revealing one vice after another world-wide.

4.

Hume wrote a six-volume history of England, which was immensely successful and made him rich. The first volume he published was about the reigns of the first Stuart monarchs, James I and Charles I. The sixth chapter of the first volume made "a pause; and departing a little from the historical style [about public men and public events], to take a survey of the state of the kingdom, with regard to government, manners, finances, arms, trade, learning." This was the defining "philosophic history" of the Enlightenment. This was the beginning of social history, the basis of Macaulay's famous third chapter in his *History of England*.[5] Hume continued, "Where a just notion is not formed of these particulars [government, manners, finances, arms, trade, learning], history can be very little instructive, and often will not be intelligible."

It gave him a mirror to see the manners of his own time: "industry and debauchery, frugality and profusion, civility and rusticity, fanaticism and skepticism."[6] Two things need to be said about these characteristic "manners" of the time. First, these were not manners as we understand the term but social forces whose causes likewise were social. Second, they were contradictory, and as such arose from the dynamics of class conflicts. Great riches confounded the ranks of men "and render money the chief foundation of distinction." He describes prices of corn, the growth of cities, the expansion of empire, the export of woolens, &c., topics now familiar to economic and social history. "The chief difference in expense between that age and the present consists in the imaginary wants of men, which have since extremely multiplied," or what we call "consumer society." He noted that the disappearance of small proprietors had begun to be replaced by the expansion of the gentry (a condition in which human nature at long last attained, he wrote, happiness!).

The phrase, "mode of production," may have two meanings. One meaning refers to the entire social formation, the whole country or society. This is what Hume described in his "philosophic history." The other, second, meaning refers to the characteristic business model, such as the workshop, the cottage, the factory, the mine, the foundry, the office, the quarry, the fishing ground, the plantation or the field. What Adam Smith accomplished with David Hume's help was to show how these two meanings were tied to each other and reflected changes that were taking place around him. Karl

Marx produced an extended, researched analysis of this second meaning of mode of production in his chapters on cooperation, manufactures and machinery (Chapters 13–15) in Volume I of *Capital*. This second meaning opens us up to the labor process and from thence to the working class. Class is no longer posed as Haves versus Have-Nots (distribution) but as the creators of what's worth having (production). That process of creation becomes exploitation under a specific organization of work and technological application. Marx adopted this stadial theory, or these four stages of history, by positing a fifth, communism, which was to supersede the commercial or capitalist mode of production.[7]

5.

Now back to money. If money was to be a lever in the transition from "barbarism" or the defeated clan society of the Highlands to the "commercial civilization" of England as the victory at Culloden required, how was it to work in the new "stage," capitalism, which required a proletariat or working class? If there was not yet a working-class philosophy of money, there was a practice. To understand that practice, we need first outline the change mode of production, which in Britain occurred first in textiles.

The gradual collapse of cottage industry and the accompanying immiseration of the putting-out system led to the condition of manufacture which itself was the antecedent to the factory. The woollen and worsted industries—the traditional source of English exports and wealth—were centered in the West Riding of Yorkshire. The handloom weavers were controlled by the merchants who put out to them credit for loom rental and supply of wool. "By the turn of the nineteenth century the transfer of woolen and worsted production from workers' homes to central shops enabled clothiers to impose direct supervision and discipline over the workplace." Productivity increased from perhaps two pieces a week to "six, eight, or ten." This included controlling the work process, and eliminating local, informal and low-priced markets for semi-finished goods. It also heightened the importance of cash.

The form of production mixed agriculture and handicraft. The process of enclosing domestic looms into the workshop was directly parallel to the enclosure of common fields. The handloom weavers were poor but proud people. By occupation, they were charcoal burners, draw boys, shuttlemakers, stuff makers, cow keepers, shalloon weavers. They lived at home, in hillside or terraced cottages, with big windows for the weaving room. They had many forms of commoning. A weaver's family might keep a cow; a son might burn charcoal in the woods; yet criminal law will deem them "loose and disorderly persons."

Families combined handloom weaving with agricultural pursuits. In particular kersey, a coarse cloth used for army uniforms and for the poor, was produced among these hills and dales. Their work depended on the export market, especially to north America. Many accepted the King's shilling and went to war, only to return to the valleys when peace and unemployment came, as happened in 1763. Peace brought slump. Slump brought illegalities.

Slingeing was the practice of taking yarn or waste. End-gatherers were persons who collected wefts, fents and thrums from the sorters, carders, kembers, spinsters and weavers. Thrums were an example of such waste. They were the nine-inch endings of the weaver's warp after the woven piece was cut from the loom. As far away as London, the newly created police blamed "rag and thrum shops" for supporting workers' takings.[8] Production was taken out of workers' homes "principally to prevent embezzlement," said a witness from Huddersfield to an 1803 Parliamentary committee investigating conditions in the woolen industry.[9] Becker says "labor's takings were transformed from a customary right into a public wrong." He reminds us that "Notions of property and ownership were re-conceptualized during this era, conforming to altered imperatives of capital." It was known as "a woman's offence," because women were at the center of the household of the domestic economy.

The criminalization was achieved by worsted clothiers, who initiated a system of inspection as part of the new economic morality, an industrial police. No clear distinction between waste or surplusage and finished piece.[10] Outworkers who embezzled materials were detected by an industrial police recruited and paid by large merchants. These police provided the backbone against the Yorkshire coiners. They operated by secrecy, bribery and provocation.[11]

6.

Once again we return to money. The Prime Minister, Lord North, opened Parliament in May 1774 saying "that nothing can better deserve the attention of Parliament than the state of the Gold Coin." Ten years earlier, what was called "the yellow trade" had begun in earnest. It combined clipping and coining. Guineas were clipped and moidores were coined. A half crown (or two and a half shillings) could be clipped from each guinea. All that was needed was a strong pair of shears, what every wool comber would have in any case (in London it was thought that "almost every wool-comber in the North kept a file for that purpose"). A hammer was needed to flatten the melted buttons, which were then inserted between a pair of dies to make an impression of the moidore. Clippings from twelve guineas were required to produce one moidore at a time when a weaver made 7s. a week. The 'philosopher's stone' of the alchemist was replaced by the craft knowledge of skilled engravers and metal workers.[12]

The debasement of the national coinage began in Yorkshire; the coining heartland lay between Halifax and Rochdale. At the other end of the country, in Norfolk, the byword for a "broken" coin was a "Yorkshire guinea." "Massive public support" for the clipping and coining of Yorkshire.[13] Juries acquitted against the evidence. The supervisor of the excise in Halifax, William Deighton, built an intricate web of bribery and betrayal to penetrate the nearly opaque weaving communities in the narrow valleys of Yorkshire's West Riding. In November 1769, he was murdered.

Marquess of Rockingham was prime minister in 1765–1766 when he distinguished himself by the suppression of food riots in Sheffield, and he became prime minister again in 1782. In between, he led a concerted attack on the "yellow trade" in 1769. Broken coin might be accepted in the local exchanges around Halifax but not in London, in national and international markets. By Christmas, thirty suspects had been arrested. One hundred fifty-six people were accused between 1765 and 1773.

In the coming year, three coiners would be executed in Yorkshire, including David Hartley, "well-known by the Name of *King David*, or *Chief of the Coiners*." He was known and admired for his skill even among those who disapproved of the end to which it was put. A people's remembrancer writes "that David Hartley was so nimble with his tools he could drill a hole edgeway through a sixpence." Making money to these people was not only a family affair, it also bespoke another concept of loyalty and sovereignty. King David's title signified another notion of monarchy obvious to all. A letter to *The Leeds Intelligencer*, August 29, 1769, explained that the title was "an honorary reward for saving his country from the formidable enemy—Poverty."

James Oldfield was also hanged in April 1770 for coining. He had founded an Independent church. The parish of Halifax was a stronghold of Methodist "enthusiasm." Linked by kinship, neighborhood, employment, and shared struggle they became a law unto themselves, and that—law—was how they came to my attention. David Hume's list of subjects of social history did not include law or crime. These were the subjects of the social history I practiced in a collective organized by E.P. Thompson.

I had accepted from Marx that the working-class was the historical agent of communism (the fifth "stage" of history) and I had accepted from Engels that crime was a characteristic form of resistance before the working-class "made itself" as a conscious historical agent.

But not before they had an important hand in "the making of the English working class," meaning an autonomous class of proletarians in England, no longer subsisting by means of the commons and crafts, but at the mercy of an array of powers church and state, capital and money. Indeed, E.P. Thompson emphasized them in his 1963 book of that title, *The Making of the English Working Class*. The years of that making were from 1792 to 1832. We came to know that the story began earlier in the brutalizing violence of the eighteenth century, when governance was by starvation (political economy) and hanging (law).

At the time, Thompson resided in midland comfort in Leamington Spa and still missing the accent and politics of Halifax where he had written *The Making of the English Working Class*. Among the first things he wanted to tell me was the following story, which would help our common research agenda about crime and class. Whether elders had told the story to him (members of the Communist Party had access to a rich but internal oral history) or he learned it from the researches of the curator of the Bankfield Museum, Halifax, H. Ling Roth, who published the documentary evidence in 1906, I cannot tell.[14]

Thomas Spencer, brother-in-law to King David and prime mover to the murder of Deighton, was hanged in 1783.[15] He led the rioters in Halifax in June 1783 in seizing large quantities of grain and forcing its sale at traditional prices. He was hanged for theft in August 1783.

[A] mass of people thronged the narrow road that led from Halifax to the village of Mytholmroyde. Old people stood at their doors with uplifted hands, and children looked eagerly with the impatience of youth at the approaching crowd, expecting their parents to be amongst them. But anxiety mingled with awe marked the features of all.

Mrs. Walton was an aged witness, eighty-one years old, by the time F.A. Leyland, the noted antiquary had a conversation with her in 1856. Ten years later, he will lecture on the coiners at the Halifax Literary and Philosophical Society. She remembered Isaac Hartley, brother to King David, "as a 'likely' tall and gaunt man, although he was old when she was a girl." Another ancient witness was Mr. Howarth who at the age of eighty spoke to Leyland (whose son passed his father's papers to H. Ling Roth). As a boy, Howarth had struggled through the crowd up the steep hill outside Halifax where the hangings of Spencer and Saltonstall took place. "Spencer, without a sign of emotion, looked from the elevation where he stood, over the distant hills and valleys he had known from his childhood, and where in his advanced years he had passed a life notorious for its iniquity." He made a short speech declaring his innocence as a dying man. There was much that Howarth did not say, because he still lived in the region and there were family reputations to protect. But he did say this about the body of the other victim of the gallows.

The people of Heptonstall, and the inhabitants of the farm steads that were scattered over the surrounding heights, seated on the slopes, and crowding the tortuous and narrow way which led to the church of St. Thomas the Martyr, waited in pitying sadness, the arrival of Saltonstall's body. With difficulty, the cart was drawn and pushed up the long and steep ascent to Heptonstall; and, as it neared the place, the crowd thronged the road, many following the corpse from the valleys, raising their hands with loud murmurings and lamentations that were carried afar by the winds which rarely cease in these northern heights.

Those winds continued to blow, and the story flew with them, so Thompson could convey how a community grieves.

Glimpses of human exchanges which are not monetary can be seen in incidental comments in the judicial record of the coiners. A woman will ask for the piece in the loom to pay the debt incurred earlier from the milk and butter she had supplied. She had a cow; he had a weaving. The cow had grass, the grass grew on common land (common of herbage). They bicker and talk in the cottage, standing on flagstones (commons in the quarry), sitting on chairs made from timber from the woods (common of estovers),

> in the frost-blue flames
> Of the handloom weaver's rushlight the heroic shadows leap

to quote E.P. Thompson writing in Halifax in 1950. He refers to commons of rushes.[16] The poem is called "A Place Called Choice"—against the Bomb, the grime, the poverty, the violence of post-war England with the sordid victory of "the man of business." It is a profound recollection of earlier times brought into the present of the poet's mind by the wind which blows "heroic," presenting England with a choice if only it will recognize its past. Already in 1950, Thompson expresses a choice, not the inevitability of the fifth "stage."

7.

As for that fifth stage, I returned to the USA in 1972 to join the struggle for it not knowing whether it was true communism or actual commoning. That is when my path and that of George Caffentzis crossed. We were in dire need of his "enthusiasm" and philosophy and at last, here it is!

Writing forty years after Caffentzis conceived his project in 1971, David Graeber concluded his study of the first 5,000 years of debt with the year 1971, "The Beginning of Something Yet to Be Determined."[17] Neither Graeber's epic nor Caffentzis' philosophical critique reveals that "something." A clue however is suggested by the fact that following Nixon's uncoupling of gold and dollar in August 1971 the prisoners of the maximum security prison in Attica, New York, went on strike and were slaughtered in the blood bath ordered by Rockefeller. He too is remembered as "the Butcher." The coincidence (butcher Cumberland = butcher Rockefeller) is not causal; however, it is suggestive of things to come within a regime which treats people as meat.

Caffentzis concludes with a note of radical doubt. None of his philosophers opposed slavery, none opposed the unpaid labor of women. What will a philosophy of struggle look like? Are there any tools from the master's house we may use to demolish it? It seems unlikely. He concludes with a coda on Marx's eleventh thesis on Feuerbach, "the philosophers have only interpreted the world in various ways, the point is to change it." Caffentzis found the contrary to be true, namely, that in point of fact the philosophers actually did try to change the world in various ways, their theories of money being one of them. They guided the capitalist class, the bourgeoisie, to whom their philosophies were directed and to whom their philosophy belongs. We might alter the eleventh thesis: social historians have only *described* various actions from below when the point is *to avenge* them as the means *to nourish* seeds of change?

Peter Linebaugh
Ann Arbor, Michigan
August 2020

An Autobiographical Preface

One's point of origin for a life-long project must always be arbitrary and fictional, since a project's origin is never identical with its conscious inauguration while the determination of its true temporal location is beset by a Zeno-like process forever denying uniqueness and completeness. Therefore, when I claim that this book (and the trilogy on the Philosophy of Money it completes) really began on August 15, 1971, please receive this claim with some sympathetic skepticism, attributing it at best as a by-product of my own autobiographical myth-making intended for better self-understanding (or vice versa).

That date, August 15, 1971, is not a personal one, of course, for it picks out the moment President Nixon announced to the world that he had just "closed the gold window," unilaterally revoking the rules of the Bretton Woods system and ending, as it seems to have turned out, the crucial role of gold in the world of money. This announcement affected me more theoretically than practically, since I was then a poor graduate student studying the philosophy of physics at Princeton University, living off grants and the financial assistance of my wife. But I was also involved in a book project dealing with money. For I had joined two other Princeton University graduate students (one in philosophy, Julius Sensat, and the other in political science, Marc Linder) in writing a critique of bourgeois economics (later called *Anti-Samuelson*). This "grand" project in turn had its own "origin" (with the appropriate caveats) in the nationwide student strike of 1970, provoked by the US military's invasion of Cambodia and government's killing of protesting students at Kent State and Jackson State Universities.

During that strike and in the semester preceding it, activist students demanded "counter-courses" and "counter-texts" in a number of fields, especially in economics. Some veterans from the anti-war movement (Julius, Marc and myself included) decided that the time had come to put together a "counter-course" and a "counter-text" to the standard introduction to economics course taught at Princeton (and countless other colleges and universities) that then invariably used Paul Samuelson's *Economics* as its textbook. This political project had been on the agenda of Students for a Democratic Society (SDS) for a while, but it had not yet been put into action by graduate students influenced by SDS who had recently organized the Union of Radical Political Economists (URPE). These budding professional economists decided to write new introductory textbooks on radical economics, instead of critiques of economics. But we philosophical amateurs of economics at Princeton continued working on the idea of producing a total critique.

We worked in the summer of 1970 to come up with a preliminary draft of a counter-course assuming that the undergrads coming back from the previous spring's battles would be ready to take on the double work of studying Samuelson's textbook and creating a critique of it. Here our optimism (or our rage against the system that was killing millions of Vietnamese and thousands of US youth) got the better of us. The enthusiasm for counter-courses among Princeton's undergraduates had diminished by the fall of 1970, but our passion to critique and blaspheme the bourgeois fetishism called "economics" was still strong. Moreover, we had the sense that the world was going through a revolutionary transformation shaking capitalism to its roots. So we continued on the project even though the immediate pedagogical purpose was becoming moot. We "knew" that its time would come again soon.

The project required a careful study of Marx's critique of political economy and so in the following summer (1971) it so happened that we were studying Volume III of *Capital* page by page, including the famous discussion of the monetary and credit system, in preparation for writing a critique of Samuelson's views on money. This reading also prepared us to appreciate the gravity of Nixon's decision. Marx (like Georg Simmel and many other nineteenth- and early twentieth-century commentators on money) was convinced that capitalism could not eliminate the role of gold in its monetary system, even though it posed a continual threat to its self-expansion. In the hot, humid summer of 1971 we pondered passages from *Capital III* like the following:

…with the development of the credit system, capitalist production continuously strives to overcome the metal barrier, which is simultaneously a material and imaginative barrier of wealth and its movement, but again and again it breaks its back on this barrier.

(Marx *Capital III*: 574)

But it should always be borne in mind that, in the first place, money—in the form of precious metal—remains the foundation which the credit system, by its very nature, can never detach itself. Second, that the credit system presupposes the monopoly of social means of production by private persons (in the form of capital and landed property), that it is itself, on the one hand, an immanent form of the capitalist model of production, and on the other hand, a driving force in its development to its highest and ultimate form.

(Marx *Capital III*: 606)

It is well known that Engels stitched together Marx's hastily written notebooks and incidental scraps to create the text of *Capital III*, with the result that many pages are both ponderous and obscure. However, these passages on the role of gold, as well as many others in the rest of *Capital*, are not obscure at all. They clearly show Marx's unequivocal yet ambivalent inscription of gold and other precious metals into the heart of capitalism. In them, he recognizes both "hard" money's attraction (i.e., in times of crisis, gold becomes the only certainty) and repulsion (i.e., in moments of expansion, the credit system desires only to negate and transcend the stifling gold barrier). Marx aptly captures both capitalism's recognition of (and humiliation before) its own "golden chains."

But in the light of *Capital III*, Nixon's August 15, 1971 decision casts him as capitalism's liberator. For he did not present the closing of the gold window as a temporary expedient (like the numerous suspensions of gold backing of currency during war and economic depression since the American and French Revolutions). Nixon declared the equivalent of a permanent "state of exception" for the world economic system, given the continuous central presence of specie in monetary systems since the time of King Croseus.

When Marc, Julius and I met on Monday morning, August 16, 1971 our question was: could capitalism be liberated from gold? There was no doubt in our minds that Nixon's action bespoke an epochal crisis of capitalism, perhaps deeper than the one posed by the Great Depression of the 1930s. We knew we were definitely living through interesting times. Were these capitalism's end times as well? We had reason to think so, since we were convinced that Nixon's striving "to overcome the metal barrier" was doomed to failure, *if Marx was right.* Or, to put it in the theological terms that Marx ironically used to describe the relation between the monetary and credit systems: could "Protestantism" (the credit system built on "faith") emancipate itself from "Catholicism" (the monetary system based on "works")? Marx's answer was a definitive "no."

We, at the time, were committed to this answer as well. It seemed that we merely had to wait for the system to unravel with the first economic or political shock, confident that the ensuing crisis would either force the system back to gold (with all the contractions that it would cause) or it would lead to an out-of-control worldwide inflation (with all the political turmoil that would follow). Either way, the ensuing crisis would show capitalism's inability to provide a plausible future for humanity or even a basis for the USA's national economy.

By the summer of 1973, our little Anti-Samuelson collective amicably broke up after working on the book for three years. Marc went to Germany, Julius went to Texas and I went to Brooklyn. Marc then translated the material from our work into German and published the book in four volumes in Germany (under his name as main author with Julius and I as collaborators) in 1974. By that time, however, I had grave doubts as to our interpretation of Marx, capitalism and the class struggle. For in the fall of 1973 I was simultaneously introduced to wages for housework perspective (the work of Selma James, Mariarosa Dalla Costa and Silvia Federici) and the theoretical work at the foundation of the Italian extra-parliamentary Left (Mario Tronti, Sergio Bologna, Antonio Negri, Oreste Scalzone, etc.). Reading these texts and meeting some of their principal authors constituted a theoretical revolution for me. It took me years to digest the impact of this "one-two punch" of politics and theory, but one thing was immediately clear to me: my work on *Anti-Samuelson* was not adequate either theoretically or politically to the insights these new perspectives afforded. *Anti-Samuelson* was much too much a reflection of "average" Marxism of the day, and was not an adequate response to the new quality of the class struggles of the 1960s and early 1970s and their impact on capitalism.

It was at this time I helped form a new collective with the provocative, but ambiguous, title, *Zerowork*, to get the news of this new work emanating from Europe known to the anti-capitalist US Left. However, the conviction that capital was facing an irresolvable monetary crisis—the basic assumption of the first work I did on money in *Anti-Samuelson*—continued into the second phase of my thinking in *Zerowork*. The events of the following decade seemed to both verify this assumption and to put into question Marx's assumption of the logical dependence of the credit on the monetary system. In retrospect, I see that the question of the ability of capitalism to free itself from the "fetters" of gold (and implicitly, of labor) was basic to my political thinking throughout this period and it influenced my eventual work on the philosophy of money.

Certainly a dispute about the nature of money was at the bottom of the split I helped initiate in the Zerowork Collective that followed in 1977. Christian Marrazi had sent an article for the second issue of *Zerowork* where he argued that Nixon's ability to detach the dollar from gold was a sign that the value of money was no longer determined by work and that capitalism had actually achieved the state that Marx envisioned in the "Fragment on Machines" in the *Grundrisse*, namely, production would increasingly be laborless. Marrazi argued that, not accidentally, capital was reaching a point of "zerowork" at the very moment when the industrial working class in the USA and Europe was transforming "refusal of work" from a slogan to a demand. I took exception to Marrazi's argument, since I was increasingly convinced that though capital might be able to transcend gold, it cannot do so without the exploitation of labor. Marrazi's (and as I was later to see, Antonio Negri's) eliding of the "end of gold" with the "end of work" was a fatal error at the very moment when the feminist and anti-colonial movements were showing us the vast amount of work done by wageless workers in the "home" and in the fields and shantytowns of the Third World that capital was exploiting. In effect, Marrazi's argument denied the coherence of the theoretical revolution that I thought the Zerowork Collective was trying to disseminate.

THE PHILOSOPHY OF MONEY PROJECT: 1979–1983

The theoretical and practical contradictions that Marrazi's article opened up within the Zerowork Collective led to its breakdown in 1977. This split led to a political question for me: How could I use my developing knowledge of economics into an effective critique of bourgeois economics that was both academic and rigorously anti-capitalist? After many fits and starts, I finally consciously formulated a "philosophy of money" project in the fall of 1979. I was then a visiting assistant professor of Millersville State College (now known as Millersville University) near Harrisburg, Pennsylvania and only about ten miles from the Three Mile Island nuclear power plant that had nearly suffered a meltdown in the spring of that year. The Philosophy Department asked me to teach a new elective course in the Spring Semester of 1980 and I decided that the best way to bring together my work on economics, politics and philosophy was to give Simmel's 1900 effort to create a field called "the philosophy of money" a new (and somewhat different) impetus. I also knew that the topic of money would be especially interesting to the students, since it had been in the news so prominently, often topping the other two sources of news in that period: the crisis of the world oil market and the danger of nuclear power plants. After all, 1979 was the year that the US inflation rate hit its historic peak of 12 percent and, as I was putting the finishing touches on the course syllabus, the price of gold rose from $534 an ounce on January 1, 1980 to its historic high of $850 an ounce on January 21, 1980. The whole country was abuzz with monetary questions at the time.

My original Philosophy of Money course covered topics like primitive money and the crisis of the Bretton Woods System, we read and discussed texts by Freud and Marx, by anthropologists (like Levi-Strauss and Michel Mauss), by economists (like Smith, Ricardo, Jevons and Keynes), and by philosophers (like Plato, Aristotle, St. Thomas Aquinas, Locke, Berkeley, Hume, Simmel). Although the readings were difficult, the students seemed to be excited by the course. Most important, they were surprised to realize that philosophy could contribute to the understanding of complex and contemporary socio-economic issues. I resolved to teach this course on a regular basis, if and when I landed a regular teaching position. That turned out to take a longer time than I expected. It was only after teaching at Bentley College in Massachusetts between 1980 and 1983 and in the University of Calabar (Nigeria) between 1983 and 1987 that I returned to the USA as a tenure-track assistant professor at the University of Southern Maine (USM), where I have been ever since and where I have taught the Philosophy of Money course at USM a number of times.

In the meantime, I was beginning to sketch out the trilogy of books on the philosophy of money in the early 1980s. They were to focus on three philosophers of the "long eighteenth century" who were often grouped together under a variety of rubrics including "the British Empiricists": John Locke,

George Berkeley and David Hume. I chose them and this period for many different reasons, of course. First, I knew even by this level of my research that they had written important texts about money deeply connected with their philosophical "systems." More crucially, they were confronting for the first time in history the question the whole world was fully facing on August 15, 1971—was a monetary system not dependent upon the "backing" of specie possible?

I began to write the first part of the philosophy of money trilogy on Locke in Nigeria in 1983. I finished that book in 1985 and began to work on the Berkeley book immediately afterwards.

The method and problematic of my work in these books was quite different from Georg Simmel's in his *Philosophy of Money* (1900), the philosopher/sociologist who first articulated the possibility of a "philosophy of money." I saw myself as continuing his work almost a century later, but my methodological approach to the philosophy of money was very different from his. Simmel was a neo-Kantian (among other things) and so his approach to money in his book was inspired by the structure of Kant's *Critique of Pure Reason*. Kant begins his critique by locating the transcendental conditions of experience (what are the conditions for applying the concepts of space, time, causality and the self) and he ends his critique by exposing the paradoxes and antinomies arising from any attempt to apply these categories as actual totalities. Simmel follows Kant by first articulating the transcendental conditions required for the functioning of a monetary society and he ends by specifying the paradoxes and antinomies arising from the total monetarization of society on human life. In between, Simmel provides many different sociological, psychological and philosophical sketches of great acuity, often presented with a deep, dry and dark humor. Furthermore, although the *Philosophy of Money* was a book of great erudition, Simmel had very few direct references to the philosophical and economic literature on money.

I, of course, was not a Kantian (nor even a Simmelian) and consequently I rejected the viability of a project that would provide a transcendental deduction of the categories (even if, as in Simmel's case, this deduction was historicized). My method instead starts with particular texts published by Locke, Berkeley and Hume concerning money and shows how they were "caused" by the confluence and confrontation of the philosophers' class problematic concerning money, their philosophical systems (especially their work on language, semantics and semiotics), and the monetary strategies they proposed to resolve the monetary problematic posed at their historical conjuncture.

This method required the study of the very particular situation of Locke in the England of the 1690s, of Berkeley in the Ireland of the 1730s, and of Hume in the Scotland of the 1750s, instead of assuming Simmel's almost God-like extra-historical gaze on the history of money. It also rejected the view that philosophy is a procession of apologetic ideologies provided by intellectuals for the occasional use of ruling classes taking (and losing) their perches on the top of history's transient heaps of events. Philosophers like Locke, Berkeley and Hume had to solve real (and dangerous) contemporary social problems leading to crises, and their philosophies were important tools in their attempts to resolve these crises. Thus philosophy in the case of Locke, Berkeley and Hume, at least, had to confront social reality, help transform it, and, in the process, be transformed by it. In other words, my method assumes that Marx's critique of philosophy in his *Theses on Feuerbach*—"Philosophers have merely interpreted the world, the point is to change it"—does not apply to the "British Empiricists," for they were actively involved in using their philosophical systems to "change the world."

This method led to many paths I had not trodden down before. After all, my graduate training was in the philosophy of physics. I was hardly a student of tithing in eighteen-century Ireland before embarking on this project, nor was I familiar with the forms of communal agriculture and pasturage to be found in the Scottish Highlands in the seventeenth century. These, and dozens of other topics needed to be researched in order to adequately deal with the form of explanation I was embarked upon.

Inevitably, in the course of the project, a phenomenon that Simmel described so poignantly in his *Philosophy of Money*, appeared: the triumph of means over ends. I "originally" embarked on this trilogy to throw light on an important contemporary compound political question: Was capitalism without specie possible and, if it was, what does this mean for the possibility of transcending capitalism? I thought that a study of the initial phase of bourgeois thought on this question—posed by the formation of the Bank of England, by the Law System in France and the growth of "free banking" in Scotland during the "long eighteenth century—would be a means to the end of answering the question posed. But I must admit that in the course of the last quarter century, the problem of applying the method I outlined above to explaining the texts before me at times displaced my attention and became an end-in-itself. I still believe, however, that the project as initially envisioned can produce knowledge that is useful to us in answering the question posed by the possibility of a specie-less capitalism.

Introduction
Who is a Philosopher of Money?

WHO IS A PHILOSOPHER OF MONEY?

For the last thirty years, I have been writing a trilogy on Locke's, Berkeley's, and Hume's philosophies of money. With the publication of *Clipped Coins, Abused Words and Civil Government: John Locke's Philosophy of Money* and *Exciting the Industry of Mankind: George Berkeley's Philosophy of Money* and with the end of the volume on Hume before you, the trilogy is now almost completed.[1] But as I near the end of the project, I realize that I have not been as precise as possible in defining who a philosopher of money actually is, especially given the fact that there are a number of different plausible definitions in the field. Nor have I made it clear in what particular sense Locke, Berkeley and Hume qualify as philosophers of money while, I would say, Bertrand Russell does not. In Berkeley's case, for example, my lack of clarity is especially egregious, since I wrote a 450-page book on *The Querist*, a supposedly "marginal" text of eighty pages consisting all and only of 1,000 questions.

Why was my philosophy of money trilogy written as it was? I will address this question (and provide an apology for myself and a synopsis for the reader) in the Introduction by first answering the general question, Who is a philosopher of money?, and then, in conclusion, I will go on to show that Locke, Berkeley and Hume fit the definition.

TWO MODELS OF WHAT IT IS TO BE A PHILOSOPHER OF MONEY: (A) BEING A PHILOSOPHER *AND* BEING A MONETARY COMMENTATOR; (B) SIMMEL'S NEO-KANTIAN PERSPECTIVE ON BEING A PHILOSOPHER OF MONEY.

One easy way to define who is to be a philosopher of money is as a *conjunction* of being a philosopher *and* being a monetary commentator. A surprising number of philosophers have commented on money, often profoundly and perceptively, from Heraclitus to Heidegger. In fact, it would not be difficult to edit a substantial anthology of philosophers' writings on money from the pre-Socratics to the postmoderns.

Such an anthology would be useful to both philosophy and economics. Such an anthology would undoubtedly give pride of place to the monetary writings of Locke, Berkeley and Hume. For these philosophers devoted substantial pamphlets, essays and books to money. Their contributions are not just passing metaphorical use of monetary phenomena as, for example, Kant's use of the example of the "actual" *taler* in the pocket versus the concept of the *taler* to make the point that existence is *not* a predicate or in his evocation of commercial life to make the same point:

> the attempt to establish the existence of a supreme being by means of the famous ontological argument of Descartes is merely so much labor and effort lost; we can no more extend our stock of [theoretical] insight by mere ideas than a merchant can better his position by adding a few noughts to his cash account.
>
> (quoted in Shell 1982: 139)

Although contemporary philosophers are rarely mentioned in the standard histories of economics (e.g., Derrida's work on money and the gift has received little notice in economics journals), important contributions to monetary knowledge (laws, observations, concepts) are often attributed to philosophers of the past like Locke, Berkeley and Hume in these texts (Derrida 1994).[2] At times, connections are even drawn between their philosophy and their monetary theory. This tradition goes back to the nineteenth century and Marx's writings on the history of political economy, from his *Contributions to a Critique of Political Economy* to *Theories of Surplus Value* (Marx 1963b). In those texts, Marx occasionally referred to Locke's, Berkeley's, and Hume's contributions to the theory of money along side their philosophical efforts. For example, he wrote: "Very fittingly, it was Bishop Berkeley, the advocate of mystical idealism in English philosophy, who gave the doctrine of the nominal standard of money a theoretical twist" (Marx 1970: 78). This type of crocheting with philosophy—where the conjunc*tion* between philosophy and monetary theory is taken as a temporary conjunc*ture*—continues to be found in the literature on the history of economics and money in the twentieth century. For example, Joseph Johnston in his essay,

"Locke, Berkeley and Hume as Monetary Theorists," characterizes Locke's attitude toward gold and silver in the following words: "[Locke] regarded the value of money as inseparably associated with the precious metals—a primary quality of theirs, so to speak" (Johnston 1970: 84).

This "so to speak" approach can be found in many other works in the history of economics but it does not reveal any commitment to unearthing conceptual structures common to a philosopher's metaphysics or epistemology and his/her theory of money. However, this conjunction model has been recently taken to the limit by a postmodernist effort to read philosophy as symbolic production and to argue that all philosophy written in a monetary society is a sort of philosophy of money. This rather expansive approach to the philosophy of money is attractive, since it makes it possible to create a rich intertextual field of literary, philosophical and economics writing as an object of study. Marc Shell, one of the founders of this field, writes of his approach:

> This participation of economic form in literature and philosophy, even in the discourse about truth, is defined neither by what literature or philosophy talk about (sometimes money, sometimes not) nor by why they talk about it (sometimes for money, sometimes not) but rather by the tropic interaction between economic and linguistic symbolization and production. A formal money of the mind informs all discourse and is as unaffected by whether or not the thematic content of a particular work includes money as by whether or not the material content of the ink in which the work may be inscribed includes gold.
>
> (Shell 1982: 4)

Thus, the "tropic interaction" between economics and philosophy that was unleashed by the development of monetary economies in the early modern era affects philosophical writings on *any* subject. The interpreter is then free to create interesting monetary readings of apparently non-monetary texts since, as Shell reveals, "my argument is not that money is talked about in particular works of literature and philosophy (which is certainly the case), but that money talks in *and* through discourse in general" (Shell 1982: 180).

In that sense, every philosopher in a monetary society is a philosopher of money whether s/he designs to be or not. The occasional conjunction of philosophy and money is, in this approach, taken as a superficial sign of a deeper universal conjuncture.

The second model for a philosopher of money arises from the urtext of the field, Georg Simmel's *The Philosophy of Money*. This book, published in 1900, not only gave a name to a discipline, but it provided the discipline with a methodological structure rooted in the Kantian tradition (justifying Simmel's place in the canon of Neo-Kantian philosophers).

Simmel follows the structure of the *Critique of Pure Reason* (1781) as literally as possible in his *Philosophy of Money*. Kant organized his *Critique of Pure Reason* in two major divisions (reserving the Transcendental Aesthetic as an antecedent to the first division): the transcendental analytic and the transcendental dialectic. The transcendental analytic was directed to determining the necessary preconditions for the creation of objective experience. Hence, Kant's analysis of substance, causality and simultaneity discovers something like "a new storey beneath" empiricism (to use a Simmelian metaphor out of context).

The transcendental dialectic is based on the critique of the major ideas that have populated philosophy from its beginning: soul, cosmos and god. In this division, Kant attempts to demonstrate via paralogisms, antinomies and impossibility proofs that any attempt to treat these ideas as objects with fixed properties is doomed to failure. They are "transcendental illusions" even though they are the natural result of the operation of reason. Kant, therefore, sees the proper role of philosophy as dealing with the lower and upper bounds of objective experience and not the details of this experience itself.

Simmel begins *The Philosophy of Money* on the vertical dimension with a nod to Kant: "Every area of research has two boundaries marking the point at which the process of reflections ceases to be exact and takes on a philosophical character" (Simmel 1978: 53). He rephrases this point on the horizontal dimension a bit later on in his exposition: "If there is to be a philosophy of money, then it can only lie on either side of the economic science of money" (Simmel 1978: 54). In fact, he disclaims any confrontation with the discipline of economics (which was just beginning to find its own autonomy in his era) that lies between the philosophical areas: "Not a single line of these investigations is meant to be a statement about economics" (Simmel 1978: 54).

Just as Kant did in his *Critique*, Simmel divides his work into two parts: an "Analytical Part" and a "Synthetic Part." The former "present[s] the pre-conditions that … give money its meaning and practical position" (Simmel 1978: 54). It definitely evokes Kant's Transcendental Analytic and the deduction of the pre-conditions of objective experience, for Simmel is not interested in the origin and realization of money in history, but in the "mental states, in social relations and in the logical structure of reality and values" that constitute money's preconditions (i.e., what makes money possible). The Synthetic Part takes the place of Kant's Transcendental Dialectic in that it too deals with totalities like "life in general," "the inner life," "culture in general," and "the ultimate values and things of importance in all that is human." It attempts to make them intelligible from the "effectiveness of money" (Simmel 1978: 54).

So, for example, "the fact that two people exchange their products" is not only an economic fact; it is also "the object of philosophical study, which examines its pre-conditions in non-economic concepts and facts [the Analytical Part] and its consequences for non-economic values and relationships [the Synthetic Part]" (Simmel 1978: 55). Simmel practiced this Neo-Kantian methodology by first analyzing the necessary conditions for the categories of value, substance and the sequence of purposes to appear and create a monetary universe. He then proceeds to deal with the contradictions and dilemmas created by money for totalities like the self and the style of life.

A CRITIQUE OF THESE MODELS: THE FIRST IS TOO BROAD, AND THE SECOND TOO NARROW AND THE PROPOSAL OF A THIRD

Although very attractive, I found these two models for defining what it is to be a philosopher of money to be problematic. The first is too broad in scope and invites one to interpret every reference (and, as will be shown below, non-reference) to monetary phenomena in a philosopher's work as a contribution to the philosophy of money. But that is no more defensible than taking a philosopher's reference to the cat on the mat as a contribution to the philosophy of biology. Indeed, given the ubiquity of monetary references, almost every philosopher in history would become a philosopher of money according to this definition.

The postmodern "tropic interaction" approach of Shell and others that extremizes the "conjunction" approach cannot be dismissed so easily; it requires a methodology that is determined by the text's literary quality (its tropic force and extension) and not by its philosophical character. In a monetary society, as I read Shell, just as every poet is a poet of money and every dramatist is a dramatist of money, so too is every philosopher a philosopher of money.

This might very well be true, that is, the figurative power of money is so deeply embedded in the collective imaginary of monetary societies that every other symbolic production is either directly or, more likely, indirectly affected by it, philosophical writing included. However, this approach does not provide a distinctive role for philosophical thought and writing. One is a philosopher of money simply because one is a philosopher … it all happens behind everyone's back. But, conversely, in such a night there is no reason to discern any particular philosopher *as* a philosopher of money either. In the very moment that this approach defines the philosophy of money, the field disappears in a fog of metaphor, allusion and, at best, brilliant association.

The second model—based on Simmel's *The Philosophy of Money*—has the opposite problem, that of over-specificity. Not only do we have in Simmel's model a specific Neo-Kantian conception of philosophical analysis—a study of money's preconditions and the dilemmas it poses for associated totalities—but there is also a strict separation between economic facts and philosophical investigations.

This strict separation is problematic both philosophically and historically. As Quine, Sellars and Kuhn (among many others) taught us in the last philosophical generation, there is no defensible dichotomy between the analytic and synthetic, between science and philosophy, between fact and meta-fact that Simmel's Neo-Kantianism presupposes. In particular, the science of economics cannot be hermetically kept at a distance from "philosophical contamination" for two reasons: (a) this dichotomy is anachronistic; and (b) it does not recognize the fact, even down to our time, that money itself is not a fixed concept defining a definitive object of study, that is, there are continual revolutions in the theory and practice of money.

The assumption's anachronism can be caught in noting that the very name of the field that we now call "economics" did not exist in its contemporary meaning until the later part of the nineteenth century. "Political Economy" was the disciplinary name that existed immediately before "economics" to refer to the study of (roughly) exchange, production and money while, since Xenophon's time, "oikonomia" largely meant the study of the management of the home-based enterprises. But neither "political economy" nor "oikonomia" are synonymous with "economics." Therefore, any attempt to separate philosophy from "economic" facts and theories would be inoperative for philosophers working before the 1870s and would make a Simmelian definition of a philosopher of money inoperative.

An even more important historical point of criticism is that money itself has undergone many transformations and revolutions both in its theory and practice that have incorporated philosophical concepts and methods. Philosophy has played a role in monetary revolutions as it has in the scientific revolutions of physics and other natural sciences. That is inevitable, since philosophy has specialized in the production of concepts like value, fairness and equality that the creators of a monetary institution must possess and apply both reflexively and mutually. Dichotomizing philosophy and money (as Simmel's methodology requires) makes these monetary revolutions unintelligible. It puts one in a position similar to a historian of science trying to understand the origin of Einstein's relativity theory without a study of the philosophical debates concerning space and time current in the late nineteenth century. In other words, though money might, as Shell claims, "talk in and through discourse in general," philosophy has at times "talked in and through" money itself and one cannot understand money without attending to this philosophical talk.

This last criticism of a Simmelian definition of what it is to be a philosopher of money provides a good segue to the definition I have been using in my work. I argue that philosophers of money are those philosophers who actually try to "change the (monetary) world." Neither are they just "influenced" (or spoken through) by money nor do they simply "reflect" on the monetary world at an infinite distance. They are neither unconscious and passive ideologists nor totally conscious and detached observers of the monetary universe.

Philosophers of money (including the monetary nihilists like Diogenes) are committed to a monetary program of action. Their philosophy constitutes and subsumes a monetary act. Consequently, one can only understand their philosophy by contextualizing it and explaining it the way every other historical act is explained. That is why establishing whether a philosopher is a philosopher of money requires historical evidence and a historical explanatory structure (a context, a set of collective interests and association, an oppositional force, etc.)

THIS APPROACH LEADS ONE TO SEE THE PHILOSOPHY
OF MONEY AS A STRATEGIC SCIENCE THAT CONSTRUCTS
CATEGORIES TO DEAL WITH MONETARY CRISES AND
REVOLUTIONS. THE PHILOSOPHER'S SYSTEM OF CONCEPTS
IS APPLIED TO THE CONSTRUCTION OF THE THEORY OF
MONEY AND MONETARY REALITY HAS AN IMPACT ON THEIR
PHILOSOPHY

A corollary of this definition is that a philosopher of money's philosophy (ontology, epistemology, metaphysics and ethics) must have a strategic character and be deployed in the promotion of a monetary program. Indeed, if there were no evidence of such a deployment, there would be no reason to identify a philosopher as a philosopher of money. It is exactly in the use of philosophical concepts in the development and justification of monetary forms that the work of the philosopher of money is done. It is here that the analytic work of the student (and practitioner) of the philosophy of money reveals itself and proves its explanatory worth. For philosophical argument can change the (monetary) world because of the conceptual character of money itself.

The relationship between a philosopher of money's philosophy and monetary reality is not solely active, however; for a philosopher of money's philosophy must also be affected by money. Again, if there were no evidence of this impact of money on his/her philosophical categories, then s/he would not be a philosopher of money. I am not hypothesizing a universal "money of the mind" here. For there can be philosophers who have commented more or less extensively on money but have not had their philosophies deeply impacted by monetary crises and revolutions.

On the basis of this definition of what is a philosopher of money, not every philosopher who writes about money is a philosopher of money, but a philosopher who does not write about money is, *pace* Shell, *not* a philosopher of money. Thus there is a definite categorical problem when asking "Is X a philosopher of money?" (where X might be Plato, Georg Simmel, John Stuart Mill, St. Augustine, Isaac Newton, Simone de Beauvoir, or Martin Heidegger). Its answer requires both philosophical analysis and historical investigation of the following questions: (a) What is the philosopher's monetary program and strategy? (b) How are his/her philosophical categories deployed in the construction and defense of his/her monetary program? and (c) Does the category of money play an important role in his/her philosophy?

In the conclusion, I apply this definition to the cases of Locke, Berkeley and Hume.

PART I
Hume and his Class's Problematic

Part I addresses the crises that the period following the rebellion of 1745 posed for the Scotch bourgeoisie—particularly for young "second sons" like Hume who were without either inherited capital or landed property, a situation which undoubtedly provoked Hume's own thoughts toward money.

For Hume and his milieu, money was a necessary aspect of the civilizing project, for besides being a store and measure of value and a vehicle of value exchange, it also shaped and transformed the money user. It was this later function of money beyond its objective character as a store and measure of value and medium of exchange, which would most concern Hume in his mature philosophical works. The great debate concerning the proper monetary system—specie or paper—for a global capitalism that took place throughout the "long eighteenth century" among the intellectuals of Europe and North America concerned the varied estimations of the superiority of one or the other system in carrying out these functions. There was also an open question as to what kind of person would be shaped by a paper-based monetary system versus a metallic or specie-based one. David Hume entered this debate with a highly developed set of categories created to make it possible to assess complex explanations of monetary phenomena.

Part I will analyze the problematics Hume faced with the rest of the Scottish Enlightenment in determining and being determined by civilizing money, that is, what was the impact of his Newtonian methodology applied to money?

1
On the Scottish Origins of Civilization

I have not consulted books; indeed I have not books to consult! But as well as my memory serves me, let us see, my lords, how the facts and the law stand. ... It appears most clearly to me that not only every man may legally interfere to suppress a riot, much more to prevent acts of felony, treason, and rebellion, in his private capacity, but he is bound to do it as an act of duty.

—Lord Mansfield, 1780
(Quoted in Campbell 1878)

In order to understand how money becomes "civilized," it is important to examine the term "civilization." The term "civilization" is commonly used in English to describe a set of positive, even ideal, social and historical values. "European Civilization," "Western Civilization," "Industrial Civilization": to most people, any use of the word signifies a positive achievement. Indeed, who would want to be labeled "uncivilized"? And who would not want to be a member of a "civilized" society?

There are scholars, however, who declare that they "have for some time rejected the notion of civilization" because of its discriminatory implications, as civilization is "by necessity defined by reference to the uncivilized" (White 1987: 40).[1] Questions have also been raised concerning the ethical content of civilization, for it is apparent that the perpetration of horrid crimes is not sufficient to make an individual or a society uncivilized. If this were not the case, never, after the witch-hunt, the slave trade, Auschwitz and Hiroshima, could we bring ourselves to speak of "Western Civilization."

Many circumvent the problem by enclosing "civilization" within protective quotation marks, highlighting the distance between the ideal and its historical realizations. But this use of the term heightens the value of civilization, as it suggests that none of the peoples and countries defined as civilized are genuine embodiments of this ideal state. Indeed, that civilization is something to be aspired to is a "truth" few ever question, even among those prone to discard the term because of its exclusive meaning. This, I argue, is because the genesis of the concept is generally ignored, civilization being viewed as a timeless ideal, rather than a specific historical process. If the history of "civilization" were better known, we might be more cautious in granting this term our unquestioning seal of approval, even though we might still conclude that Europe, and "the West," are indeed civilized.

To investigate the development of the term "civilization" in the English vocabulary—that is, its trajectory from its origin to its final destination, as a term characterizing the highest form of social existence—is the purpose of this chapter. I do this in order to show how closely money and civilization were tied together in David Hume's philosophy of money. As I will show, the development of "civilization" is genetically intertwined with that of the British financial system, with the subjugation of Scotland to the British Crown, and the eighteenth-century social struggles in and out of Scotland. Thus, "civilization" originally referred to three different but interconnected processes: the rationalization of intra-capitalist relations (civilization *qua* reason); the disenfranchisement of the English workers from their "traditional" rights and liberties (civilization *qua* wage-repression); and the destruction of communal relations in the Scottish Highlands, resulting in the integration of Scottish society into the orbit of Britain's imperial economy (civilization *qua* progress from barbarism). Fundamental to each of these processes was the assimilation of the English Common Law to the Scottish Civil Law,[2] the first meaning, in the English vocabulary, of the term "civilization."

ETYMOLOGICAL DEVELOPMENT OF "CIVILIZATION"

The word "civilization," with its roots in the ancient Roman experience (from the Latin *civis*, citizen), is not to be found in Middle English. "Civilization" entered the language in the early eighteenth century, as a technical legal term possessing both a specific and a general meaning. In its more limited sense, it defined "A law, act of justice, or judgment, which renders a criminal process civil; which is performed by turning an information into an inquest, or the contrary" (*Oxford English Dictionary*, 1989). Generally, however, the word referred to the process of "assimilating common law to civil law" (Jowitt 1959). So it stood in 1755 when, Samuel Johnson, the editor of the most famous eighteenth-century English dictionary, gave the term a specific legal definition. Up to this time, "civilization" was cognate with "civilian," which meant a professor of Roman or Civil Law guided by the principles of Equity.

The term's definition changed in the last half of the eighteenth century. The 1828 edition of Noah Webster's *American Dictionary of the English Language* defined "civilization" as "The act of civilizing, or the state of being civilized, the state of being refined in manners, from the grossness of savage life, and improved in arts and learning." Webster made it clear that the legal definition was a secondary one, and he placed next to it a cautionary "not used." We catch sight of this semantic change in one of the entries of James Boswell's *Life of Johnson*:

> On Monday, March 23 [1772], I found [Johnson] busy, preparing a fourth edition of his folio *Dictionary*. Mr. Peyton, one of his original amanuenses, was writing for him. I put him in mind of a meaning of the word side, which he had omitted, vis. relationship, as father's side, mother's side. He inserted it. I asked him if humiliating was a good word. He said he had seen it frequently used, but he did not know it to be legitimate English. *He would not admit civilization, but only civility. With great deference to him, I thought civilization, from to civilize, better in the sense opposed to barbarity, than civility*; as it is better to have a distinct word for each sense, than one word with two senses, which civility is, in his way of using it.
>
> (Boswell 1934: 466, italics mine)

Why did "civilization," which originated as a legal term, become a synonym of "refinement" and "improvement" and the antonym of "barbarity" and "savage life"? An answer to this question will take us to that thin strip of Scotland bordering England called the "Lowlands," to that eighteenth-century flourishing of bourgeois thought that goes by the name of "the Scottish Enlightenment,"[3] and to that peculiar institution which is Scottish law.

The Scottish legal system has differed from that of England since the sixteenth century. Modern Scottish law came into existence with the introduction of the Calvinist *Institutes*, the pillar of the Presbyterian Kirk during the Reformation. This law was patterned on Roman Civil Law and incorporated the legal wisdom of the most successful empire Europe knew until the modern period. It relied on "principles," "reason," and "certainty," and thus stood in marked contrast to English Common Law, which was based on judicial precedent and was shaped by the indigenous struggles on the commons.

A sharp distinction between the Civil Law and the Common Law cannot be drawn on all grounds. "Those who contrast the Civil Law and the Common Law traditions, by a supposed non-use of judicial authority in the former and a binding doctrine of precedent in the latter, exaggerate on both sides" (Merryman 1969: 48). But there was a significant difference in the way the two systems were viewed in the eighteenth century, north and south of the Scottish border. In England, the Common Law was identified with the peculiarities of "English Liberty," while in Scotland it was taken as an example of English insularity, and contrasted to the universalizing Roman ethos of which Civil Law seemed to be the carrier. There was also a methodological difference between the Scottish and the English legal traditions: "[We have] a contrast between the two rival ways of constructing a legal system the logical and deductive Scottish method formed upon Roman models, and the empirical and inductive English method built up by decided cases on native lines" (Holdsworth 1938: XI, 16).

These contrasts were to have fatal consequences for the women of Scotland in the late sixteenth and early seventeenth centuries; for as we now know, the civilization of the Scottish legal system in the course of the Reformation was built on the stakes and gallows of the witch-hunt. The Scottish witch-hunt was notoriously much more intense and horrific than the English. Perhaps as many as three Scottish women were executed as witches for every English woman, even though England had a population four times that of Scotland (Levack 1987: 184; Federici 2004: 171). In the past, the special severity of the witch-hunt in Scotland was attributed to the remoteness of the place, but the records show that the truly remote places in the Highlands and the Hebrides suffered no witch-hunt (Larner 1981: 80; Smout 1972: 189). The executed lived in Fife, Moray, Aberdeenshire, the Lothians and the Borders, that is, in the Scottish Lowlands where the central government was in greater control (Larner 1981: 72). In fact, the witch-hunt was due not to a lack but to a surfeit of civilization. There is now a scholarly consensus that explains the course of the witch-hunt in Scotland by pointing to the profound difference between the English and Scottish legal codes (Larner 1981: 200; Levack 1987: 184; Quaifee 1987: 146). It is generally agreed that: (1) Scottish law was inquisitorial, English law was not; (2) local, unsupervised magistrates often tried women as witches in Scotland, this did not happen in England;

(3) judicial torture was rare in England, not in Scotland; (4) English juries required unanimity, Scottish juries required only a majority; and (5) English law was flexible in sentencing, Scottish magistrates applied the stipulated capital sentence with few scruples. Christina Larner, who contributed much to forging this consensus, summarized it in the following way:

> The Scottish system was Roman, inquisitorial, and theoretical; the English based on statute law and pragmatic. A person accused of witchcraft under an inquisitorial system was tortured to confess and to name accomplices. The naming of accomplices produced the mass hunts characteristic of Scotland and parts of the Continent.
>
> (Larner 1981: 77)

The witch-hunt in Scotland gave the English a graphic display of the differences between their legal systems, for tracts describing the Scottish witch-trials were popular with the English reading public throughout the seventeenth century. This perhaps accounts for the aura of severity that the Scottish law had in the English social imagination in the eighteenth century.

Even the 1707 Act of Union fell short of unifying England and Scotland with respect to the law.[4] Although Scotland at the time was underdeveloped economically and politically in comparison to England, the Scottish bourgeoisie prided itself in its older, imperially rooted legal institutions and strove to ensure their continuance. This was guaranteed by several provisions of the Union Treaty. The most crucial provision in this regard was Article XXII, which stipulated:

> that the laws which concern public right policy and civil government may be made the same throughout the whole United Kingdom; but that no alteration be made in laws which concern private right except for evident utility of the subjects within Scotland.
>
> (Walker 1976: 125)

Allowing Scotland to retain its legal system was an important concession on the side of the English ruling class. It was an eloquent sign of its desire to win the support of the Lowland Scottish bourgeoisie who, it was hoped, would help them break the might of the Scottish Highlanders, whose military prowess England had learned to fear, after their invasions of

England in 1715 and 1745, and their two aborted attempts of 1708 and 1719. The Scottish Highlanders posed a unique threat for the British Empire, which by the first quarter of the eighteenth century controlled parts of the Americas, India and Africa. For they exposed its rear door to an uncolonized population who, in refusing English rule, also refused integration in the expanding circuit of capitalist relations. The Act of Union showed that an alliance between the London rulers and the Lowland bourgeoisie was profitable to both parties. Thus, for the sake of the treaty, the English politicians bowed to the jewel of Scottish nationalist pride: the Civil Law tradition. In time, however, they themselves perceived the superior advantages of Scottish Civil Law as a principle of social organization. In view of the meaning the term was to acquire in this period, we could say that they themselves were "civilized."

SCOTTISH CIVIL LAW VERSUS ENGLISH COMMON LAW

The Civil Law was highly valued by the eighteenth-century Scottish ruling class, who believed it provided the foundations for their social and political life. A legal career was a "must" among the bourgeoisie and the landed gentry alike, for anyone intending to participate in economic and political activity; it was a guarantee of prestige. When in the 1770s one of the first street directories was assembled in Edinburgh, the list of names placed the advocates first, then, in order, their clerks, the writers to the signant, their clerks, the nobility and gentry with town houses, and finally the remainder of the middle class, without much further distinction (Smout 1972: 350). As late as the early nineteenth century, the dominant social and economic group in Edinburgh was the jurisprudential aristocracy, whose ranks produced the main figures of the Scottish Enlightenment. Lords Kames and Monboddo were eminent judges, John Millar and Adam Smith were legal scholars, and David Hume's only institutional position in Scotland was that of librarian at the Edinburgh Advocates' Library.

In the eighteenth century, the importance of mastering the Civil Law was so widely recognized among the upper-class Scots that every year many directed their steps to the law schools of the continent, most often to Holland. Boswell did his legal studies at Utrecht and, in the seventeenth and eighteenth centuries, about 1,600 Scottish lawyers studied in Leyden alone.

Among the Advocates' Library's 1,500 law books, only about 100, in 1692, were not from continental presses (Holdsworth 1938: XI, 15).

> From their sojourn in Holland the aspirants to practice in the Parliament House brought back with them not only the principles they imbibed from the masters of the Roman-Dutch law, but also the treatises with which the law schools of the Dutch Universities were so prolific. No Scot lawyer's library was complete in those days which did not contain the works of Grotius, Vinnius, the Voets, Heineccius, and other learned civilians.
>
> (Walker 1976: 134)

Such knowledge, Scottish law scholars believed, had much to contribute to the improvement of Britain's legal system, whose adherence to Common Law they viewed as perniciously flawed. English Common Law was too "peculiar" and was thus unfit for the management of international economic relations and too sensitive to pressure from popular struggles. In one word, it was too prone to "liberty." Why then, it was asked, had it prevailed in England over the rationally superior Civil Law? Two among the most eminent historians and legal philosophers of the Scottish Enlightenment, John Millar and David Hume, tackled this question.

In *An Historical View of the English Government* (1803), Millar argued that, since the late Middle Ages, Roman Civil Law had been associated with the institutional conflict between the universities and the court inns of Westminster (London), where (municipal) Common Law was taught. The tension between the nobility in Parliament and the clergy, who had run the universities, had reached a breaking point with the Reformation, when Civil Law had been improperly (in Millar's view) associated with "Roman despotism," in both the ancient (imperial) and modern (catholic) sense of the word. The victory of the Reformation in England had sealed the fate of Civil Law (Millar 1803: 316–340).[5]

The "unnecessary" association in the Middle Ages between the Civil Law and the Catholic Church is also the focus of Hume's account of its marginalization in England. Hume deplored the fact that the English laity, covetous of the Church's possessions, should have rejected, together with the Catholic clergy, the Civil Law as well, viewing it as the tool of this discredited class. His objective was to remind the English of the immense social benefits Civil Law provided. In this process, he explicitly identified "civilization" with the principles of Civil Law (or as principles of Equity) as well as with the principles of commercial society. He argued that it had been the discovery of Justinian's *Pandects* that had restored Europe, after a centuries-long interruption, to its progressive path to civilization.[6] Civil Law had given "security to all other arts" and had acted as a "mild" but persistent historical force; for the judgments made on the basis of its "general and equitable maxims" had gradually improved not only the legal decisions, but the judges as well (Hume n.d.: 510).

Hume and Millar did not despair of the possibility of civilizing the English legal system. Millar believed that it would soon be possible "for the enlightened judges of the present age to estimate the system of Roman jurisprudence, according to its intrinsic merits" (Millar 1803: 338). Hume as well, despite his contempt for the English intellectuals and commoners, saw new possibilities in his age. He admitted that "a great part of [Civil Law] was secretly transferred into the practice of the courts of justice," so that English law was rescued from "its original state of rudeness" (Hume n.d.: 509).

"Secret transmission" is a major theme in Hume's social theory. Like other intellectuals of the Scottish Enlightenment, he considered "secrecy," "invisibility," "mildness," "custom," "habit," and "unintended consequences" as crucial tactics for social change, particularly when the interlocutors were the traditionalists in the English courts, who themselves were often besieged by the riotous English working classes.

The Scottish Enlightenment's "secret transmission" of civilization had three main objectives. The first was to turn English law into a more efficient vehicle for the management of exchange relations, through an injection of continental juridical wisdom. Scotland might be an underdeveloped country, but the best among its ruling class had been trained in the Netherlands, which at the time was *the* model of an advanced capitalist nation. It was in Amsterdam's banks and counting houses (as well as in Utrecht's law schools) that Scottish students learned how Civil Law was instrumental to the creation of a system of social exchange characterized by abstractness and regularity. Hume was confident that this knowledge would be valued by the English entrepreneurs (whether aristocrats or bourgeois), who frequently recognized their economic provincialism and turned to the Netherlands for inspiration.

The civilization of English law would also serve to thwart the English urban proletariat, who demanded a more egalitarian legal system, reflecting the "ancient rights of Englishmen," that is, a system ensuring more popular control over the courts (through the extension of the right to trial by jury), over Parliament (through a widening of the electorate), and over the military (through restrictions on press-ganging and the use of martial law). Such demands were a challenge to the "thanatocratic" state England had become by the eighteenth century.[7] But the "civilization" of English law would void any appeal to traditional rights and to the judgment of sympathetic or easily pressured jurymen. Under Civil Law (with courts operating under the "principles of Equity," judgments would be shaped by "general and equitable maxims."

Finally, the aim of Scottish civilization was directed north of Edinburgh and Glasgow, at the Scottish Highlanders, who still lived under the law of the Celtic clan and constituted a threat to the commerce and government of the Scottish Lowlands and to the development of capitalism in Britain, especially the functioning of the monetary system. They had to be defeated, possibly with the aid of the English army; but, most important, the Highlanders had to be civilized.

CIVIL LAW AND THE RATIONALIZATION
OF ENGLISH CAPITALISM

The "civilization" of English law was most urgently needed for the regulation of commercial international exchanges, where the application of Common Law proved disastrously inadequate. Based on precedents and drawn from the workings of a domestic economy, Common Law could not provide a legal framework for international trade, nor could it cope with the increasing sophistication and velocity of currency exchange in Britain. David Hume's philosophical research and experiment sought to bring the monetary system into the realm of money. For example, the Common Law's preference for particularized contractual relations, that is, its tendency to understand contracts as occurring between concrete persons—and not abstract entities like corporations and the state—thwarted the creation of credit-based bank notes. In early eighteenth-century England, the conflict between the Common Law and the development of finance and trade was escalating. The "financial revolution," launched after the "Glorious Revolution" of 1689, had led to the expansion of "symbolic" or "imaginary" forms of money (Caffentzis 1989). But the monetary sphere's invasion of the imaginary was not easily comprehended. As Sir Albert Feavearyear notes:

> … in the first half of the 18th century the customers of the London banks made use to about an equal extent of the notes of those banks and of drafts upon cash accounts kept with them. Between these two documents at the outset there was really very little difference. The notes were generally for large, and often for broken, amounts, were frequently made out, not to "bearer," but to "order," and in the latter case passed current by endorsement like a cheque. It is not surprising, therefore, to find that the early writers upon paper currency drew no distinction between the various forms in which they found it. They grouped them all together as "paper credit," and held that all of them drove out and took the place of metallic money. There was no important difference between the note signed by Francis Child, the banker, which said: "I promise to pay to Mr. John Smith or order, on demand the sum of £186. 14s. 2d.," and the draft signed by John Smith and addressed to Francis Child which said: "Pay to Robert Brown or order the sum of £186. 14s. 2d." No one regarded the former as in any way more entitled to be considered money than the latter. Davenant, Hume, and Sir James Steuart all spoke of notes, bills, drafts, bank credits, and even securities, as though they were a part of the circulating money of the country.
>
> (Feavearyear 1963: 258–269)

In 1700, however, Chief Justice Sir John Holt declared that "promissory notes" were not negotiable. This meant that a John Smith would not be able to transfer his right to the payment of £186. 14s. 2d. to another person, and this in turn to another one. This measure provoked a crisis in the commercial and banking practice of England. Holt defended his decision, arguing that a note could not be a bill of exchange because:

> the maintaining of these actions upon such notes were innovations upon rules of the Common Law; and that it amounted to the setting up of a new sort of specialty, unknown to the Common Law, and invented in Lombard Street, which attempted in these matters of bills of exchange to give laws to Westminster Hall.
>
> (Holdsworth 1926: 172)

In effect, Holt was claiming that the "promise" implied in a "promissory note" was legally valid only between identifiable individuals, and not between an individual and an abstract, interchangeable bearer of the note, as allowed by Civil Law (Rotman 1987). "Lombard Street," however, did not appreciate Holt's defense of the Common Law's prejudice for nominalism, nor did it welcome his suspicion of "continental innovations." Its spokesmen in Parliament overturned Holt's decision and confirmed as negotiable all notes payable to *A* simply, to *A* or order, to *A* or bearer. This is how Sir William Holdsworth, the twentieth-century legal historian, sums up this conflict between the defenders of Common Law and the spokesmen for the city's trading and financial interests:

> This episode taught the courts that they could not wholly ignore approved mercantile custom; they must adapt the rules to such customs; that in fact there were cases in which "Lombard Street must be allowed to give laws to Westminster Hall." And the eighteenth century was to show that the courts had learned the lesson.
>
> (Holdsworth 1926: 176)

In this context, the changes introduced by Scottish jurists, who frequently worked their way into English courts, gradually undermined the authority of Common Law. Evidence of this development can be found in some technical, but significant, points of law, such as the "doctrine of consideration" and that of "quasi-contract." Both areas show the mounting influence of capitalist relations on social life and the growing dominance of abstract, general considerations in the regulation of social transactions.

The doctrine of "consideration" in Common Law served to distinguish two kinds of agreements: enforceable contracts and unenforceable "pacts." In the Common Law tradition, some "consideration" had to pass between two parties, in order for an enforceable contract to exist between them. (An unenforceable pact would be my promising to give my car to *X* simply because I like *X*, and without any "consideration" on *X*'s part.)

In the course of the eighteenth century, this view was challenged by a new doctrine postulating that a "moral obligation," grounded on principles of equity, was a sufficient basis for the existence of a contract. Thus "consideration"—that is, the passing of values from one party to another, in the new Civil Law approach—became merely evidential, ceasing to be the criterion for the existence of a contract. As Sir F. Pollock pointed out, if this view had been accepted, the whole modern development of English contract law would have been changed, "and its principles might have been … assimilated to those of the law of Scotland" (Holdsworth 1926: 34). More than that, had this view been accepted, then the question of who would decide what was a moral obligation would have become vital, and the distinction between moral reason and legality would have been in danger of collapsing.

A similar situation developed in the area of "quasi-contracts," these being obligations implied but not explicitly stipulated by law. The change here would have affected that increasingly gray area of contractual life, where one was under the obligation to pay, despite the lack of a contract (Harding 1966: 285). Take the example of a merchant whose cargo was scattered in a storm, retrieved by another merchant's vessel and returned to the first merchant. Was the first merchant obligated to pay the costs of retrieval? Not necessarily, according to Common Law, since there was no explicit contract between the two merchants, but, under the rubric of "quasi-contract," one could argue that the first merchant had an implied obligation to pay the second. As Lord Mansfield, the leading theorist of such an extension of the law, put it, depending on the circumstances, "there are ties of natural justice and equity that compel one to pay or refund the money" (Holdsworth 1926: 97).

As one can see from these encroachments of Common Law, the leading probe was the notion of "equity." As Lord Kames wrote, "It appears now clearly, that a court of equity commences at the limits of the common law … [thus it] enforces every natural duty that is not provided for at common law" (Lord Kames 2014: 22–23). "Equitable principles" and "equitable maxims," abound in the writings of the Scottish Enlightenment. It was here that the Scottish "secret transmission" achieved its most "civilizing" impact on the English legal tradition.

From the Middle Ages to the eighteenth century, England had two courts and two legal systems: the King's courts with their highly developed Common Law; and the courts of Chancery, whose code of equity was historically rooted in the Civil Law. In the eighteenth century, the decision to go to the courts of Chancery was based on the possibility of having one's case judged outside the network of precedent. The courts of Chancery thrived in the marginal and undecidable aspects of the Common Law but this practice generated a conflict between the two branches of the law, which Scottish jurists were quick to detect as the weak link in the English legal system.

Thus, Lord Kames, in his *Principles of Equity* (1760), calling for the end of this division, stressed the superiority of Scottish law where principles of equity were fully integrated into the legal system. For "Equity, in the proper sense, comprehends every matter of law that by the Common Law is left without remedy" (quoted in Lehmann 1971: 212). It is not insignificant that, as an example of the application of equitable principles, Kames mentions the suppression of workmen's combinations (MacCormick 1982: 157–158).

CIVILIZATION AND THE REPRESSION OF POPULAR JUSTICE

For my part, my Passions are very warm for the Memory of King Alfred, who hang'd 44 Judges in one year, as Murthers of the Law.
—North Briton Extraordinary, no. 83

While the British ruling class hailed the civilization of mercantile law, the civilization process was to find a formidable obstacle in the London "lower sorts," for whom the defense of Common Law was of prime importance. Being based on the trial by jury system, Common Law was more responsive to popular pressure, as the jury was almost independent of the judge.

It was for this very reason that Scottish jurists in England and their disciples labored to abolish this system, which was still used in both civil and criminal cases. In promoting this change, the Scottish jurists took the opposite path from that pursued by lawyers and philosophers on the continent. Here the "Enlightenment" inspired a juridical reform that was to eliminate the more inquisitorial aspects of Civil Law procedure, such as judicial torture, whose abolition was promoted by the Italian jurist Cesare Beccaria.[8] By contrast, the Scottish jurists strove to limit both the power of the jury and the right of the "populace" to interfere in matters concerning law and government.

What criteria inspired their work can be seen in a politically important libel case, *The Dean of St. Asaph's Case*, which was tried in 1783. The judge, Lord Mansfield, ruled that the jury only had the right to determine whether the accused wrote and published the document, and whether the document referred to the offended parties. Beyond that, it was the judge's prerogative to determine whether the publication was libelous. This refusal to grant the jury the right to make a "general verdict" well expresses the civilizing effort in England. "Civilization" meant that the juries would not be "intrusted with

a power of blending law and fact, and following the prejudices of their affections or passions" (Holdsworth 1938: 679). None fought more strenuously
against jury trial than the same Scots-born Lord Mansfield who, in response
to an effort to introduce the system in Scotland, wrote:

> The partial introduction of trials by jury seems to me big with infinite
> mischief and will produce much litigation ... It is curious that fraud,
> which is always a complicated proposition of law and fact, was held in
> England as one of the reasons for a court of equity, to control the incon-
> veniences of a jury trying it.
>
> (Campbell 1878: 554)

Mansfield's words must be read in the context of the increasingly sharp
confrontations between the state and the London proletariat, which, year
after year, led to a dramatic increase in the use of "summary proceedings" (i.e., trials without jury against offenders of parliamentary statutes,
especially in the areas of taxation and "public peace"). "Of late," William
Blackstone drily noted in his *Commentaries*, "[this procedure] has been so
extended, as to threaten the disuse of trials by jury" (Blackstone 1892: 676).

Born in the Scottish Lowlands in 1705, Lord Mansfield (originally William
Murray) was the main agent of legal civilization in England. For more than
fifty years, from the late 1720s to the mid-1780s, Mansfield worked at the
civilization of English Common Law, and he nearly succeeded in "civilizing"
the principles of commercial and mercantile law.

He met the consequences of his work, however, in the form of a riotous
resistance by the London proletariat, which he helped to repress. This aspect
of his work is often underplayed by the increasingly Thatcherite scholarship
of our times. In a hagiographic biography, Edmund Heward concludes that
"Lord Mansfield's greatest contribution to the law of England was establishing principle both as the mainspring of Common Law, and as a means of
threading through the thickets of particularity" (Heward 1979: 170). But
Heward fails to inform us that many in the streets of London viewed Mansfield's "principle" as juridical despotism.

Resistance to Mansfield's civilizing efforts came from two sources. On
the one side, there was the "middling sort": the merchants and artisans,
whose affairs were centered in London and the main provincial towns. On
the other was "the inferior set of people," those whom Sir John Fielding

described as "the infinite number of chairmen, porters, labourers and drunken mechanics" (Rude 1962: 6). Both were excluded from the surplus generated by the system of slavery, extermination and trade later known as "the British Empire." Their confrontation with Mansfield intersected with a period of struggle that has passed into British history as the "Wilkes and Liberty" days (1763–1774).

John Wilkes was a leading organizer of the "Society of Supporters of the Bill of Rights." He was a flamboyant politico who embodied the resistance to the threat civilization posed to English law. The Wilkites demanded: the total accountability of magistrates, from the king to the local J.P., before the law; the elimination of class-based discrimination in legal practices; the institution of trial by jury in almost all legal proceedings; and the gaining of public consent before military force could be used in controlling social crises (Brewer 1980: 140). William Moore, a contemporary of Wilkes, thus summarized the Wilkite position:

> the greatest happiness any nation can enjoy, is being governed by laws by the consent of the people, either collectively or representatively, and of having a right to call the principal magistrates intrusted with the execution of those laws to an account for maladministration.
>
> (quoted in Brewer 1980: 142)

Naturally, the Wilkites found their nemesis in Lord Mansfield. *The North Briton*, the major organ of the Wilkites, continually countered Mansfield's assault on public accountability, equality, jury trial and deference to public consent in times of crisis:

> the judge has little more to do than to superintend the trial, and to preserve inviolate the forms of justice. … But can this compliment be paid to a judge, who confounds, controuls and browbeats a jury? Who changes, garbles and packs a jury? Who in all his speeches, is perpetually talking of supporting the measures of the government, that is the prerogative of the crown, but never once of supporting the privileges of the people.
>
> (quoted in Brewer 1980: 158)

At the peak of the Wilkite campaign against Mansfield, an anonymous letter writer appeared on the London scene to challenge the chief justice.

Under the pseudonym "Junius," in November 1770, he published an open letter "To The Right Honourable Lord Mansfield," whose beginning reflected the anti-Scot sentiment pervasive in London and the major provincial towns at the time: "I own I am not apt to confide in the professions of gentlemen of that country, and when they smile, I feel an involuntary emotion to guard myself from mischief" (Junius 1978: 207). The letter points to the struggle between Common and Civil Law, which had reached a climax during the reign of James I, the Scottish king (Levack 1987: 122–123):

> In contempt or ignorance of the common law of England, you have made it your study to introduce into the court, where you preside, maxims of jurisprudence unknown to Englishmen. The Roman code, the law of nations, and the opinion of foreign civilians, are your perpetual theme; but whoever heard you mention Magna Carta or the Bill of Rights with approbation or respect?
>
> (Junius 1812: 162–163)

Junius bemoaned the introduction of the rules of equity:

> Instead of those certain, positive rules, by which the judgment of a court of law should invariably be determined, you have fondly introduced your own unsettled notions of equity and substantial justice. Decisions given upon such principles do not alarm the public so much as they ought, because the consequence and tendency of each particular instance, is not observed or regarded. In the mean time the practice gains ground; the court of King's Bench [Mansfield's court] becomes a court of equity, and the judge, instead of consulting strictly the law of the land, refers only to the wisdom of the court, and to the purity of his own conscience (Junius 1812: 164). … But what kind of conscience is it that is "making the trial by jury useless and ridiculous" and would like "to introduce a bill into parliament for enlarging the jurisdiction of the court, and extending your favorite trial by interrogatories to every question, in which the life or liberty of an Englishman is concerned"?
>
> (Junius 1812: 174)

The letter, which Horace Walpole called "the most outrageous I suppose ever published against so high a magistrate by name" (quoted in Junius

1978: 206), ended with a warning concerning the possible consequences of Mansfield's civilizing project: "It is remarkable enough that the laws you understand best, and the judges you affect to admire most, flourished in the decline of a great empire, and are supposed to have contributed to its fall" (Junius 1812: 181).

Junius' defense of the "traditional rights of Englishmen" undoubtedly appealed to the "middling sort," who feared the advance of civilization on the level of property transactions. But Mansfield's work was known in a more carnal way by the London proletariat and those who appeared at the sites of the provincial assizes.

Judicial hanging, as a means of class intimidation, was an essential element of the restructuring of mercantile law that Lord Mansfield was responsible for (Hay 1975). In his twenty-nine Sessions at the Old Bailey, Mansfield personally ordered twenty-nine people for branding, 448 for transportation and 102 for hanging (Linebaugh 1992: 360). He was also for twenty-two years on assize (the court sessions periodically held outside of London), where he treated the provincials to the same terror he meted out in London (Heward 1979: 66–70). Thus, Mansfield was popularly considered a reincarnation of Judge Jeffreys, the hanging judge of the first period of judicial thanatocracy; and "the *cheveux de frise* [the eighteenth-century equivalent of barbed wire], atop the wall of King's Bench prison, was known as 'Lord Mansfield's teeth'" (Linebaugh 1992: 360). Mansfield's principles of equity stopped at the debtors and thieves. Even in his seventy-sixth year (1781), he demanded in the House of Lords that both the families of imprisoned debtors and spiritous liquors be kept out of prison, so that "imprisonment should in future be more rigid" (Heward 1979: 61). His request was likely stimulated by the events of the previous year, which were crucial for the fate of civilization in England.

In June 1780, the London proletarians took to the streets in what became known as the Gordon Riots. Their main objects were juridical: the "delivery of Newgate," the freeing of the debtors, the attack on the Old Bailey and, last but not least, the destruction of Lord Mansfield's house.[9]

In the days after June, the "savagery" of the London poor was much decried, by poets and politicians alike, as an ominous sign of imperial fall. The crowd left a burning Newgate Prison reinforced by the liberated prisoners and Lord Mansfield heard that:

an immense multitude, carrying torches and combustibles, were marching down Holborn, and entering Bloomsbury Square ... when they began to batter his outer door, he retreated by a back passage with the Countess; and he had hardly escaped from their fury when their leaders were seen at the upper windows, tearing down and throwing over furniture, curtains, hangings, pictures, books, papers, and every thing they could lay their hands on, likely to serve as fuel for the fire that was already blazing below. In this instance resembling a Paris mob, [ironically] they declared that there was to be no pillage, and that they were acting on principle. Pilfers were punished; and one ragged incendiary, to show his disinterestedness, threw into the burning pile a valuable piece of silver plate and a large sum of money in gold, which he swore should not "go in payment of masses."

(Campbell 1878: 524)

The reference to "masses" is due to one typical reading of the riots as primarily motivated by anti-Catholic sentiment. But after the research of Rude and Linebaugh, the class dynamics of the riotous events have come to the fore (Linebaugh 1992: 334; and Rude 1962: 334).

Figure 1.1 Contemporary engravings showing the Gordon Riots and burning of Newgate: An engraving published by Alexander Hogg circa 1781 in London. Collection of the author.

Figure 1.2   Contemporary engravings showing the Gordon Riots and burning of Newgate: A satirical print condensing many events from the riots published in London in 1781. Collection of the author.

Two opposing principles of justice met in Bloomsbury Square on that day. On the one side was Mansfield's transmission of the Civil Law of Rome into the sinews of the emerging global empire, and on the other was a proletariat who demanded a justice beyond and against the universalization of mercantile law. This conflagration of civilization is thus described by Campbell: "Flames were speedily vomited from every window; and, as no attempt was or could be made to arrest their progress, long before morning nothing of the stately structure remained but the bare and blackened skeleton of the walls" (Campbell 1878: 524).

The lawyer-poet, William Cowper, thus lamented over the burning books of civilization:

> So then the Vandals of our isle,
> Sworn foes to sense and law,
> Have burnt to dust a nobler pile
> Than ever Roman saw!
>
> (Quoted in Campbell 1878: 525)

Figure 1.3 "Sawney Bean the Cannibal": The *Newgate Calendar* was originally a monthly bulletin produced by the keeper of Newgate Prison releasing sensationalist, spurious accounts of executed inmates. By the mid-eighteenth century, the bulletin's form and title had been appropriated by a host of publishers. Among the most popular creations of this industry was the myth of "Sawney Bean," a bold attempt to capitalize on Anti-Highlander sentiment, following the Jacobite uprisings of 1745. According to the tale, Sawney a Highlander-son of a ditch digger, having no taste for honest labor, ran away with a witch named "Black Agnes Douglas." The newly weds took up residence in a coastal cave where, through their own ferocious copulation and incest, were said to breed a forty-five-member clan. This happy commune was sustained through the nightly robbery, dismemberment, and devouring of local travelers. According to the myth, Sawney and his clan robbed and ate some 1,000 persons before their capture and execution. Image courtesy of Wikicommons.

None lamented, however, those shot by the soldiers who came on the scene two hours after Mansfield's books began to burn. Nor, until recently, have John Gray, Leititia Holland, and Mary Gardiner been mourned, who were sentenced to death for taking part in the assault on "the noble pile" (Linebaugh 1985). Their notion of "right" was not included under Blackstone's categories, and their "wit and genius" have not been inscribed in well-purchased pages. Yet their power was decisive. The Gordon Riots put an end to the civilization of English law. Within a decade, Mansfield's innovations began to be rejected in the areas of contract and punishment by the very lawyers and judges who had stood before him in awe. This contraction from the Civil Law was done in the style of jurisprudence. But behind the rejection of Mansfield's civilization of law lay the "bare and blackened skeleton" of his home. His library was not strong enough.

SCOTLAND AND THE CIVILIZATION OF THE HIGHLANDS

Somebody observing that the Scotch Highlanders, in the year 1745, had made surprising efforts, considering their numerous wants and disadvantages: "Yes, Sir, [said Johnson] their wants were numerous; but you have not mentioned the greatest of them all the want of law."

(Boswell 1934: 126)

Johnson's joking remark pointed to a contradiction that plagued the lawyers and philosophers of the Scottish Enlightenment. At the very time when they were striving to civilize the courts and streets of London, their own countrymen, if not blood relations, were the most "barbarous," "lawless" people in eighteenth-century Britain. Johnson, however, was wrong. The Scottish Highlanders had laws. They were the laws of the clan, pivoted on communal identity and communal land property, with the land and laws administered by the clan chief and the heads of the septs, the chieftains, who governed without the blessing of a king, archbishop, or chief justice. The chiefs were "a law unto themselves"; they were also owners of clan land, as land tenure in the eighteenth century was becoming increasingly privatized.[10] But although they rented to "tacksmen," who in turn sublet to clansman tenants, clannish obligations still subsisted. The chief was expected, in times of collective or personal crisis, to extend his surplus to his clansfolk. And the rents the chiefs exacted were tempered by a sort of "war communism," as

33

the chiefs saw in their clansmen not only a source of labor but also a source of military strength.

This unstable combination of tribal communalism, feudalism and private ownership called for a military loyalty that was no longer known to the press-ganging English. Chieftains, tenants, and subtenants all were expected to join in military enterprises, whether they involved cattle-rustling, inter-clan feuds, or the attempt to seize state power in the world's largest empire. Such an attempt was made in 1745, the year referred to in Johnson's joke, when the Scottish clansmen marched from Inverness to put "Bonny Prince Charlie" on the English throne.[11]

Their gestures became the marvel of the age, inspiring much reflection on the civilization process. But the spectacle of the 1745 invasion of the Lowlands and England (like the one in 1715 and the aborted ones in 1708 and 1719) was as distressing to the Scottish civilizers as to the English. "How could they have done it?" More crucially, "How could they be stopped from trying again?" was a question on everyone's mind in Edinburgh and Glasgow (as well as in London) decades after the event. This is how Adam Smith answered the first question in his 1766 *Lectures on Jurisprudence*:

> Another bad effect of commerce is that it sinks the courage of mankind, and tends to extinguish martial spirit. In all commercial countries the division of labour is infinite, and every ones thoughts are employed about one particular thing. ... Each of them is in a great measure unaquainted with the business of his neighbour. In the same manner war comes to be a trade also. ... The defense of the country is therefore committed to a certain sett of men who have nothing else ado; and among the bulk of people military courage diminishes. ... This is confirmed by universal experience. In the year 1745 four or five thousand naked unarmed High-landers took possession of the improved parts of this country without any opposition from the unwarlike inhabitants. They penetrated into England and alarmed the whole nation, and had they not been opposed by a standing army they would have seized the throne with little difficulty.
> (Adam Smith 1978: 540–541)

The invasion was blamed on civilization, that is, on the increasing "refine-ment," "luxury," and "effeminacy" brought about by the commercial spirit whereby "[t]he minds of men are contracted and rendered incapable of elevation, education is despised or at least neglected, and heroic spirit is almost utterly extinguished. To remedy these defects would be an object worthy of serious attention" (Adam Smith 1978: 541).

The task was either to strengthen the heroic spirit of the civilized Lowlanders, or to "refine" and "effeminize" the Highlanders. The Scottish intellectuals realistically opted for the latter course. Their first task was to create the conditions whereby the Highlanders could become civilized. This posed the problematic of historical stages—Savagery, Barbarism and Civilization—which, not surprisingly, became a major theme in the thought of the Scottish Enlightenment.[12] Adam Ferguson, David Hume, Lord James Burnett Monboddo, Lord Kames and Adam Smith were among a host of chronographers who expatiated on "how from being a savage, man rose to be a Scotsman," as Walter Bagehot later quipped (quoted in Bryson 1968: 89). While their approach differed, they agreed that these clannish "Irish" roaming the Highlands were a model of barbarism. (The Lowlanders were frequently unwilling to admit that the Highlanders were Scots.)

In the anthropological scheme of the Scottish Enlightenment, "barbarism" was an intermediate stage between "civilization" whose essence was law and convention, providing order and stability for the protection of property and "savagery," which was characterized by the absence of property. Savages were hunters and fishermen. Barbarians came into being with movable property (they were herders living in small clans), while only with unmovable property could "civilization" take off. As Ferguson put it (echoing Rousseau): "He who first said 'I will appropriate this field; I will leave it to my heirs'; did not perceive, that he was laying the foundation of civil laws and political establishments" (Bryson 1968: 48).

How could one transform these "Irish" Highlanders from barbarians into civilized "Scots"? A social "contract" struck with the clan leaders, or among the Highlanders themselves, would be unthinkable. To Locke's assumption of an "original contract," Scottish philosophers unanimously objected that this would first require the formation of individuals capable of contracting. Adam Smith rejected John Locke's theory with a thick blanket of sarcasm:

Ask a common porter or a day-labourer why he obeys the civil magistrate, he will tell you that it is right to do so, that he sees others do it, that he would be punished if he refused to do it, or perhaps that it is a sin against

God not to do it. But you will never hear him mention a contract as the foundation of his obedience.

(Adam Smith 1978: 402–403)

For Adam Smith, civilization originates not from the private consent of independent individuals but from the principles of authority and utility. Hume's rejection of contract theory was even more decisive. He wrote in 1752:

> 'Tis vain to say, that all governments are, or should be, at first, founded on popular consent, as much as the necessity of human affairs will admit … I maintain … that conquest or usurpation, that is, in plain terms, force, by dissolving ancient governments, is the origin of almost all the new ones, which ever were established in the world.

(Hume 1768: 499)

Here in essence was a strategy for the civilization of the Highlanders. Its premise was that it would be impossible to negotiate with them, for no agreement would be binding on them. Another plan was necessary, grounded on a healthy dose of Humean force and followed by measured injections of Smithean authority and utility. The plan called for a military defeat of the Highlanders, the co-optation of the remaining leaders, and the application of "utility" for the transition to civilized life. The first part of the plan was put into place with the defeat of the clans at the Battle of Culloden in 1746 and the massacres that followed:

> Some five thousand men had risen under their chiefs for the Pretender: they were physically smashed as fighting units by the battle and by the atrocities which followed it. Legislation then consolidated the work of the army throughout the Highlands. No one anywhere in the Highlands was allowed to carry firearms (a significant exemption was made for cattle drovers), or to wear Highland dress or to play the pipes which were associated by the Government with barbarous habits and martial deeds. … A committee of Edinburgh lawyers was constituted to administer the estates forfeited from rebel leaders in all parts of the Highlands. Though not in any way vindictive, they worked on the assumption that Highland

peasants were ignorant, idle and culturally savage, and they therefore strove to do all they could to eliminate the mores of the clan.

(Smout 1972: 321)

On this committee sat Lord Kames and others familiar with Hume's writings and Smith's lectures. They were in a position to transform the Highlands because the forfeited estates would only be sold to chiefs who supported the government. In 1752, legislation annexed thirteen forfeited estates "unalienably" to the Crown. All rents and profits were to be used for "Civilising the Inhabitants upon the said Estates and other Parts of the Highlands and Islands of Scotland," and for promoting among them "the

Figure 1.4 The Battle of Culloden/Blàr Chùil Lodair and its aftermath: "Scotch Pride Humbled or the Rebellion Crushed" an engraving from the Oxford Magazine 70 (1771). The image depicts Highlanders in tartan kneeling before the Duke of Cumberland following their defeat in the battle of Culloden. Image courtesy of WikiCommons.

Protestant religion, good Government, Industry and Manufactures and the Principles of Duty and Loyalty to his Majesty, his Heirs and Successors" (Youngson 1973: 27).

Figure 1.5   The Battle of Culloden/Blàr Chùil Lodair and its aftermath. The final confrontation of the Jacobite uprisings in 1745 as represented by David Morier in 1746. Image courtesy of WikiCommons.

The task of "civilizing" the Highlands thus fell to Scottish lawyers. Now other aspects of Hume's and Smith's concept of civilization came to the fore. "Utility," that is, the cultivation of self-interest, commerce and the division of labor, would undermine, once and for all, clannish communalism and martial spirit. The financing of an extensive education system and the construction of roads in the post-1745 era further tamed the Highlands. Later, a combined policy of enclosures, transportation and factory work drove the Scots out of the Highlands into the capitalistic world where the language of money talks. Through these processes, pre-capitalist Scotland ceased to exist, and a new "civilized" society took its place. How quickly this civilization process occurred can be seen by Johnson's description of the Highlands forty years after Culloden:

There was perhaps never any change of national manners so quick so great and so general, as that which has operated in the Highlands by the last conquest and the subsequent laws. We came hither too late to see what we expected a people of peculiar appearance and a system of antiquated life. The clans retain little now of their original character: their ferocity of temper is softened, their military ardour is extinguished, their dignity of independence is depressed, their contempt of government subdued, and their reverence for their chiefs abated. Of what they had before the late conquest of their country there remains only their language and their [rural] poverty.

(Johnson 1971: 57)

Those too were lost with "the Clearances," the popular name for the land enclosures that took place in Scotland in the 1790s and early nineteenth century. Indeed, famines and clearances were the final result of the civilization of the Highlands.

CONCLUSION

Although the Scottish civilians and their allies made much progress in the eighteenth century on the path to civilization, Hume and Millar's hopes were never fulfilled. Commercial law in England proved to be the one area where civilization was most successful. Demands arising from England's domination of world trade and the increasing commodification of everyday life were a powerful propellant to the rationalistic ideology of Roman law. But in the post-1789 period anything Roman began to smack of subversion. Suddenly "theories," "reason," and "equality" (i.e., the virtues of a transition into a monetary world became symptoms of revolution, and the credit of the Ancient Romans (along with their legal system) began to diminish. Thus, in his *Reflections on the Revolution in France*, Edmund Burke depicted the Romans as the "harshest of that harsh race" of conquerors, who modeled for the French revolutionaries the use of rationalistic terror (Burke 1961: 199).

In such a changed climate, the vaunted universalistic, rationalist Civil Law lost its luster. The civilization of the criminal law in England was even less successful. The great political tumults of the Wilkites and the premonitory rumble of the Gordon Riots stopped the efforts to eliminate jury trials and to introduce inquisitorial methods in criminal proceedings in England. The ideological winds were changing direction. The implicit argument of Edward Gibbon's *The Decline and Fall of the Roman Empire* (1776) was that the Roman state, although equipped with the most severe and equitable legal system, had not been able to defeat the insurrectionary movement of Christianity in its midst (Gibbon 1952 [1776]: 204). Thus, a refined skepticism as to the value of Civil Law as a defense of property and the state undermined this keystone of the civilian's argument.

Finally, the extirpation of the Highlanders succeeded beyond the expectations of the Edinburgh legal aristocracy. The Highlanders were more decimated than civilized. The communal and feudal power of the clan chiefs was broken and the population scattered, but the legal structure of the Scottish land law did not undergo a complete civilization. In early nineteenth-century Scotland, George Joseph Bell could write that:

> A double system of jurisprudence in relation to the subjects of property has arisen in Scotland, as in most European nations the one regulating land and its accessories according to the spirit of Roman jurisprudence which prevailed before the establishment of *feus*.
> (quoted by T.B. Smith 1961: 38)

And Smith could echo him in the mid-twentieth century: "the land law of Scotland remains the most feudal in the world" (T.B. Smith 1961: 181–82). Although feudal obligations attached to land tenure were monetarized after Culloden, resistance to absolute "freehold" ownership of land won the day and in the Scottish lawyers' own backyard.

These failures sealed the fate of total legal civilization. Roman law, following a period of renaissance in the mid-eighteenth century, began to lose its social and ideological power after the Gordon Riots in Britain. This decline was never again reversed. The Civil Law's separate institutional existence ended in 1867 with the reform of the ecclesiastical and Admiralty courts and the destruction of the Doctors' Common (Levack 1987: 201). However, 1867 was only the time of the burial—the project of legal civilization had died long before.

It appears in conclusion that the other definition of "civilization," which Boswell had urged Samuel Johnson to introduce in his *Dictionary* in 1772, in the sense of "opposed to barbarity" was prescient. As a Scotsman trained in Civil Law, Boswell perhaps sensed that the time for legal definitions was passing, but nevertheless the transformation of the Scots from clans people and cattle rustlers to bankers and merchants (a transformation that was congruent with his life) needed a name. "Civilization" was a most appropriate term, as it blended the French concern for manners (Civility) with the Scottish commitment to Civil Law, and it suggested a strategy that combined military terror with economic and monetary development, a strategy indeed that would be used again and again at the service of the British Empire. We will not investigate here what motivated Johnson to refuse the term. Whatever his motives, it is sufficient to recognize that the collapse of the Civil Law tradition in the nineteenth century gave the Boswellian version of "civilization" the power to expand and dominate the linguistic and ideological field.

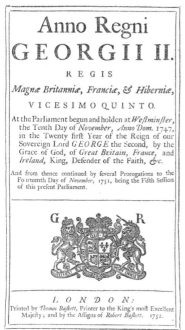

Figure 1.6 The Annexing Act: The frontispiece of the "Act for annexing certain forfeited estates in Scotland to the crown unalienably" as published in pamphlet form by Thomas Baskett, printer to the Crown, in London, 1752.

Figure 1.7 The Annexing Act: The first page of the "Act for annexing certain forfeited estates in Scotland to the crown unalienably" as published in pamphlet form by Thomas Baskett, printer to the Crown, in London, 1752.

Figures 1.8 and 1.9   The Highland Dress Act and Disarmament Act: Images of Highland soldiers in regimental garb published in London in 1743, two years before the Scottish rebellion by John Bowles. The selection shown here was published in 1776 as a pamphlet by the King's printer Thomas Baskett.

An ABSTRACT of an Act for the more effectual difarm-
ing the Highlands in *Scotland ;* and for more effectually
fecuring the Peace of the faid Highlands; and for re-
ftraining the Ufe of the Highland Drefs ; and for further indemnifying fuch Perfons as have acted in Defence
of His Majefty's Perfon and Government, during the
unnatural Rebellion ; and for indemnifying the Judges
and other Officers of the Court of Jufticiary in *Scotland,*
for not performing the Northern Circuit in *May,* One
thoufand feven hundred and forty fix ; and for obliging
the Mafters and Teachers of Private Schools in *Scotland,*
and Chaplains, Tutors, and Governors of Children or
Youth, to take the Oaths to His Majefty, His Heirs, and
Succeffors, and to regifter the fame.

Anno decimo nono GEORGII II. *Regis.*

THE Preamble fets forth, That by an Act of 1 Geo. I. intituled, *An Act for the more effectual fecuring the Peace of the Highlands in Scotland,* it was enacted, That after the 1 *November,* 1716, no Perfon or Perfons (except fuch as are therein men-tioned and defcribed) within the Shire of Dun-tue, on the North Side of the Water of Lt-ven, *Stirling* on the North of the River *Forth,* *Perth, Kincardin, Aberdeen, Inverneſs, Nairn, Cromarty,*

Figure 1.10   The Highland Dress Act and Disarmament Act: The abstract for "An Act for the more effectual securing the peace of the Highlands" often referred to as the "Disarmament Act" or "Dress Act" which included a prohibition on traditional Highlander dress, forbade schools unaffiliated with the crown, forbade bearing of arms by the Highlanders and made allowances for recompense of those loyal to the crown during the rebellion. The selection shown here was published in 1776 as a pamphlet by the King's printer Thomas Baskett.

On the Scottish Origins of Civilization

Figure 1.11   Satirical anti-Jacobite broadsides from1745: the personification of
industry is abandoned by Britannia who, having dropped her shield dances to
a French fiddle tune with the personification of folly who carries poverty on his
back. On the right, men in Highland garb kneel before the devil, the pope and the
"pretender" Prince Charles Edward Stuart clad in tartan.

Figure 1.12   Satirical anti-Jacobite broadsides from1745: An image of Prince
Charles in Roman armor with a foolscap and tartan leggings, to the left, on a
cloud, Time holds a mask removed from the Prince's face. While the mask speaks
(disingenuously) of its desire to renew the nation, the real Charles tells of his
desire for vengeance while, in the background, a troop of Scottish soldiers and a
clergyman are burnt at the stake.

43

2
Civilizing the Highlands:
Hume, Money and the Annexing Act

*... if the disaffected chief be turned out of the possession of his estate, and
the estate vested in the crown, and leased out to those of the clan upon long
terms and at an undervalue, every such lessee's self-interest will operate
directly against his clannish spirit.*

—Duke of Newcastle (1752)

Marx complained in his *Theses on Feuerbach* that "Philosophers have merely
interpreted the world, the point is to change it." But his generalization about
philosophers is mistaken when it comes to the "British empiricists": Locke,
Berkeley and Hume. These philosophers were deeply involved in changing
the capitalist world's great changer: money. They all developed a philosophy of money and attempted to change the form of money, the character of
money users and monetary institutions accordingly.

In my works on these philosophers, I cite a number of different efforts at
intervention they used to "change the world." Locke's most important intervention in the monetary sphere is almost self-evident: the recoinage crisis of
the mid-1690s (Caffentzis 1989). The case of Berkeley is less obvious, since
his effort was a failure. But it is clear that in 1737 he launched (with the help
of a circle of "monetary activists") a campaign to institute a paper currency
and National Bank in Ireland (Caffentzis 2000). He realized in short order
that his campaign was going to fail, so he did not bring his plan (outlined and
justified in his quizzical work on money and banking, *The Querist*) before
the Irish Parliament as he intended. Finally, I argue that Hume presented his
views on the relation between money and civilization in his *Political Discourses* in 1752 in order to intervene in the debate concerning "civilizing
the Highlands" that was precipitated by the Annexed Forfeited Estates Act
which passed in that year in the British Parliament (Caffentzis 2001). This
Act "nationalized" thirteen estates of Jacobite Highland chiefs charged with

(and one executed for) treason. It assigned a Crown-appointed Commission to run these estates and use the profits to "civilise the Highlands."

In this chapter, I will bring more evidence to bear on this hypothesis concerning the 1752 publication of Hume's *Political Discourses*.[1] It remains a hypothesis simply because Hume does not literally say, "I am writing to address the issue of the fate of the forfeited estates and the problem that the Annexing Act was meant to solve." In the introductory remarks in the first essay of *Political Discourses*, Hume claims only to be dealing with "general" reasoning and subjects. He explicitly eschews deliberations on particular cases like the Annexing Act. When he uses historical examples in the text, for example, they are largely about ancient nations, Western European states (including England) or a generalized Great Britain. He rarely directly mentions Scotland, either the Lowlands or the Highlands.

This is not unusual for Hume until his latter years. He was very careful not to take particular political positions concerning Scotland in print. Aside from his anonymous pamphlet on the Stewart case, *A True Account of the Behaviour and Conduct of Archibald Stewart, Esq: Late Lord Provost of Edinburgh, in a Letter to a Friend* (1748), which was plainly motivated by the mortal peril of a friend, his published work did keep to the methodological dictates of the *Political Discourses'* introduction.

My effort "to read Hume politically" with respect to *particular* issues (and not whether he was *ideologically* more Tory than Whig, more Court than Country) is not new. John Robertson (1985) in his *The Scottish Enlightenment and the Militia Issue* carried out a similar reading of the *Political Discourses*, but in his case it dealt with the much discussed Scottish Militia issue, that is, whether the Scots would be allowed to form their own militias after the '45. Most immediately, the Scottish ruling class and "literati" were largely concerned for their own safety without having a trained militia under their control on hand. But the issue was also important as an index of the trust English politicians placed on the Scottish lairds, merchants and lawyers' ability to manage the affairs of Scotland and not let the genie of Jacobite rebellion out of the Highland bottle. Certainly Scottish politicians of the time were almost unanimously for the Annexing Act. As the Duke of Newcastle said to his colleagues in the House of Lords, "Your Lordships see, that all those of that country [Scotland] who have seats in either house of parliament are strenuous for the bill's being passed into law" (Scots Magazine 1752c: 470). The reason for this unanimity is that both

the Annexed Estates and Militia issues were motivated by the same convenient "problem" for them: the rebellion *from* the Highlands. The reality
was much more complex, however. After all, there were many Lowlanders
who joined the rebellion and Jacobite sentiments could be found in many
an English manor and tavern as well.[2] But it pleased the powers that be in
mid-eighteenth-century Edinburgh and London to describe the "problem"
in such terms. Hume was certainly complicit in reinforcing this identity in
his *A True Account* mentioned above. For he described the Jacobite Army
in the pamphlet as consisting of Highland soldiers, even though he must
have known better, since many of the Scots he met in France during his days
writing the *Treatise* in the 1730s were Lowland Jacobites exiled after 1715
and he corresponded with many exiled after Culloden. Further, Hume and
his circle knew that there were many Lowland estates that were forfeited due
to their owners' treason in the '45.

Hume certainly was careful *not* to confront either the Annexed Forfeited
Estates and the Militia Acts squarely in his writing. Thus, in order to support
my case, I refer to evidence that might show that Hume's involvement in the
debate both in the text and context of the *Political Discourses*. Let me begin
with the contextual evidence and then present the textual.

THE ANNEXING ACT: THE HOUSE OF LORDS DEBATE

Hume, as an avid participant in Edinburgh political life at the time, must
have appreciated the importance of the Annexed Forfeited Estates Act to the
Scottish intelligentsia and ruling class in 1752. Given the inability to pass a
Militia Act that would grant to the Lowland ruling class the right of collective self-defense, the Annexing Act's passage was a specific expression by the
most powerful of their English "elder brothers" of a trust in their efforts (or,
at least, a chance to gain that trust). If the contents of the *Scots Magazine* is
any measure of what was being foregrounded in the Scottish concerns of the
day, then the Annexing Act was clearly primary. The *Scots Magazine* of that
time was a monthly and, of the twelve issues in 1752, three dealt with the
Annexing Act in their lead articles.[3]

The Act received the signature of George II on 26 March 1752 and in the
April issue of the *Scots Magazine* printed an abstract of it beginning with a
synopsis:

An act for annexing certain forfeited estates in Scotland to the crown unalienably, and for making satisfaction to the lawful creditors thereupon; and to establish a method of managing the same, and applying the rents and profits thereof, for the better civilizing and improving the highlands of Scotland, and preventing disorders there for the future.

(*Scots Magazine* 1752a)

In its September and October issues, the *Scots Magazine* published a transcription of a debate in the House of Lords concerning the Act. Together they indicated the evident concern, hesitancy and suspicion major English politicians had toward the Scots, both Lowland and Highland. For the passage of the Annexing Act into law marked the transition from what Macinnes has called "punitive civilizing" to "exemplary civilizing" in Scotland or what Hume, in his *Of the Original Contract* (1748), referred to as the transition from a period of "force and violence" to one of "allegiance" to the laws and government (Macinnes 1996: 211, 217; Hume 1768: 491–511). The latter being rooted on a recognition that "men could not live at all in society, at least in a civilized society, without laws and magistrates and judges, to prevent the encroachments of the strong upon the weak, of the violent upon the just and equitable" (Hume 1768: 505). But this transition was by no means uncontested. The "butcher of Culloden," the Duke of Cumberland, did not trust that the Humean period of force and violence had adequately turned the Highlanders into the faithful subjects full of allegiance to the Crown.

The *Scots Magazine* chose the contributions of John Russell, the Duke of Bedford, and William Pulteney, the Earl of Bath, as the voices opposing the Act and Philip Yorke, Lord Hardwicke, and Thomas Pelham-Holles, Duke of Newcastle as the supporters.[4] These were among the most powerful English figures in the Parliament and so their debate on the bill undoubtedly would have been known, at least in general terms, by Hume and his circle even before the September and October issues of the *Scots Magazine*. Some of these arguments were probably developed in Edinburgh and London when the drafts of the Act were being circulated and discussed. They are worth considering, for they define the political coordinates Hume must have considered in his own thought on the Act.

John Russell was one of the leading figures in opposition to the Newcastle government then in power and, at the time, he was in alliance with the Duke of Cumberland. He had a long history of anti-Scottish activity: in 1734, he moved a resolution in Parliament against the alleged corrupt practices used in choosing the Scottish peers; during the '45, he personally raised and led a regiment of foot soldiers against the Jacobite rebels. His arguments against the Annexing Act were often non-sequiturs and *ad homonyms*, but they did touch on the standard English Lords' suspicions of their Scottish ruling-class colleagues. First, there are the accusations of rampant corruption and unscrupulous power-seeking in Scotland. He pointed out that the Act would inevitably open up an endless number of opportunities for gain for the Commissioners, the majority of whom would inevitably come from Scotland:

> We all know the nature of public undertakings; we know how apt they are to be made a jobb of by those that are employed in the execution; and the project to be established by this bill looks as like a jobb, and is, in my opinion, more liable to made a jobb of, than any public undertaking I ever heard of.
>
> *(Scots Magazine* 1752b: 418)

The Act would not only increase the possibilities for corruption, he argued, but it would lead the already powerful Scots Commissioners to become even more powerful (and potentially more dangerous) with the help of the English taxpayer. Russell responded to a hypothetical retort in the following way:

> 'Tis true, it may be said, that the former possessors were disaffected, whereas those to whom their power is to be transferred are well affected to our present happy establishment. My Lords, affection may be pretended, and the most dangerous of all enemies is he who pretends to be a friend.
>
> *(Scots Magazine* 1752b: 419)

He then pointed out that the ends of the Act—the civilizing and improving of the Highlands—have no time limit or limit of resources: "so that the great work of improving this country, and reforming the people, is to be always doing, but never done" (*Scots Magazine* 1752b: 420).

Russell concluded that it would be far better to simply sell the forfeited estates to English or Lowland Scottish buyers who, in their purchase of land, "would not think of increasing their power, but their rental" (*Scots Magazine* 1752b: 421). For only such private owners would be interested in "root[ing]

out that clannish spirit which prevails in the highlands, and to propagate a spirit of industry among the people" (*Scots Magazine* 1752b: 422).

William Pulteney's speech against the Act was much more reserved and did not have the wit and fire that characterized his performances at the height of his orational power in the struggles against Walpole's administration in the 1730s and early 1740s. He was by 1752 something of "an aged raven" (see the article on Pulteney in [Stephen and Lee 1917]). Although he echoed some of the Russell's Scotophobic themes, he did hit a nerve in pointing out that the Act introduced a form of "Turkish" rule in Scotland, which was counter to the improving spirit developed in England:

> The wide-extended empire of Turkey is a melancholy instance of the bad policy of vesting the lands of any country in the hands of the crown; and it is well known, that the great improvement of all our lands in England has arisen from their being made alienable, and in consequence divided amongst a vast number of private men, every one of whom took all possible care to improve that part of which properly belonged to him, and which with its improvement he had a power to transmit to his own posterity, or to such other sons as he pleased to name.
>
> (*Scots Magazine* 1752c: 467)

Indeed, Pulteney, evoking his old "country" ideology, argued that the Act was anti-constitutional because it would disenfranchise the tenants and put them at the mercy of "bashaws [the Commissioners] appointed and removable at the pleasure of the Crown" (*Scots Magazine* 1752c: 468). Thus, in Parliament's zeal in repressing the clannish spirit, he argues, it was allowing the Crown to take on the dictatorial character of the Highland chiefs!

The *Scots Magazine* editors chose two of the most powerful figures in contemporary British politics, the Duke of Newcastle and the Lord Chancellor Hardwicke, to defend the Act. They certainly trumped the opposition, if not in argument, then in terms of status. Newcastle was the most prominent politician of the immediate post-Walpole period while Hardwicke was the leading legal official in the House of Lords. Hardwicke was apparently one of the craftsmen of the Annexing Act as well of the barrage of post-'45 legislation designed to disarm, disrobe and disinherit the Highland clan elite.

What is remarkable about Hardwicke's defense of the Annexing Act is how much he agreed with its and Scotland's critics. Like them, Hardwicke assumed that the Scottish elite would manage, through fraud or force, to put the Jacobite owners of the forfeited estates back in control, if they were allowed. Hence, he argued, it is only by annexing them that they would be kept from the hands "of those who never have, nor ever will make use of them, but for disturbing the tranquility of their country" (*Scots Magazine* 1752b: 425).[5] For he echoed Russell and Pulteney in saying that the sin of the Highland elite is rooted in their thinking which "affected military power rather than riches" (*Scots Magazine* 1752b: 426).

Newcastle's approach was much more sophisticated than Hardwicke's. He reiterated Hardwicke's line of argument, that is, that the Annexing Act is effectively the only way the Jacobite owners can be stopped from surreptitiously taking over their forfeited estates, but then went on to analyze the positive effect of the Act on "the people in the highlands of Scotland." He saw in them a struggle between "the clannish spirit" and "self-interest," for clan chiefs used their self-interest, through favors and threats, "for propagating among them a warlike and rapacious spirit" (*Scots Magazine* 1752c: 472). But if the chiefs could be "turned out of the possession of [their] estate," then people could take advantage of the long leases offered by the Act and "every such lessee's self-interest will operate directly against his clannish spirit." With this spiritual calculus in hand, Newcastle then argued that the individual Highlander on the annexed estates would be incentivized to improve his leased land (as previous generations of non-gentry farmers did in England). Newcastle concluded his speech in a "vision" statement:

> The improvement of the land of these forfeited estates is not therefore expected to arise from commissioners or managers to be appointed by the crown, but from the lessees for long terms under the crown; and it is by such lessees under ground-landlords, that the lands of England, and indeed in all countries have been improved.

Thus, the Act would drive a wedge between the Highland people, who would discover a new prosperity under the Crown, and their former clan leaders, who could only offer more uncertainty and war.

THE ANNEXING ACT: ITS CONTENTS

Parliament passed the Annexing Act, but its text reflected the English Lords' suspicion of the Scottish elite, expressed by both defenders and critics in the debate.

The Act is divided into two parts. The lengthier one deals in much detail with the actual transferring of the forfeited estates into the Crown's "unalienable" possession and the management of the estates once they are so transferred. It clearly was written as a response to the previous experience of forfeited estates after the 1715 rebellion, which eventually led to the return of many of these estates back into the hands of the Jacobite families. In fact, the Crown's act of inalienably annexing of a number of these estates was intended to literally put them beyond the reach of such a fate. Similarly, the length of the leases was to be standardized—twenty-one years, unconditional leases and up to forty-one years, conditional leases—to encourage investment, but not a sense of ownership. They were also not open to subleasing or absentee tenure. For the tenants were not only to be reliable rent payers, they were also to be "bulwarks" of government policy in the "wilds of the Highlands." Finally, factors were prohibited from charging the usual commissions (or bribes) for the leases: no one "shall pay or cause to be paid any gratuity or annual presentation for obtaining or holding such lease, other than the rent in the lease expressed" (*Scots Magazine* 1752a: 164).

In other words, the authors of the Act were conscious of the possibilities of conniving and corruption in the Highlands above and beyond the standard of eighteenth-century bureaucratic practice. They viewed the Highlands (if not all of Scotland) as a place of clannish loyalties, Jacobite politics and easily hidden (because distant) corruption. They also knew that the provisions of the Act might inadvertently reward treason and idleness under the guise of civilizing the Highlands and promoting improvement. To escape future accusations of coddling Jacobites or encouraging the Scottish will-to-power, they wanted to be as cautious as possible.

Consequently, though the Annexing Act and the work of its Commissioners is seen as one of the legislative achievements of the Scottish Enlightenment, there was a surprising lack of detail concerning the authors' of the Act mediate and long-term plans for the Highlands and, later, of the Commissioners as well.[6] For example, in Gilbert Eliot's papers devoted to his role as a Commissioner of the Annexed Estates over two decades the most complete plan is titled "Hints Toward a Plan for Managing the Forfeited Estates." Within it, there is a self-criticism, for the author of the plan writes that these are "outlines of a Proper Plan. But outlines are not sufficient."[7]

The effective structure of the Act is that the "clear produce of the [annexed] estates" (i.e., the rent and profit) was to provide the revenues necessary:

to the purposes of civilizing the inhabitants of the highlands and islands of Scotland, the promoting amongst them the Protestant religion, good government, industry and manufactures, and the principles of duty and loyalty to his Majesty, his heirs and successors, and to no other purpose whatever.

(*Scots Magazine* 1752a: 163)

How was the "civilizing and promoting," in this passage of the Act, or the "civilizing and improving," in the Abstract's synopsis, to be achieved? The Act's civilizing and improving mechanisms are the trinity of kirk, school and prison.

The Act's provision for the Highland *soul* deals with the possibility that the Commissioners might see it fit to set up new Presbyterian Church of Scotland parishes by dividing old ones, since some of the parishes on the estates were so large that even a hard-working minister could not reasonably deal with his "flock." The Act gives Commissioners rules to follow under such a circumstance which include the size of stipends for the new ministers (not more than £50 sterling per annum), what to do with the incumbent ministers (they continue on with their stipends even if they are above £50) and the division of the tithes (to be decided by the Court of Commission for Plantation of Kirks).

The Act's provision for the Highland *mind* was to support the erection of public schools in the Highlands "for instructing young persons in reading and writing English, and in the several branches of agriculture and manufactures." Additionally, the "produce of the estates" can be used to pay the salaries of teachers and the clothing, room and board of the students. Finally, the Commissioners are given permission to buy land for these schools (if they are not on the annexed estates) and "utensils and materials for agriculture and manufactures."

The Act's provision for the Highland *body* was to direct the Commissioners to:

cause prisons [to] be erected on the aforesaid estates, or other parts of the highlands or islands of Scotland; which shall be lawful prisons: and the commissioners are empowered to appoint jailors, with reasonable wages, and a proper allowance for indigent prisoners.

CIVILIZING AND/VERSUS IMPROVING

The institutions—kirk, school and prison—and their accompanying personnel—ministers, teachers and jailers—might provide the minimum matrix for the processes of civilizing and improving, but they hardly constitute a plan for a type of transformation that would "prevent disorders [in the Highlands] for the future." Was this lacuna simply due to the obvious nature of the processes involved or was it due to the lack of connecting links that the authors of the Act assumed the Commissioners would provide?

The answers to these questions are complex. The improving side of the project was no mystery to the English or Lowland Scottish authors of the Act. This was the "age of improvement," after all. Many members of Parliament and potential Commissioners were improving landlords and some even members of the "Honorable Society of Improvers" founded in Scotland in 1723. Improvement is an ideology that "had long been in use in the narrow economic sense of enhancing profitability, but its emergence as a wider cultural concept dates from the later seventeenth century" (Borsay 2002: 184). Even in the mid-eighteenth century, however, "improvement" was most directly identified with practices that increased agricultural productivity. Consequently, in this sense, the phrase "improving the Highlands" in the abstract of the Act would simply mean that by changing the conditions of land tenure (from the feudal and communal arrangements prevalent before the '45) and using the rents to increase the education of the next generation of farmers, agricultural productivity in the Highlands should increase. The Commissioners, as collective managers of the Crown's annexed estates, would be expected to demand from the tenants there the application of the same improving practices they instituted on their own lands.

In effect, the Act was meant to transform the Crown (via its representatives and agents, the Commissioners) into an ideal improving landlord who was to model on the annexed estates (which formed only a small, though central fraction of Highland territory) for the remaining Highland lairds the kind of estate management necessary to integrate their properties—their *oighreachd*—into the still largely agrarian capitalist system of Britain.[8]

The integration had to coordinate transformations on two levels. Many of the previous prevailing *relations of production* (from communal runrig farming to the multiple forms of land tenure—including ward, socage, mortification and blench) had to be abolished to be replaced by a form of land property open to swift and final alienation. This process was spurred by a legislative assault on Highland land tenure and legal practices after the '45 (or "lawlessness" as seen from the perspective of English landlords whose land had become completely commodified). Thus, the Act for the abolition of Heritable Jurisdictions in Scotland (20 Geo. II, c. 43) along with the Disarming Act, the Highland Dress Act and the Vesting Act that were immediately passed after Culloden—was meant to weaken the power of the local lairds who had almost monarchical powers in their clan lands. Heritable jurisdiction was a local authority that the clan leaders had to "mete out justice" among their clansmen independent of the national system of law courts. In effect, the "laws of the land" ended at the boundaries of the *duthchas*—the land settled by clan members who pledged allegiance to the chief. The abolition of the heritable jurisdictions shifted the legal authority in Scotland to "the court of session, court of justiciary at Edinburgh, the judges in the several circuits, and the courts of the sheriffs and stewards of shires or counties, and other of the King's courts in Scotland" (Horn and Ransome 1957: 189). Similarly, the institution of wardholding or "military tenures," that is, right to land tenure to be exchanged for military services, was also abolished with the effect that any presumed obligation to follow the chiefly landlord into war was legally nullified (although such a purely military basis for land tenure "had become anachronistic prior to the advent of Jacobitism" [Macinnes 1996: 215]).

The change in *relations of production* were to be matched with an increase in the agricultural *forces of production*. This too was no mystery to the authors of the Act and the potential Commissioners. The technological path to increased agricultural production and profitability had been tested for more than a century. The rotation of crops, the extensive and intensive use of manures (dung, lime, shell and potash), plowing where appropriate, the planting of new crops like turnips and flax, the draining of moors and many more techniques studied by improving Commissioners like Lord Kames were undoubtedly to be incentivized (Annette Smith 1982: 88–107). They certainly were to be taught to the children of the tenants of the annexed and other Highland estates. Since improving also involved commodification, the increased crops had to find a market. So the building of roads, bridges and inns were also going to be on the agenda of improvement of the Highlands.

These moves of improvement in the Highlands, explicit or implicit, inscribed in the Act were clear, but the means and ends of the project of "civilizing the Highlands" were less obvious. *For civilizing and improving are not the same thing.* Civilizing was not a process rooted in the economic experience of individual landlords in England and the Scottish Lowlands. It was a systemic social transformation. Neither did it operate estate-by-estate, field-by-field and tenant-by-tenant nor did it have a simple index like profitability. It might have happened to the English and to the Lowland Scots, but it was not planned by anyone. Improving of estates can be planned, but can the civilizing of a people? Were more kirks, schools and prisons enough?

The Annexing Act, however, made civilizing the Highlands the goal of state policy, the assumption being that there were plan-based "road maps" for both improving *and* civilizing. But was the assumption justified? If the Act had been passed in the 1760s, that would have been the case. By then there was a clear conception of the meaning of the verb "to civilize," which was formalized as a transition to the last stage (i.e., civilized or commercial and monetary society) of the classic "four stages" theory of social development—typified by the hunter, the herder, the farmer and the merchant—that is often identified as a central doctrine of the Scottish Enlightenment. That stadial formula was to be enunciated by Kames and Smith in a variety of works in the late 1750s and 1760s (Berry 1997: 116). The Highlanders, of course, were always confined in these works or others they influenced to one or more previous stages of history, or as Peter Womack put it, "what once we were" (Womack 1989: 23). But the Act was written at the very moment that the notion of civilizing was undergoing a profound change due to the work of David Hume. Kames, Smith and the other Scottish Enlightenment thinkers later formalized Hume's conceptual innovations.

By 1752, "to civilize" had a rather complex semantic genealogy. On the one side, the notion had its roots, as Norbert Elias has shown us, in the court and bourgeois cultures of the fifteenth through eighteenth centuries (Elias 1978). The key to the civilizing process was Simmelian mediation and the classic example being the increasing use of cutlery in refined eating that put the eater at a distance from the object of his/her consumption. This is the usage that is associated with politeness and civility as opposed to rudeness and brutality. On the other side, "to civilize" had roots in Civil or Roman Law, for it literally meant "to turn a criminal cause into a civil one" or a "common law into a civil law process," and was cognate with "civilian," that is, a teacher of Civil Law.[9]

What connection existed between the civilizing process as one that creates more and more moments of mediation between subject and object (ranging from hunger to sexual desire) and the process of transforming Common Law and criminal processes into Civil Law and processes? What brought together the polite court of Louis XIV and the Civil Law-dominated courts of Edinburgh? It was the work of the Scottish Enlightenment, especially David Hume's, that posed this question and answered it. For Hume, at least, the mediator of mediators was money. Thus, at the very moment when the project of civilizing the Highlands was becoming the object of the British state, Hume was fashioning a meeting point for these two meanings of civilizing.

MONEY AND CIVILIZATION

And I shall finish this essay on money, by proposing and explaining two observations, which may, perhaps serve to employ the thoughts of our speculative politicians. For to these only I all along address myself.
—David Hume, *Of Money* (1752)

The *Political Discourses* was largely written after the '45, when the discussion of "civilizing the Highlands" was reignited by the defeat of the Jacobite rebellion. Barely had the bodies of Cumberland's genocidal march across the Highlands been buried when General Bland, the Commander-in-Chief in Scotland, sent a paper titled "Proposals for Civilising the Highlands" to the *Caledonian Mercury* in June 1747. In the ensuing years, a draft bill that eventually became the Annexing Act circulated in the political circles of Scotland (Annette Smith 1982: 19–23). It was at this time that Hume finished and published his *Enquires*, the first in 1748 and the second in 1751, and the *Political Discourses* where he expressed his sensitivity to questions of intellectual division of labor and where he, as a philosophic second son, ought to "fit in."

Hume's job, as he expressed it, in debates concerning civilizing the Highlands or any other particular political issue was to interject "general reasonings" and "general principles" which, "if just and sound, must always prevail in the general course of things, though they may fail in the particular cases; and it is the chief business of philosophers to regard the general course of things" (Hume 1955: 4).[10] Thus, if Hume was to discuss the civilization of the Highlands, he would properly deal with it by discussing civilizing as a general process and not just as a matter concerning the Highlands alone.

Hume's primary prescription in *Political Discourses* for any civilizing planner is "Improvement is not enough!" That is, any plan that limited itself to agricultural elements of improvement, especially in terms of technique, would not alone lead to the civilizing of the Highlands. As if envisioning the spread of crofting and consequent Highland Clearances of the nineteenth century, Hume warns in *Of Commerce* that there is a disastrous trap in improvement without civilization. If the bulk of the people in question apply themselves to agriculture and increase their skill and productivity without having access to commodities "which serve either to their pleasure or vanity," then "a habit of indolence prevails" (Hume 1995: 10).[11]

Three elements are needed beyond agricultural improvement in order to launch a civilization process: reform of the laws of property (justice), refinement of the arts (luxury), and monetary excitement and diffusion. Hume wrote extensively about property and refinement in his pre-1752 writings, but the *Political Discourses* put property and luxury in a monetary context and transformed the understanding of both. For money is neither luxury nor property *per se*, in the sense that it is not a source of pleasure in itself and its power is only actualized in its alienation.[12] But money brings the rules of property (justice) and the enjoyment of consumption (luxury) together in order to create the conditions for civilization. Thus, Hume in the *Political Discourses* warns the future Commissioners and other civilizers of the Highlands that, along with the abolition of pre-capitalist forms of land tenure and increased agricultural education, they must provide for a monetary strategy that would link up any agricultural productivity increases attendant on this abolition and education with an industrial and trade policy that would provide beyond-subsistence luxury commodities to the Highlanders.

More profoundly, Hume argues against what appeared to be a self-evident description of the problem of the Highlands to the Lords in Parliament—the conflict between "power and rentals" for the chiefs or between the "clannish spirit and [economic] self-interest" for the people. Lords like Newcastle and Russell assumed that there was a given dichotomy in the "breast" of each Highlander—clansman/*homo economicus*—and the point of Crown policy was to strengthen the side that would lead to "preventing disorders [in the Highlands] for the future." But, the point that Hume develops in his works from the *Treatise* to the *Discourses* is that there are no given dichotomies in a realm of artificial virtues (embodied in rules concerning property) and there is no given self to have an interest in before the establishment of the rules of property. *Homo economicus* is not a natural given, it must be constructed.

The famous "inconsistencies" of Hume's writings on money in the *Political Discourses* can be best understood in the context of the debate concerning the Annexing Act and the civilizing project. For Hume is often taken to be a quantity of money theorist, who then overwrote his theory by giving money an activist role in changing economic reality.[13] But this is to forget that Hume is a philosopher who, in the moral realm, sees money as a force in human life that can only be observed in accelerative action, for example, collisions and gravitational fields; for one of the key features of Newtonian mechanics is the importance of the difference between relative and accelerative motion. As long as there is no change in the rate of change, the quantity of money operates as if it was inconsequential—a "mere convention" like the decision to use Arabian or Roman methods of notation (Hume R 37)—just as the sense of motion disappears when the objects around one are moving at a uniform motion in the same direction. Once the quantity of money is changing, its forceful effects can be discerned. But there is no more inconstancy between the principles appropriate to money in a constant state and in an accelerative state than between the laws of kinematics and dynamics.

Hume in *Of Money* examines the impact of money when it is increasing *intensively* and when it is increasing *extensively* (R 37–40 and R 40–43 respectively) or, as he puts it in the conclusion of the essay, money *qua* the precious metals has an impact through their "gradual encrease, and their thorough concoction and circulation through the state" (R 46).

Thus, he argues that simply taking into account the monetary stuff and the commodity stuff in a country can never account for the prices in that society. For what is crucial is the extension of the field where money and commodities "meet" and "affect each other." Hume's application of this principle concerning the impact of the increase in the number of "contracts" "coin enters into" begins with the contrast between "rude, uncultivated ages" and "times of industry and refinement." In the former,

ere fancy has confounded her wants with those of nature, men, content with the produce of their fields, or with those rude improvements which they themselves can work upon them, have little occasion for exchange, at least for money, which, by agreement is the common measure of exchange.

(R 42)

In such a state, it appears that there is a scarcity of money, but the appearance is merely a consequence of "the manners and customs of the people." The scarcity of money is a "collateral effect" (i.e., there is little use of and for money) rather than a cause. But in the age of refinement, no one is satisfied with "what can be raised in their neighbourhood," and so "in this situation of society, the coin enters into many more contracts, and by that means is much more employed than in former [age]" (R 43). Thus, the crucial question is not how much money stuff there is in a society during the transition from an uncultivated to a refined, civilized state, but how many "collisions" between money and commodities in a given period and area there are; for the money supply can easily be expanded when needed, since "it is easy to mix gold or silver with a baser metal" (R 41).

The planner of civilization must provide for "the encouragement of trade and manufactures" not simply because of the usefulness of these activities in themselves, but as a spur to increasing the extension of the monetary field into the agricultural world which inevitably overshadows these sectors in the beginning of the transition. For the availability of foreign luxuries and manufactured commodities stimulate the fancy—the transcendent and transgressive element in human nature—to create the surpluses that make it possible for the farmers to bring an "overplus" to market. Without it, "They have no temptation, therefore, to increase their skill and industry; since they cannot exchange that superfluity for any commodities, which may serve either to their pleasure or vanity. A habit of indolence prevails" (R 10).

Hume also informs his audience of speculative politicians, some of whom are destined to be chosen Commissioners of the Annexed Estates (and, therefore, become magistrates), that "the good policy of the magistrate consists only in keeping [money], if possible, still increasing" (R 39). Although this is a general principle, it applies especially to the transition from a savage state to a refined one. For the problem with the conditions of the savage stage (dominated by hunters and fishers) and the subsistence agricultural stage is that they do not "excite the industry of mankind," to use George Berkeley's phrase. But increasing the quantity of money definitely has this effect whether it is "imported" or it comes from "operations on the money" (i.e., debasement). As Hume argues, "because, by that means, [the magistrate] keeps alive a spirit of industry in the nation, and encreases the stock of labour, in which consists all real power and riches" (R 39–40).

Hume provides a powerful description of excitation circuits activated by the "import" of money into a society.[14] At first, it is "confined to the coffers of a few persons," but soon it diffuses through the economy as increased wages, sales, investment and profit. Hume then asks the speculative politicians in his audience to step back and observe the whole: "It is easy to trace the money in its progress through the whole commonwealth; where we shall find, that it must first quicken the diligence of every individual, before it encrease the price of labour" (R: 21). The terms of the passage—"willingly submitted," "better," "greater," "with alacrity," "only whetted"—reveal a new level of excitation evoked by the flow of money which shifts the proportions between action, pleasure and indolence in the direction of action. Savage and barbarous nations tend to indolence, interrupted by fits of violence (which often cannot even be called "war") while civilized ones tend to keep people in "perpetual occupation" interrupted by "those pleasures which are the fruit of their labour" (R 21). Thus, the civilizing Commissioner must find a way to keep an increasing flow of money directed to the Highlands, otherwise all efforts to civilize the Highlanders will be imperiled. For a decreasing level of money will likely lead to a return to "the poverty, and beggary, and sloth" that typified the Highlands before the '45 (at least in the imagination of the typical Lowlander and the Londoner) (R 40) (Womack 1989: 14–20).

Variations in the quantity of money and its field of impact are not the only financial elements relevant to the civilization process, the interest rate is crucial as well. Hume argues that this rate is determined not by the absolute quantity of money in a society, but "on the habits and way of living of the people" (R 50). The period "when people have emerged ever so little from a savage state" and proprietors of the land are dominant is typified by high interest arising from three conditions: "a great demand for borrowing; little riches to supply that demand; and great profits arising from commerce" (R 49). With the coming of commerce and the dominance of merchants, a low interest rate prevails due to exactly the opposite circumstances. Hume notes that in the transition from the age of landlords to the age of merchants there is an increase in the amount of money available in a society, as well, but it is not the cause of the fall of the interest rate. The increase in the quantity of money along with low interest is a collateral or concomitant effect of another cause: the flourishing of "luxury, therefore, manufactures, arts, industry, frugality" (R 57 and 59). Consequently, if the Commissioners try to impose low interest rates in the Highlands, they would be mistaken, since the interest rate is an index of civilization, not its cause: "And thus, if we consider the whole connexion of causes and effects, interest is the barometer of the state, and its lowness is a sign almost infallible of the flourishing condition of a people" (R 55).[15] But like the barometer (and unlike the ruler), the interest rate measures a complex quantity whose main significance lies in its relative readings.

Hume instructs the civilizer to attend to property relations and to be sure that there is effective demand for and supply of manufactured luxury goods. But the civilizer must also be sure that there is an appropriate monetary climate, with an increasing quantity of money and an ever-expanding monetary field. Hume warns, however, that the average rate of interest would be his measurement of success or failure, not a lever to bring about civilization, any more than a barometer can change the air pressure.

CLANNISH SPIRIT AND SELF-INTEREST: THE MARRIAGE OF THE WIDOWED MOTHER

My father ... died when I was an infant, leaving me, with an elder brother and a sister, under the care of our mother, a woman of singular merit, who, though young and handsome, devoted herself entirely to the rearing and educating of her children.
—David Hume, *My Own Life* (1777) [Hume 1987: xxxi–xli]

Why should money, commerce and luxury play such an important role in the transition from a savage to a civilized society (in Hume's terms) or in the destruction of the clannish spirit and the development of civilized self-interest (to put it in the terms of Newcastle's House of Lords speech)? Hume in his *Treatise* created the tools for an answer to this question which he applied a decade later in the *Political Discourses*. For the contrast between civilized and pre-civilized society is not simply one of unadulterated good versus evil. Hume clearly preferred commercial civilized society, but he did understand societies based on the power of family and friendship and the gift economy that sustained them. He contrasted, for example, "interested" and "disinterested" commerce in the *Treatise* in the following way:

> But tho' this self-interested commerce of men begins to take place, and to predominate in society, it does not entirely abolish the more generous and noble intercourse of friendship and good offices. I may still do services to such persons as I love, and more particularly acquainted with, without any prospect of advantage; and they may make me a return in the same manner, without any view but that of recompensating my past services.
>
> (T 335)

Much of this disinterested commerce, however, arises from the limited generosity that arises from the family and "the natural appetite betwixt the sexes" that produces it. But, as it often occurs in Hume's thought, this limited generosity of the family, though the "original principle of human society" is at a certain point the greatest block to the development of society:

> But tho' this generosity must be acknowledg'd to the honour of human nature, we may at the same time remark, that so noble an affection, instead of fitting men for large societies, is almost contrary to them … [each person's] love to others bears the greatest affection to his relations and acquaintance, this must necessarily produce an opposition of passions, and consequent opposition of action; which cannot but be dangerous to the new-establish'd [social] union.
>
> (T 313)

Undoubtedly, the clannish spirit that Newcastle evoked in his remarks is rooted in a familial experience of a common life of production and protection in the Highlands. It bears for Hume, however, all the signs of a stage of society that is original (even honorable and noble), but which is an enemy of a large commercial society for its monetary basis emphasizes abstractness and universality.

As Macinnes notes, "*A'Chlann*/the clan, literally the children, as a political, social and cultural entity was the collective product of feudalism, kinship and local association … the primary value of clanship was protection" (Macinnes 1996: 1–2). There was a patriarchal (and, at times, matriarchal) character within the clan along with a communal one. But whatever their proportions, there was an undeniable (and, for many, attractive) "family feeling" in the Highland clans as late as the eighteenth century.

Any strategy to end the clannish spirit must take into account this love of relations and affectionate sense of kinship that animates it. One can destroy the clan through genocide, but anything short of its physical elimination would have to consider this love and find a way to turn it into hatred, indifference or distraction. If the destruction of the clan spirit (and not its body) is essential to monetary civilization, then Hume needed a theory of the clan *qua* family.

Hume implicitly outlined a path to the disintegration of the clannish spirit in Book II of the *Treatise* in the section on the family, "Of the love of relations." For in that section Hume points out:

> Whoever is united to us by any connexion is always sure of a share of our love, proportion'd to the connexion, without enquiring into his other qualities. Thus the relation of blood produces the strongest tie the mind is capable of in the love of parents to their children, and a lesser degree of the same affection, as the relation lessens.
>
> (T 228)

Is this love of family natural and beyond manipulation? If that were the case, then the genocide of the clans or the transport of the members to the colonial world would be the only way to civilize the Highlands. But family feeling is not a given, it is rooted in the idea of ourselves which "conveys a sensible degree of vivacity to the idea of any other object, to which we are related" (T 229). If the objects we are related to change, then so do our feelings of love. But in most cases that involves a physical transportation away from the previous objects of our relation. In lieu of such a violent transformation, Hume notes a more subtle way to change the mental environment.

According to Hume's passionate dynamics, in order for two ideas, A and B, to "produce a perfect relation" not only must the imagination be conveyed from A to B by resemblance, contiguity or causation, "but also that it return back from [B] to [A] with the same ease and facility" (T 230). It would appear that each of these relations are "reciprocal," and indeed they are; so it would appear that their bond is not open to change. But then Hume locates a mistake in this reasoning:

> For supposing the second object [our B], beside its reciprocal relation to the first [our A], to have a strong relation to a third object [C]; in that

case the thought passing from the first object to the second, returns not back with the same facility, tho' the relation continues the same; but is readily carry'd on to the third object, by means of the new relation, which presents itself, and gives a new impulse to the imagination.

(T 230)

The "new" situation can be seen in Table 2.1 (where the numbers are the transition weights):

Table 2.1 Diagram of Hume's theory of the transition of energetic states

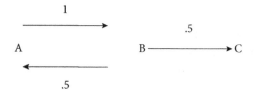

The imagination passes from A to B and then, instead of automatically going back to A, it often goes on to C, thus breaking the self-enclosed loop—"the double motion is a kind of double tie, and binds the objects together in the closest and most intimate manner"—kinship (the clannish spirit) imposes. "This new relation, therefore, weakens the tie betwixt the first and second objects" (T 230).

Hume uses a powerful quasi-Oedipal example to illustrate this breaking of the kinship loop: the differential impact that the remarriage of a widowed father and a widowed mother has on their children. The children of the remarried widowed mother no longer think of their mother and then return to think of themselves as they did before her remarriage, but "the ties of interest and duty bind her to another family and prevent that return of the fancy from her to myself, which is necessary to support the union" (T 230). This does not happen with the marriage of a widowed father,

when my imagination goes from myself to my father, it passes not so readily from him to his second wife, nor considers him as entering into a different family, but as continuing the head of that family, of which I am myself a part.

(T 231)

Without the ability of providing a "third object" to the members of the clan, the kinship loop will never break down by itself. "Disinterested commerce" would forever delay the flourishing of "interested commerce." This is why the introduction of trade, luxury and money are so important to the civilization process for Hume. They provide a potential infinity of pleasurable "third objects" and a universal method of access to these pleasures; their presence makes it possible for the clannish system to disintegrate from within. For once one's imagination passes from one's self to one's clan relation and then, instead of returning, it goes on to the other clan member's possessions and money which give him the power of acquiring new property that pleases outside of the clan environment, the circuit is broken. In this situation, one no longer gets that clannish excitement of loving, protective self-reflection from the other, but another kind of excitement, that of opening to a realm of pleasures and the spirit of action in a world of strangers. As Hume points out in *Political Discourses*, in transitions from a clannish society to a civilized one, foreign trade is always crucial:

> If we consult history, we shall find, that, in most nations, foreign trade has preceded any refinement in home manufactures, and given birth to domestic luxury ... And this perhaps is the chief advantage which arises from a commerce with strangers. It rouses men from their indolence; and presenting the gayer and more opulent part of the nation with objects of luxury, which they never before dreamed of, raises in them a desire of a more splendid way of life than what their ancestors enjoyed.
>
> (R 13–14)

Money is crucial in this transition, for it *is* the language of strangers. Since it provides a common representation not only among a world of previously undreamed of objects of luxury, but also between previously unmet people. The clan cannot not speak it (Wennerlind 2001: 145).

HUME AND THE ANNEXING ACT

Given the connection between civilization and money as expressed in the *Political Discourses*, can we conclude that Hume approved of the Act? The fact, attested to by the Duke of Newcastle, that the whole Scottish Parliamentary delegation supported the Act does not necessarily imply anything about Hume's views, nor does the fact that two of his oldest friends, Lords Kames and Minto, became active Commissioners of the Annexed Estates. Although Hume shared many of the immediate and long-term goals of his Scottish Enlightenment and ruling class colleagues, he was no conformist. For example, Hume was suspicious of branch banks and paper currency, and he was positively apocalyptic about the threats posed by Britain's public debt even though most of the members of his circle were quite positive about these aspects of contemporary economic life.

The Annexing Act is one of the earliest examples of what now is called "nation-building," that is, the conquering power takes the planning of the vanquished society into its hands. It was most familiarly practiced by the USA in West Germany and Japan after World War Two and in Iraq and Afghanistan at the beginning of the twenty-first century. Although we know that Hume approved of civilizing the Highlands (among many other places), some commentators like R.H. Campbell would argue that Hume *qua* member of the Scottish Enlightenment should be doctrinally opposed to an exercise of "nation-building" which relied on nationalized property (Campbell 1982). But we must be careful not to impose the ideological debates of the twentieth century on Hume. For him, the principled political divide is not between a free market versus a state-regulated economy, but between the republican and the monarchical parts of the British constitution represented by the Country and Court parties respectively (Hume 1768: 61–62). Clearly, the Annexing Act was a major extension of the "monarchical" power and it is not surprising that an old Country politician like Pulteney would use harsh terms like "Turkish empire" and "bashaw" in describing it. On the other side, the drafters of the Act and its defenders emphasized the "national security" aspects of the legislation, that is, "preventing disorders [in the Highlands] for the future," since such a concern is clearly in the realm of the monarch prerogative.

Thus, Hume's attitude to the Annexing Act's appropriateness and effectiveness would be determined by his attitude to the republican/monarchical divide in British politics. But the political thrust of *Political Discourses* was meant to promote a "coalition of parties" (which is Hume's post-Culloden version of "the end of ideology"). By 1752, he was anxious to undermine the philosophical and historical disputes between the parties that led to civil wars and revolutions like the '45. That effort required keeping a balance between the divided constitutional principles and rejecting "the spirit of innovation [which] is in itself pernicious, however favourable its particular object may sometimes appear" (Hume 1768: 520). Hume's criterion of judgment would then be not whether the Act was republican or monarchical, but whether it was *destabilizing* the balance between these two constitutional elements.

The Annexing Act was certainly an innovation with a favorable object, that is, civilizing and pacifying the Highlands. But it could be seen as pernicious to the constitutional balance, since it put the Crown in direct control of a sizable territory and population with an open-ended brief that, as Russell put it, "is to be always doing, but never done." Hume was already deeply concerned about the impact of the national debt which was tending to make the king "absolute master," since he was the only power in the state capable of negotiating with the increasingly powerful annuitants (Hume 1955). The Annexing Act would intensify the tendency to overstimulate the king's power and make him a Turkish "Grand Signior" with his own lands, "bashaws" and a new bred of tenants who receive their access to land at the King's pleasure. Consequently, there is good reason to believe that Hume supported his colleagues on the Militia issue, but he was probably dubious about the Annexing Act's means, even though he undoubtedly supported its civilizing ends.

3

Hume's Monetary Education in Bristol

Students of Hume's life invariably take his approximately six months in Bristol (roughly between March and August 1734) as an inconsequential moment in his life. The Bristol period is usually treated as an odd way station between his early life in Scotland and his time of intensive thought and writing in France that led to the publication in 1739 of the first two books of *A Treatise of Human Nature*.

However, given the focus of this book, Hume's *first and only* direct experience of international trade (assuming that the eighteenth-century book trade in Britain that Hume was deeply involved in was largely oriented to the domestic market) must loom much larger. Indeed, given the recent revaluation of the *Treatise*, Hume's writings on commercial life and the impact of international trade on human nature are no longer relegated by Hume scholars to the 1752 *Political Discourses*. The *Treatise* is itself seen as a major contribution to the development of the conceptual infra-structure crucial for the kind of self-reflection necessary to live in a commercial capitalist society (Finlay 2007; Wennerlind 2005). Consequently, there is good reason to believe that many of Hume's intellectual projects were shaped by his experiences in Bristol immediately before his intense period of work on the *Treatise*.

In this chapter, I am presenting evidence for a fuller portrait of how Hume's position in Michael Miller's sugar trade (and hence slavery-based) establishment might have affected the twenty-three year old, who came to Bristol thinking to escape the psychological crisis he faced in 1733–1734. He wrote to an unknown physician, perhaps Arbuthnot or Cheyne, about this crisis and his therapy:

> I therefore fix my choice upon a considerable Trader in Bristol, I am just now hastening thither, with a Resolution to forget myself & every thing that is past, to engage myself, as far as is possible, in that Course of Life,

& to toss about the World, from one Pole to the other, till I leave this Distemper behind me.

(Mossner 1954: 88)

This entrance into the active life of international trade was intended to be for the young Hume a sort of behavioral shock therapy.

It appears that Hume, if he stayed true to his Resolution in his letter, found a way to leave his Distemper behind him in Bristol and return to his studies and writing for five years (1734–1739) in France. This is not a small matter, knowing the potentially destructive consequences of depression on young adults. So what did Hume find in Bristol that had such a salubrious effect?

1. MICHAEL MILLER, "AN EMINENT MERCHANT" IN BRISTOL

The first thing he confronted on arriving in Bristol was his boss, Michael Miller. What impressions would Hume have received in meeting this "considerable Trader"? For example, how old was he? I have no clear evidence of the date of his birth, but he died in 24 May 1785 (Minchinton 1957: 26).

There is also good evidence that he was the father of Michael Miller, junior, on the basis of a 1789 document in the National Archives (AC/S/38) that states: "Release George Tierney of Burton St., London, and Anna Maria his wife (granddaughter of Michael Miller the elder and d'ter of Michael Miller the younger...). Michael Miller the younger joined the Merchant Venturers of Bristol in 1765 (on payment of a "fine" of 150 pounds sterling), he later became "Master" of the Venturers in 1778 and the next year he became mayor of Bristol. He died in the middle of his mayoral tenure in 1780.

Michael Miller, Senior in 1734 had another fifty-one years of life and he also had a son who was to be of a mature age thirty-one years later (i.e., ready to take over his father's business and so anxious to join the Merchant Venturers, an organization that his father was either unwilling or unable to join). Given these circumstantial bits of evidence, Michael Miller was probably in his thirties in 1734, vigorous and decisive, a man from the "active" side of life that Hume was interested in investigating since, after all, Hume came from people with landed property and a metropolis, Edinburgh, centered on the business of state (especially the law, as his father and many of his closest associated practiced it).

69

Michael Miller was a no-nonsense business-first fellow, if we can tell from his letters and his voting behavior. We have a number of letters from him to his MP representative, Sir Jarrit Smith, for example, where he reveals himself to be "no respecter of persons." Thus, in a letter of 1761 he writes to Smith that he, Smith, will be expected to pay as "a fund for future services in defending our Society as their Stock had been entirely exhausted for your election" and suggesting that some of this money be found from our "Tyger privateer" (a letter from Michael Miller to Sir Jarrit Smith, MP, in AC/C/110_1–24). The "society" referred to here was the society of Bristol merchants, somewhat akin to today's Chamber of Commerce, which having sponsored Smith's election expected recompense. The "Tyger privateer" in question referred to the mercenary forces given a pass to attack and pillage enemy ships; in effect practicing a form of state-sanctioned piracy.

We also know something about him due to the fact that there was a Parliamentary election on May 14–24, 1734 that was contested and so there was an official Parliamentary inquiry into the election results (see Latimer 1970 [1893]: 188–189). The election took place in the aftermath of the Excise Crisis and Walpole's retraction of the Excise Scheme in 1733. (The Excise Scheme being Walpole's dramatic expansion of the number of commodities that would be subject to a "sales tax." In order to police the tax collected, a whole new division of "excisemen" was to be recruited.) Most of the merchant class in Bristol opposed the scheme (at least as applied to sugar and molasses, the principal commodities of the port). However, John Scrope (also known as John Scoope) was an MP from Bristol and had been Walpole's Secretary to the Treasury. Inevitably, he was an energetic supporter of Walpole's scheme. Miller voted for Scrope's opponent Thomas Coster, who openly rejected the Excise Scheme. Examining *An Alphabetical List of the Freeholders and Burgesses of the Several Parishes of the City and County of Bristol whole Polled at the Election in the Year 1734 ...* (London 1734), I find there are almost *no votes for both Scrope and Coster*, but there are many votes for both Scrope and Elton and both Elton and Coster. Miller voted only for one MP, Coster. He was not willing to vote for the popular (and vacillating?) Abraham Elton. Michael Miller apparently wanted his vote to speak for his position; he did not want to dilute it.

Thus, the man who was to be Hume's entree to the mercantile world was a tough merchant, who had his priorities and the measure of his success in achieving them clearly defined, in short, money. If he were at all typical, he would have shared the features that Kenneth Morgan presented in his collective portrait of fifty Bristol West India Sugar Merchants in the eighteenth century:

** "most sugar merchants under review were drawn from the commercial bourgeoisie and artisan classes";
** "nearly half of the recruits were channeled into merchant houses trading with the West Indies that their fathers had established";
** "All of the merchant investors were involved in mergers, sales and changes of ownership" of West Indian plantations, and half were owners of slave plantations;
** "The goals of this merchant group seem to have been familiar ones: the pursuit of wealth, respectability, and comfort";
** The sugar merchants tended to pass the ownership of their firms to their children (a characteristic not found with the tobacco merchants).

(Morgan 1992: 189, 190, 192, 200 and 202)

Less dispassionate references to typical Bristol merchants can be found in the contemporary literature. Thus, in the 1742 edition of Defoe's *Tour*, after discussing the narrowness of the streets of Bristol, the editors go on to say:

… we might mention also another Narrow, that is, the Minds of the Generality of its People; for, let me tell you, the Merchants of Bristol, tho' very rich, are not like the Merchants of London; The latter may be said (as old of the merchants of Tyre) to vie with the Princes of the Earth; whereas the former, being rais'd by good fortune, and Prizes taken in the Wars, from Masters of Ships, and blunt tars, have imbib'd the Manners of those rough Gentlemen so strongly, that they transmit it to their Descendents, only with a little more of the Sordid than is generally to be found among British sailors…

(Quoted in Marcy 1966: 29)

He, of course, would have had his prejudices about Scotsmen, shaped by the popular attitudes of the time that in their turn had been in formation for centuries. Certainly the stage Scotsmen of Elizabethan times, for example, were typically "comical, alien, dangerous and uncivilized people—as Frenchmen who spoke a form of English, perhaps" (Braumuller 1997: 9).

The Scot and Scotland of Elizabethan times were figures of fun … and fear. For example, the famous historian of that period, Raphael Holinshed, wrote of the original Scots, that Roman historians "do seeme to speake of a parcel of the Irish nation that should inhabit Britaine in their time, which were given to the eating of mans flesh" (quoted in Braumuller 1997: 11). Scots began as cannibals and continued on to be violent and treacherous "backstabbers."

Shakespeare's *Macbeth* marked the time in the English dramatic world when Scotsmen stopped being figures of fun and turned into tragic villains, who would assassinate their proper superiors "to get ahead." Indeed, Scotland itself in Shakespeare's landscape is a dark place overflowing with witchcraft, mayhem and murder. When Macduff, a refugee in London escaping from Macbeth's wrath, asks the newly arrived noble Ross, "Stands Scotland where it did?" Ross responds:

> Alas poor country
> Almost afraid to know itself. It cannot
> Be called our mother, but our grave, where nothing
> But who knows nothing is once seen to smile;
> Where sighs and moans and shrieks that rent the air
> Are made, not marked; where violent sorrow seems
> A modern ecstasy.
> (Shakespeare, Act 4, sc. 3, lines 88–95, in Braumuller 1997: 151)

A century later, this stereotype was reinforced by the invasions and risings from the north by the Covenanters in 1640 and 1644 and then by the Jacobites in 1709, 1715 and 1719. The pamphlet literature of the early eighteenth century was filled with depictions of Scots as devious and violent, and, above all, committed to undermining English interests. This negative view of Scots ebbed and flowed throughout the eighteenth century. The 1707 Act of Union certainly did not end it. As McGaughy concludes his study of English attitudes toward Scots in this period: "Scottophobia remained ensconced in the minds of Englishmen, and would color how they perceived events involving the Scots for many years following 1707" (McGaughy 2008: 93).

In 1734, this "Scottophobia" would undoubtedly have been prominent in the minds of Bristol merchants like Michael Miller because they had real anxieties concerning the competition inspired by Scottish merchants who were only at this time beginning to cut into the tobacco, sugar and slave trades some twenty-seven years after the Act of Union that opened up a duty-free zone between Scotland and England. It also designated Scottish ships to be British, hence they could trade in the Americas and be protected by the British navy. These provisions made Glasgow, for one, a direct competitor to Bristol on the Western Coast, especially given the widespread smuggling and excise evasion that was taking place in the Scottish port:

> Where the Scots excelled was in undercutting their English rivals by developing smuggling on a grand scale ... In the tobacco trade most of the systematic fraud involved conspiracies between merchants and customs officers persistently to underweigh incoming cargoes. One estimate suggests that in the two decades after the union Scottish merchants were probably paying duty on only a half to two-thirds of their colonial imports.
>
> (Devine 1993: 57)

This sharp dealing was another confirmation of the suspicions English merchants had toward their Scottish rivals who were gearing up to take a major share of the trans-Atlantic trade. In fact, it was English merchants' protest against this smuggling that led to the professionalization of the customs bureaucracy and the widespread assumption that "Scottish success was at the expense of English merchants" (Devine 1993: 59).

Given the above, one wonders why Miller decided to take on a young Scotsman as something of an apprentice. For all he knew, Hume could be training in order to return to Scotland and increase the mercantile acumen of Miller's Scottish competitors. What did he make of his new employee once he arrived on the scene? Hume had, as he wrote, "got a Recommendation to a considerable Trader, [i.e., Michael Miller]" (Hume 1932: 18). Assuming he got this recommendation from someone close to him or his family, it is a sign that Miller had Scottish connections. This should not be surprising since merchants like Miller were hard-headed enough to know that though the Scots merchants were competitors, they were also increasingly clients and colleagues.

Scots were clients of traders in the Caribbean and North America like Miller, in that by 1734 Scots were the major source of personnel in a "range of activities including planting, trading, medicine and politics" in the Caribbean (Hamilton 2005: 4). In the first third of the eighteenth century, "Scots were prominent among the grantees receiving estates of over 100 acres" in the

Caribbean while "[i]n the North American colonies, the Scottish presence grew similarly ... perhaps most notably in the Chesapeake, where Glasgow merchants played an increasingly important role in the tobacco trade from the 1740s" (Hamilton 2005: 4). Miller would undoubtedly have developed trade relations with Scottish planters in the sugar colonies, and the planters in turn would have had members of their "network" in Edinburgh who could vouch for Hume.

Scots were also becoming merchant colleagues, for many Scots who repatriated back across the Atlantic (with their profits, but without their slaves, due to court decisions that banned the presence of slaves on British soil) did not always settle back in Scotland. Indeed, they increasingly chose to continue their business in the south-west of England, which had Bristol as its commercial center. This Scottish–Bristol connection was to become a commonplace in the last half of the eighteenth century but, by the 1730s, there would be the beginning of such a connection. Scottophobe or not, Miller might have recognized the importance for his business to have a good relationship with Hume's referees who might become his neighbors.

2. WHAT DID HUME FEEL AS THE OBJECT OF SCOTTOPHOBIA?

The first thing that Hume would have experienced in Bristol was that although he was a Briton, given the 1707 Treaty of Union between England and Scotland, he was still a stranger in a strange land. His language (especially his pronunciation) and his behavior would have immediately indicated to Bristolians that he was a Scot and therefore a target of "Scottophobia." I have some objections to the term for it psychologizes, even psychologizes away, the prejudicial attitudes of English men to Scots without adding the structural forces that shaped and reinforced these attitudes. Be that as it may, the hostility Hume experienced, whatever the causes, was quite concrete. Given that Hume's stay in Bristol was the first time he spent a long period in England, the pervasive Scottophobia left a deep impression on him, and a negative one at that, which he memorialized in a number of famous quips. In fact, it is interesting that though many Scots (including many from the elite) went to the Caribbean (perhaps as many as 17,000 in the period between 1750 and 1799, Hamilton 2005: 24) comparatively few took up residence in England.

Figure 3.1 "Sawney Weatherbeaten or Judas Iscariot": An uncivilized wretch in traditional Highlander garb, the character of "Sawney" was popular in the London press throughout the eighteenth century and was often used to caricature specific political figures of Scottish origin. In this engraving, published in 1792 by William Holland, Sawney displaces a pig at a scratching post. Newly arrived to London with "fraud in his heart and famine in his face" Sawney is prepared to "sell my King and any God for gold."

Figure 3.2 Among the many racist caricatures of the Scots published from London in the eighteenth century was a popular motif representing "Sawney in the Bog House"; a Highlander come to London using the "bog-house" for the first time. This image dates from 1745, the year of the Jacobite uprisings and is associated with the workshop of William Hogarth.

Figure 3.3 Among the many racist caricatures of the Scots published from London in the eighteenth century was a popular motif representing "Sawney in the Bog House"; a Highlander come to London using the "bog-house" for the first time. This image is also from 1745 and contains a verse inscription in a parody of Scots dialect: "To London Sawney came, Who, from his Birth,/ Had dropt his Folio Gates on Mother Earth;/Shewn to a Boghouse, gaz'd with wondring Eyes;/ Then down each Venthole thrust his brawny Thighs;/ And squeezing cry'd— Sawney's a Laird I trow./Never did he nobly disembarge till now."

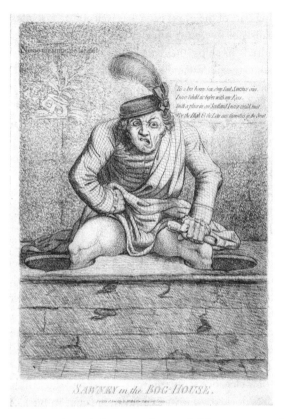

Figure 3.4 From 1745 through the 1790s, the motif of Sawney appears frequently in popular print. In this image from 1779, Sawney declaims "'Tis a bra' bonny seat, o' my saul, Sawney cries,/ I never beheld sic before with me Eyes,/ Such a place in aw' Scotland I never could meet,/ For the High and the Low ease themselves in the Street." Behind him on the wall is seen the motto and insignia of the Stewarts and Sawney clasps in his hand a document which reading, "Act for establishing Popery" a parody of the perceived Catholicism of the Jacobite rebellions. Collection of the author.

3. WHAT DID HUME SEE?

The first thing that Hume saw on arriving in Bristol was a thriving commercial town very different from the city Hume knew well, Edinburgh, which was an archaic center of political power—it was a bustling city that, however, was on the decline in 1734.

The bustling part of the impression was well attested to. Alexander Pope, on a visit to Bristol five years after Hume's arrival, wrote: "as far as you can see, hundreds of ships, their masts as thick as they can stand by one another, which is the oddest and most surprising sight imaginable" (quoted in Morgan 1993: 33).

Bristol was also being architecturally transformed during the time of Hume's arrival. The remarkable (and unlikely) rise of Bristol as the second port and second city of Britain was being finalized in stone.

Most decisive in this transformation was the construction of Queen Square that began in 1699, at a time when it was called "The Marsh," that is, a terrain of "void" and "common" space used by the commoners of Bristol in the beginning of the eighteenth century for their pleasure and subsistence. "Most of the void ground bordering the square was leased out and built upon within the period 1700–18" (Ison 1952: 143). By 1734, the Square, however, had been completely built around and Hume's employer's firm (and home) was located on 15 Queen Street (appropriately, a Barclay's Bank branch is now at that address). There was a carefully preserved uniformity in the buildings of Queen Square that William Halfpenny captures. As Ison describes it, a new "capitalist common" created by "the continuous lines of three-storied house fronts of red brick dressed with freestone" (Ison 1952: 145). Indeed, one can see the direct connection with and proximity between the new elegance acquired from "trade" and those filthy vehicles of sugar and slaves docked a few yards away in the quay in Buck's "North West Prospect of Bristol" (1734) sitting at odd angles when the tide flowed out (see Hughes et al. 1996: 21).

Indeed, when Hume would leave the premises of his employer at this time, he would be seeing in front of him the slow (some would say, agonizing) construction of an equestrian statue of King William III, the nemesis of the Jacobites and non-juring Tories, in the center of Queen Square. How is that for gender politics!

Bristol was an unapologetic city of trade and power, but it was also a city of a merchant ruling class that was in the process of facing a mercantile crisis. It is not clear how widely and sharply this crisis was recognized, either among the urban proletariat of Bristol or the ruling class camped around King William III's phallic statue in the midst of Queen Square. But there was a noticeable decline in the number of ships and their tonnage entering Bristol from transatlantic destinations. Thus, in the three year period immediately before Hume's arrival (1729–1732), there were 147 ships and 15,061 tons while, in the five-year period (1733–1737), there were 130 ships with a total tonnage of 11,914, that is, an 11 percent drop in the number of ships and a 20 percent in tonnage. After a period of uninterrupted growth, Bristol trade began to face a classic mercantile crisis. As Kenneth Morgan writes:

> Most sectors of Bristol's overseas shipping declined in the early 1730s … Shipping in the West India trade was hit hardest, the tonnage arriving at Bristol from the Caribbean fell from 8,610 tons to 6,305—a 26.8 per cent drop—between 1727-32 and 1733-7. The large dip in the volume of Bristol West India trade resulted from a decline in the production and British importation of sugar at that time…
>
> (Morgan 1992: 16–18)

(Perhaps this decline led to Miller's involvement in wine importing in an attempt to diversify). Some merchants who were conscious of this decline blamed it on the competition (in the tobacco, sugar and slave trade) that Liverpudlian and *Scottish* merchants posed by providing the commodities at lower prices and taking lower commissions (Morgan 1992: 18). It would not have been surprising for Hume to hear his boss complaining of the conditions of the trade in this unexpected moment of downturn after a long period of uninterrupted success. Perhaps Miller let loose a Scottophobic remark or two in the process.

Hume was learning from the inside the duplicity and volatility of commercial life. For the refinement of commercial society is not straightforward accomplishment, however well the transition of passions into interests is managed.

4. WHAT DID HUME DO AS A CLERK IN MILLER'S SUGAR TRADE ESTABLISHMENT?

Hume described in his "crisis" letter his version of what he would like to happen in his new employment: "to toss about the World, from one Pole to the other" in the service of a sugar merchant. In the terminology of the times, Hume was describing the role of a supercargo or factor aboard ship in the Caribbean. This was quite different from being a sedentary clerk in an office in Bristol. The supercargo would arrive in Jamaica or another sugar

Figure 3.5   Hume in Bristol: the façade of 8 Queen's Street in Edinburgh where Hume worked in the offices of Michael Miller. Image courtesy of Wikicommons.

Figure 3.6   Hume in Bristol: the equestrian statue of King William III, the nemesis of the Jacobites and non-juring Tories, in the center of Queen's Square, which Hume would have seen each day on leaving work. Image courtesy of Wikicommons.

island and try to broker the best deal "on the spot." It inevitably had more drama and élan than the routine life of a clerk!

As *The Young Shopkeeper's, Steward's, and Factor's Companion* (Donne 1768) presents the difference in the following way:

> A steward may either be considered as a kind of factor, or clerk. If as a factor, he may conduct his books without an account of stock, but as then, the Lord will lose the Satisfaction of seeing the real Value of his Estates, etc., we have rather chosen to look on the Steward as a kind of Clerk, keeping the Books for his Master.
>
> (Donne 1768: 20)

So the key difference between Factor and Clerk is the ability to autonomously trade. As a clerk, there is no opportunity to earn extra income derived from "sharp dealing" (buying cheap and selling dear). But at the same time, the Factor has to face many liabilities a clerk does not. For example,

> If a Factor sells his Employer's Goods to a Man discredited, who proves insolvent before Payment: the Factor shall pay for the said Goods, unless he can prove it was not publickly known, and that he was ignorant of it, or trusted the Man for Goods of his own also.
>
> (Donne 1768: 36)

Indeed, the dramatic differences in the allowable commissions for Factors indicates the "risk premium" that different kinds of regions presented:

> In Jamaica, Barbadoes and most of the plantations, it is often 8, and sometimes 10 per Cent. In Aleppo, Smyrna, and other Parts of Turkey, it is commonly 3 per Cent. In Leghorn and other Parts of Italy, and in Britain, it runs at 2 ½ per Cent. In Spain, Portugal, France, Holland, Hamburg and Dantzick, at 2 per Cent.
>
> (Donne 1768: 36)

As a clerk, Hume's tasks were more routine. His job was not to follow the merchant's categorical imperative to Factors, that is, "Dispose of my Goods in the same Manner as if they were your own; or, Buy or sell, such Goods for me, as the Market goes, or at the Current Price, and act in every Respect as you would for yourself…" (Donn 1768: 36), and to keep Miller's books and expedite the firm's correspondence. Indeed, the job of the Factor or super-cargo in the sugar trade at least was increasingly giving way to a commission system. As Morgan writes of this period:

> Sugar was originally bought on the spot in the West Indies either by inde-pendent merchants or by supercargoes. From the late seventeenth century onwards, however, the emergence of large estates and sugar monoculture in the Caribbean, the rise of a substantial class of planters, and the con-centration of the economic interests of the West Indies upon England all helped to develop the growth of a commission trade in sugar. Under this system planters shipped their sugar to English merchants, who were usually paid 2 ½ per cent on the sales for selling the sugar and carrying out miscellaneous services.
>
> (Morgan 1992: 193)

I am not sure whether Miller's establishment was already working on a com-mission basis, but there is good evidence that it did. If so, there would be no opportunity for Hume to become a supercargo. But this would be true not only for Miller's establishment. The Jamaica trade had been operating on a commission basis long before 1750, the year when "most Bristol sugar merchants transacted business on commission" (Morgan 1992: 195). "This was particularly true in the Jamaica trade, in which Robert Lovell, William Miles, Michael Miller, John Curtis, Samuel Munckleu, Mark Davis, Protheroe & Claxton, and Davis & Protheroe were agents serving the needs of various plantations" (Morgan 1992: 195–196).

Though Hume's dream of being a decisive supercargo in the sugar trade was doomed, from his clerk's perspective, however, he was undoubtedly impressed by the kind of trust that developed in what appeared to be an extremely rough and tumble trade. After all, sugar buyers and sellers were separated by thousands of miles of ocean, sugar was produced in violent conditions of slavery, and sugar was hauled by sailors drawn from what Hume would consider to be "the dregs of humanity."

5. WHAT OF THE SUGAR TRADE?

By the time the young David Hume took on his duties as a clerk in Miller's sugar house, the sweetest commodity had become the object of a huge trade from the Caribbean increasingly to England. As Mintz writes:

In 1660, England consumed 1,000 hogsheads of sugar and exported 2,000. In 1700, she imported about 50,000 hogsheads and exported about 18,000, By 1730, 100,000 hogsheads were imported and 18,000 exported, and by 1753, when England imported 110,000 hogsheads, she re-exported only 6,000.

(Mintz 1985: 39)

Thus, one of the most marginal of commodities from the point of view of condimental history increasingly was becoming the central pole of capitalist accumulation as well as a staple in most households, from day laborers to aristocrats.

Miller's firm was involved in the import of many commodities, but it centered on sugar, a central commodity of world trade at the time. It taught remarkable lessons to alert students of human nature. For sugar posed many paradoxes to those like Hume who loved to spin and unwind them. The first paradox arose from the fact that the most profitable edible commodity of his time was not a dietary necessity. It was superfluous, that is, production and profit in a commercial world is determined more by fancy and pleasure than by reason and healthy satisfaction. As Kenneth Morgan writes: "there is no doubt that cane sugar from the Caribbean was the most valuable British import in the century and a half down to 1820" (Morgan 1992: 184). Hume would make much of this near Mandevillian paradox in his own notion of human nature, especially in his reversal and transvaluation of the hierarchy of passions and reason.

The second paradox arose from the fact that the most profitable form of production was to be found in small areas of intensive slave-labor cultivation in a torrid insect-infested region instead of large areas of extensive wage-labor cultivation in "temperate" zones. Sugar production was by no means a salubrious enterprise. What is profitable, therefore, is not obvious and taking risks is not folly, but an inductive enterprise.

Finally, sugar is a "luxury" commodity in the eighteenth century, for it clearly is not a product of subsistence agriculture in England or Scotland. Unlike the potato, another extra-European species, sugar will not grow in their climate and soil. Nor was there a slave workforce that would sow, cultivate, harvest and process the sugar. Hume, in his later work, was clearly in favor of these "luxury" commodities, since they awoke a passion for the surplus, that is, a desire motivating action to go beyond the mere satisfaction of needs and an allied over-valuation of "indolence" (Hume 1987: 269). This connection between pleasure and action is crucial for happiness, according to a later Hume, and is an explanation of how sugar *qua* substance became the product of a vast network Caribbean plantations, African villages, and British ships and ports.

6. WHAT OF THE SLAVE TRADE?

Hume was to become, by 1752 in the *Political Discourses*, an opponent of slave production (though by no means a non-racist, on the contrary). What did he learn of the slave trade in Bristol? One thing is not clear: was Michael Miller & Co. involved in the slave trade in 1734? A four-volume study, of *Bristol, Africa and the Eighteenth-Century Slave Trade*, edited by David Richardson, reveals that Michael Miller & Co. was the owner of vessels involved in eight slave trading voyages from Bristol.[1] These voyages begin in 1760 and continue on to at least 1768. There is no mention of Michael Miller in the first two or in the final volume of Richardson's opus.

This does not mean that Hume would not have learned about the slave trade. For Bristol was filled with slave traders and slave vessels. Bristol was by 1734 the ascendant (though beginning to decline) slave port of Britain. In 1734 alone, there were 34 vessels that were cleared for African slave trading destinations. Richardson writes:

> Throughout the 1730s the slave trade continued to attract large amounts of Bristol capital. At the peak of the port's involvement in slaving in 1730–32 and 1737–38, the sums invested were probably close to 200,000 pounds sterling annually; over the decade as a whole they perhaps averaged nearly 160,000 pounds annually.
>
> (Richardson 1987: xv)

There were Africans in Bristol in Hume's time, of course. From sailors to servants brought back from the West Indies when their masters returned to the home country. The year 1734 was also long before Lord Mansfield's famous ruling in the Somerset case of 1771 that ended with a ban on the presence of slaves in public in Britain.[2] Eickelmann and Small write:

The exact size of the population [of the black population] will never be known but in the early 1770s it was suggested that there were 14,000 or 15,000 black people in the whole country. The majority were said to have lived in London, and the rest mainly in the slaving ports of Liverpool and Bristol.

(Eickelmann and Small 2004: 47)

Dresser and Fleming were only able to document the existence of about 100 Africans in Bristol in the eighteenth century (2007: 87).

Hume would have seen the thrown off fragments from a machine that was grinding up millions thousands of miles away. Undoubtedly, for such an inquiring fellow the question of slavery would have become a major one in his mind while watching the coming and going of the black people who were quite rare in Edinburgh. Undoubtedly, the recent wave of slave revolts in the British Caribbean would have served as a hot and cautionary tale.

Figure 3.7 The Sugar Trade: "Barbarities in the West Indies," a satirical print by James Gillray published in London in 1791. The inscription reads, "B-t your black Eyes! what you can't work because you're not well?—but I'll give you a warm bath, to cure your Ague, & a Curry-combing afterwards to put Spunk into you."

7. WHAT WERE THE DECISIVE ISSUES THAT WERE BEING DISCUSSED IN BRISTOL AT THE TIME?

On arriving in Bristol, Hume would have been confronted with a number of issues that helped shape his controversial mind. Consider some of the most obvious. The abolition of slavery was still off most Bristolian tables as a topic of conversation in 1734, though with the Quaker and Methodist presence, it would have made it on the list of topics worthy of debate (if not action). But the electoral campaign pitting supporters and critics of the Excise scheme would have revived the complex debate concerning the excise.

Then there was the issue of impressment. It provided a key place in the *Gloucester Journal*: "With the Most Material Occurrences Foreign and Domestic" of May 7, 1734. There is a lead article in that issue that presents an argument against impressment using the notion of opportunity costs:

> The idleness alone, which great Numbers are kept to avoid their being impressed, such Constraint being disagreeable to human Nature, and more especially to Englishmen, is such a Loss to the Nation, as well as Injury to the Individuals, that all means ought to be embrassed to prevent it … This is in Reality a Tax upon the Subject, though not in the appearance of one, for he that prevents my gaining a shilling, equally injures me, as if he took it from me.
>
> (*Gloucester Journal* 1734)

Undoubtedly, Hume would have had a chance to read the *Gloucester Journal* since it was circulated in Bristol (being quite close to Gloucester). Hume had a number of friends in Bristol including John Peach, who went on to found the Bristol Library Society (Latimer 1970 [1893]: 403).

8. THE FAMOUS LETTER

I end this chapter with an important moment in Hume's monetary education: his unemployment and departure from his job as clerk in Bristol and return to the role of itinerant philosopher. We have no details as to his wages and working conditions. Did Michael Miller fire him? Did he quit? Was it an amicable parting? Hume was very cagy (through silence) about this issue in his "autobiography." He described his departure from Bristol curtly in the following sentence: "In 1734, I went to Bristol, with some recommendations to eminent merchants, but in a few months found that scene totally unsuitable to me" (Hume 1932: 1–2).

Then there is a letter between Dean Tucker and Lord Hailes (Sir David Dalrymple) that, since the nineteenth century, has been read to imply that Hume was continually quarreling with his boss over the correct way to write business letters. There is, of course, much irony in this tale, for here we have a Scot very self-conscious of his Scotticisms in the midst of southern England telling a self-confident English trader whose business spans the Atlantic how to write in his own language. Is this not a leitmotif connecting his political economic thinking and action with respect to the English merchant class and his philosophy of money? For Hume and his circle were quite skeptical of the English merchants' capacity to successfully run a global empire. They would have agreed with Eli Heckscher's judgment that England, even in 1931, "retains so much more of what is odd, inconsistent and haphazard in its social customs and industrial practices than any other civilized country" (Heckscher 1935: 2, 464).

PART II

Hume's Philosophy and his Strategy

David Hume left Bristol in the fall of 1734 and settled for almost three years in France where he wrote *A Treatise of Human Nature*. The book, however, "fell still-borne" from the press, attracting little attention, in large part because it did not directly confront the political problematics of the day. This failure inspired Hume's turn away from the academic treatise and embrace of the essay form as well as his use of the "philosophy of money" as a tool to address pressing political issues: the Jacobite rebellion; debates over the wages of Scottish workers; and the conflicts between specie or paper as the form of currency most appropriate to world empire. Part II shows how Hume's major philosophical insights—such as the distinction between natural and artificial virtues—served to accomplish the practical resolution to these problems.

4
Why was Hume a Metallist?

"Meanwhile, my good lad, here is a trifle for you to drink Vich Ia Vohr's health." The hawk's eye of Callum flashed delight upon a golden guinea with which these last words were accompanied He hastened, not without a curse on the intricacies of a Saxon breeches pocket, or spleuchan, as he called it, to deposit the treasure in his fob...
—Walter Scott, *Waverly; or, 'Tis Sixty Years Since* (Scott 1986: 146)

FUNCTIONALISM VERSUS METALLISM?

Hume's *Political Discourses* (1752) was his first immediate commercial publishing success—three editions were printed in two years—for it spoke directly to a vital concern of his central audience: the lawyers, lairds, academics and merchants of the Scottish Lowlands and Borderlands: money. Hume's book was one of the most sophisticated and elegant analyses of the functioning of money available until then. Indeed, a number of his sketches of monetary behavior, especially his hydraulic approach to the flows of money on the international market, have been shaped into paradigmatic textbook examples of economic reasoning since then (see, e.g., Case and Fair 1999: 854–855).

But modern textbooks do not assume, as Hume is widely thought to have assumed, that money was metallic, that is, gold and silver. This metallic assumption can be plainly seen in many passages of the *Political Discourses*. For example, in "Of Money" and "Of Interest" he writes as if this assumption were so obvious to the reader that there is no reason to make it explicit. Money and specie are elided in these chapters without much fuss:

It appears, that the want of money can never injure any state within itself: For men and commodities are the real strength of any community. It is the simple manner of living which here hurts the public by confining the gold and silver to few hands, and preventing its universal diffusion and circulation.

(R 45)

And these commodities [the merchant] will sometimes preserve in kind, or more commonly convert into money, which is their common representation. If gold and silver have increased in the state together with the industry, it will require a great quantity of these metals to represent a great quantity of commodities and labour. If industry alone has encreased, the prices of everything must sink, and a small quantity of specie will serve as a representation.

(R 52)

There are times when he contrasts metallic money with its alternatives in the *Political Discourses*, but always in a derogatory way. In "Of Money," he purposely contrasts the international acceptance of gold and silver with the doubts he entertains about "paper-credit":

That provisions and labour should become dear by the encrease of trade and money, is in many respects, an inconvenience; but an inconvenience that is unavoidable, and the effect of that public wealth and prosperity which are the end of all our wishes. It is compensated by the advantages, which we reap from the possession of these precious metals, and the weight, which they give the nation in all foreign wars and negociations. But there appears no reason for encreasing that inconvenience by a counterfeit money, which foreigners will not accept of in any payment, and which any great disorder in the state will reduce to nothing.

(R 35)

In "Of Public Credit," he disparagingly contrasts public securities with gold and silver (even though he categorizes paper-credit as a "species of money"):

Public Stocks, being a kind of paper-credit, have all the disadvantages attending that species of money. They banish gold and silver from the most considerable commerce of the state, reduce them to common circulation, and by that means render all provisions and labour dearer than otherwise they would be.

(R 95)

In "Of the Balance of Trade," he argues that paper money is not "real cash" and drives the level of silver and gold circulating in a country below its "natural level" (R 68).

Due to passages like these, historians of political economy and economics from Marx, to Schumpeter, to Vickers, to Laidler have read Hume as a "metallist." For example, Vickers includes Hume's name in something of a roll call of metallists: "Child, Petty, Locke, Cantillon, Hume and Harris were prominent metallists." Of course, we must be clear about what "metallism" means as a typological term (Vickers 1959: 31).[1] To do this let us turn to Schumpeter's definitions of two kinds of metallism, theoretical and practical:

> By theoretical metallism we denote the theory that it is logically essential for money to consist of, or to be "covered" by, some commodity so that the logical source of the exchange value or purchasing power of money is the exchange value or purchasing power of that commodity, considered independently of its monetary role.
>
> By practical metallism we shall denote sponsorship of a principle of monetary policy, namely, that the monetary unit "should" be kept firmly linked to, and freely interchangeable with, a given quantity of some commodity.
>
> (Schumpeter 1954: 288)

These are, of course, two quite different kinds of commitment. The former claims a logical or "analytic" connection between money and some commodity, while the latter calls for principled (moral and/or political) relation to hold between money and a particular commodity (which, in the nature of things, might only accidentally be realized precisely).

Schumpeter includes Hume in his list of theoretical metallists, which begins with Aristotle and ends with Marx. In particular, he argues that Hume's view of money's metallic essence was typical of the average monetary view of the period. He claims that Hume's view "differs from [Sir Josiah] Child's only in explicitness and polish," while Child, a mercantilist theorist and spokesman of the English cloth industry in the late seventeenth century,

> clearly identified money with those parts of the stocks of gold and silver that fill the monetary function and held that in spite of this function gold

and silver, coined or uncoined, still remained commodities exactly like "wine, oil, tobacco, cloth and stuff."

(Schumpeter 1954: 290–291)

Indeed, in his short discussion of Hume's central monetary text, the 1752 *Political Discourses*, Schumpeter dismisses any possibility of "novelty" in Hume's work, although he recognizes its "force and felicity."

Given the weight of the passages from Hume and the commentary literature, can there be any reasons to be skeptical about Schumpeter's categorization of Hume as a theoretical metallist? In this chapter, I argue that such doubts are indeed justified. Hume was never a theoretical metallist. However, there is no single category that easily subsumes his monetary ontology, for his views on money were philosophically complex and sensitive to economic developments, especially those transpiring in Scotland. In order to best locate Hume's view of money, one must situate Hume's monetary theory more deeply in the political project that he had embarked on in the *Political Discourses* and in the philosophy of money that he created to accomplish his aims. In so doing, I conclude that Hume was, paradoxically, a practical, not a theoretical metallist *in spite of* and *because of* the developments in Scottish society after the 1745 Jacobite rebellion.

The first source of doubt as to Hume's theoretical metallism is rooted in his attitude toward the eminent philosophers of money who immediately preceded him and with whose works he was quite familiar, Locke's contributions to the "recoinage debates" of 1696 and Berkeley's *The Querist* (1735–1737). Locke was a paradigmatic theoretical metallist who argued that, even if the full-weight recoinage of England's money supply did generate a deflation, it was worth it in order to keep the whole monetary system from collapsing due to the increasing gap between the coinage's face value and its actual clipped value. In brief, he argued that the idea of money was a compound of an idea of a mixed mode and the idea of a corporeal substance. For Locke, mixed modes are "Combinations of simple Ideas, as are not looked upon to be characteristical Marks of any real Beings that have a steady existence, but scattered and independent Ideas, put together by the Mind, are distinguished from the complex Ideas of Substances," while corporeal substances are "Combinations of simple Ideas, as are by Experience and Observation of Men's Senses taken notice of to exist together, and are therefore supposed to flow from the particular internal Constitution, or unknown Essence of that Substance."[2] The mixed mode aspect of money arose from its social and cultural use, while its material substance aspect allowed for its transcultural universal exchangeability. The gold and/or silver substances (and their primary qualities) constituting money gave it an objective status, a "standard made by nature," that could elicit agreement across languages and cultures.

Berkeley's notion of money was premised on his rejection of Locke's notion of material substance. From a Lockean perspective, Berkeley's espousal of a paper money system for Ireland was an attempt to identify money as a mixed mode alone; hence, it was doomed to catastrophe. But Berkeley's critique of material substance implied that any notion of money rooted in it, like Locke's, would be a will-o'-the-wisp. For Berkeley, according to a recent student of his monetary thought, "money was a mixed-mode notion stripped of any essential dependence on material corpuscular substances. Its purpose was to stimulate and regulate action, not to measure and store a quantity of specie" (Caffentzis 2000: 274). Money, by being a ticket, a counter, a token, a tally or a mark—all metaphors that Berkeley used to describe its function—escaped the impossible Lockean expectation of being beyond all interpretation and subjectivity, for the primary function of money was to "excite the industry of mankind."

These dichotomies matched the ontologies and concepts of money, which structured the field Hume entered in writing the *Political Discourses*. Hume's acceptance of Berkeley's critique of Locke's doctrines of substance, abstraction and primary qualities should have brought Hume to question the philosophical justification of Locke's metallism, namely, specie provides money with an objective naturalized substratum that makes international trade possible. What, then, would have brought Hume to embrace metallism? Given the binary structure of the philosophical/monetary field at the time, Hume's anti-substantialism seems to be an incoherent foundation for a metallist ontology of money, which presumes the existence of intrinsic values and objective properties. This tension prompts one to ask: Was Hume coherent throughout the range of his work? Was his philosophy compatible with his political economy as it intersected the monetary field? Could he consistently be a Berkeleyan-influenced skeptic concerning substance and an adherent of Locke's metallism? To answer these questions adequately, one must study monetary texts in conjunction with his philosophical ones.

Hume's philosophical writings certainly abound with kernels of pure anti-substantialism. From his radically anti-Cartesian account of the self or mind as "nothing but a heap or collection of different perceptions united together by certain relations and supposed, though falsely, to be endowed with a perfect simplicity or identity" to his critique of the "fiction" of substance as the result of the tendency to fallaciously homogenize small differences into identities, Hume quite self-consciously made the metaphysicians of substance something of the knights errant of philosophy (N 207 and N 220).[3] Thus, he writes of the proponents of substance:

> ... they seem to be in a very lamentable condition, and such as the poets have given us but a faint notion in their descriptions of the punishments of Sisyphus and Tantalus. For what can be imagined more tormenting, than to seek with eagerness, what for ever flies us; and seek for it in a place, where 'tis impossible it can ever exist?
>
> (N 223)

This anti-substantialism has been one of most attractive features of Hume's thought to those schools of philosophy that rage against schools. Thus, earlier on in the recently past twentieth century, Hume was the darling of the autopsists of metaphysics, the logical positivists and, in the present "postist" period, he has entered into the pantheon of "schizophrenic" philosophers via the work of Gilles Deleuze.[4] Anti-substantialism immediately folds into functionalism in Hume's philosophy since what remains after the *auto da fe* of the idol of substance is a complex net of relations. Norman Kemp Smith describes this result as Hume's "Relational View of Substance":

> To view objects or selves as "substance" is not, therefore, on Hume's teaching, to view them as *self subsistent*. Like all other existents met with in experience, they are essentially conditioned modes of existence and are not, therefore, nonmodal in the traditional meaning of that term.
>
> (Kemp Smith 1941: 503)[5]

This "modalism" extends to causation itself. Hume's rejection of any necessity in the causal relation places "causation" in the wider force field of association with those curious philosophical bastards "custom and habit."

Anyone familiar with the history of the philosophy of money in the early eighteenth century and with Hume's philosophical anti-substantialism and functionalism would, therefore, find the unambiguous theoretical metallism Schumpeter attributes to him rather a surprise. If one were choosing *a priori* what ontology of money would most comfortably match Hume's functionalism, it would probably be close to Berkeley's in *The Querist* (1735–1737), that is, he would eschew any kind of metallism. But, as we have shown, the passages supporting the metallist interpretation in Hume's *Political Discourses* seem strong, even decisive. Was Hume being opportunistic here? Is this one of the famous marginal discontinuities that the deconstructionists make so much of?

There are, after all, apparent hesitations and contradictions in Hume's monetary theory that Vickers, Marx and others who categorized him as a metallist pointed out. Vickers, for example, notes, reflecting back on Locke's metallism, that "though Hume was otherwise consistently a metallist, he opposes ... the monetary restriction inherent in the previous recoinage arguments" (Vickers 1959: 223). The "previous recoinage arguments" that Vickers is referring to are Locke's, who, as mentioned above, argued, with all the authority of his position as *the* ideologist of the Glorious Revolution, that the clipped coins in circulation in England in the 1690s should be recalled, melted down and recoined to the weight of the previous unclipped coinage.

In a telling footnote, Hume explicitly rejects the Lockean metallist orthodoxy:

And as a recoinage of our silver begins to be requisite, the continual wearing of our shillings and sixpencees, it may be doubtful, whether we ought to imitate the example of King William's reign, when the clipt money was raised to the old standard.

(R 39)

(an entry in the Errata of the original *Political Discourses*). Hume claims that the best form of recoinage would have:

[a] penny's worth of silver taken from every shilling, the new shilling would probably purchase everything that could have been bought by the old; the prices of everything would thereby be *insensibly diminished* ... In

executing such a project, it would be better to make the new shilling pass for 24 halfpence, in order *to preserve the illusion, and make it be taken for the same.*

(R 39, italics mine)

It is important for our purposes to note that Hume's suggested monetary manipulation essentially uses the human mind's "tendency to fallaciously homogenize small differences into identities" that brings about the "fictions" of substance, according to Hume's account, to create a beneficent "gradual and universal encrease in the denomination of money." Thus, in this case, Hume's philosophical anti-substantialism directly supports his criticism of strict metallism, *á la* Locke.

Marx also found Hume's metallism problematic and insisted on pointing to a contradiction in his monetary views, since

[Hume] makes gold and silver enter the world of commodities as non-commodities; but as soon as they appear in the form of coin, he turns them, on the contrary, into mere commodities, which must be exchanged for other commodities by simple barter.

(Marx 1970: 164)

Hume does not distinguish, as a theoretical metallist should in Marx's view, *how* the quantity of money increases and therefore he confuses a "sudden and forcible transfer of hoarded money from one country to another," an undervalued recoinage of the sort described above, an issuing of token money or paper-credit notes, and the importation of gold and silver whose cost of production has lowered. As a consequence, Marx argued that for Hume "gold and silver are thus things without value, but in the process of circulation, in which they *represent commodities*, they acquire a fictitious value" (Marx 1970: 164). Marx is right here; this is hardly the doctrine of a theoretical metallist, but is it a symptom of Hume's general suspicion of "intrinsic value" of anything, gold and silver included?

These inconsistencies discussed by Vickers and Marx are rooted in a more basic tension in his philosophy of money that puts his ultimate theoretical metallism in question. But determining whether Hume was a metallist at all and, if he was, what kind of metallist he was, requires more than an examination of his philosophical texts. A careful study of the historical context of the first edition of the *Political Discourses* (1752) and the transformation of Hume's views on money in his writings after 1752 is also needed in order to understand the source of Hume's ambivalences and complexities.

Figure 4.1   Scottish paper and metallic currency: an early paper currency issued by the Bank of Scotland in 1723. Image courtesy of Wikicommons.

Figure 4.2   Scottish paper and metallic currency: the front and back of a 1602 "Silver Thistle Merk" from the reign of James VI (1567–1625). Image courtesy of Wikicommons.

THE SCOTTISH SETTING OF THE PARADOX

In order to examine and resolve this tension in Hume's philosophy of money, it is crucial to consider the role money played in the political project Hume confronted during the writing and publication of the *Political Discourses*. The book was published in 1752, but we know that it was conceived in the late 1740s, since a *précis* of its main themes can be found in Hume's letter to Montesquieu of April 10, 1749 (Hume 1932: 136–137).

What was the decisive political/social project occupying the minds of Hume and the other "Enlightened" *Scots* of his day that could have been the source of Hume's political-economic concern?[6] This project was complex and Janus-faced. One side of the project was long term and faced south to London and through London to the world market. After the disastrous collapse in 1700 of the Darien Company, the Scottish ruling elite's main attempt at developing its own colony in Panama, their only reasonable path to taking part in the world market was through London, and the majority of them reluctantly acceded to this bitter wisdom by accepting the offer of Union in 1707 (Devine 2000: 4–19).[7] Immediately after the Union, the circle of improving lairds, lawyers trained on the continent, and Atlantic merchants located in the corridor between Edinburgh and Glasgow exerted an impressive political, juridical and intellectual impact on London and the Empire more than commensurate to their financial and merchant capital.[8] The intellectual achievements of this elite were recognized in the eighteenth century and even today the Scottish Enlightenment is given a place of honor next to the French with the English trailing behind. The juridical impact, especially through the work of William Murray, Lord Mansfield, a Lowland Scot, literally revolutionized British commercial law and nearly threatened to do the same for its criminal law by injecting the principles of Scottish civil law into English common law.[9] The Scots also literally "invaded" the British army, its diplomatic service and penetrated into the highest levels of the executive.[10]

Hume was a ready recruit in this "invasion," for, as we have seen above, he served as a clerk in a Bristol merchant's firm, an aide-de-camp in the British army and in a number of posts in the diplomatic corps in Turin, Vienna, and, of course, Paris. But his most important thrust was intellectual. The project he took up after the publication of *Political Discourses* was *The History of England*, which became the authoritative account for the

English of their own history for almost a century. Certainly Hume's prescriptions in 1752 (especially in "Of the Balance of Trade," "Of Taxes," and "Of Public Credit") were directed against the long-established mercantilist policies emanating from London that hampered Scottish trade and industry for nearly a century.

But there was another face to the political project of Hume's circle, one that looked north to the Scottish Highlands. That aspect of the project was imperative at the time, but it has been neglected by most of Hume's commentators.[11] The 'Forty-Fiver and its aftermath clearly constituted one of the most decisive moments of Scottish history overlapping the writing of the 1752 *Political Discourses*. The year 1745 was when thousands of armed Scottish Highlanders and others, bent on overthrowing the English crown and putting Bonny Prince Charlie's father on the throne, marched into the Lowlands, taking Edinburgh and all the major Scottish towns. Then they penetrated deep into England. The invasion lost momentum at Derby, within 100 miles of London, and the Highlanders retreated back into Scotland that winter. This force defeated or outmaneuvered the official troops sent against them until, finally, they were confronted and decisively destroyed by the British Army at Culloden, in Scotland, in April 1746.[12]

The official "cause" of this remarkable political-military knife thrust into the heart of the most powerful nation state on the planet was Jacobitism, that is, the demand for the return of the Stuarts to the British Throne. And much has been made of the "romantic" (tending on "crazed") aspects of the cause of "Bonny Prince Charlie" in song and story.[13] But what made so many thousands of men and women risk so much for what appeared to be an outlandish and lost cause (and, at the same time, get so close to victory)?[14]

Hume and his Lowland Scottish Enlightenment circle knew the reasons quite well, since they were in constant touch with the Highlands and many of them, like Adam Ferguson, harkened from there. Moreover, much of the meat at their dinners came from the North. The Highland fighters' concern was no more nor less the preservation and development of their mode of life. Hume and his circle called it "barbarian" or "rude"; a little later, Samuel Johnson called it "patriarchal"; some contemporary authors call it "Celtic Feudalism"; I might add that it had elements of "runrig communalism."[15] It was a remarkably "mixed" system, composed of elements of all the known "stages" and "modes" of economic organization known to the Scottish Enlightenment.[16]

The Highland mode of life demanded that each adult male develop a generalized military capacity that was continually exercised in the internal feuds, social banditry, civil and international war the Highlanders engaged in. Moreover, there were 652,000 Highlanders in 1750, or about 51 percent of the Scottish population.[17] The Highlanders were a heavy and dangerous presence in the mind of the "modernizers" of the late 1740s, Hume included. Certainly, the Enlightened Lowland Scots could hardly achieve much headway with their subtle "invasion" of England, if their Highland cousins were erupting and threatening the whole British Empire every decade or so.

This way of life was increasingly being pressured and transformed by the expansion of capitalist relations emanating from the Lowlands. But the Highlanders' resistance to becoming a mere northern appendix of the Lowlands was not only a military concern. For this resistance might ignite the mass of the Scottish and English population's general lack of enthusiasm for the Hanoverian Whig regime some day. It is all too easy to shrug off historical might-have-beens, but there was no such complacency in Edinburgh and London in 1745/6! The 'Forty-Fiver had been the fourth large rebellion in sixty years aimed at reversing the consequences of the "Glorious Revolution," and it had very nearly succeeded. Moreover, the loyalty of Britain's other "others"—the London "mob" and the Irish "natives"—could not be counted upon if another such uprising poured out of the Highlands.

Hume himself was a worried and antagonistic spectator to the 'Forty-Fiver.[18] He was spending the year with the mad Marquess of Annandale in England, and his correspondence with his Scottish circle avoided all direct reference to "the present unhappy troubles" for fear of incriminating himself or his correspondents in case a letter was opened by the Jacobite authorities in occupied Edinburgh. But a year and half after Culloden, Hume wrote and published *A True Account of the Behaviour and Conduct of Archibald Stewart, Esq: Late Lord Provost of Edinburgh. In a Letter to a Friend* (1748) to exculpate the former Provost of Edinburgh, Archibald Stewart, from allegations that he purposely let the Jacobite forces take Edinburgh in 1745. Hume applied the now classic Scottish Enlightenment theory of stages in explaining why it was so hard for Provost Stewart to defend the city:

> When Men have fallen into a more civilized Life, & have been allowed to addict themselves entirely to the Cultivation of Arts and Manufactures, the habit of their Mind, still more than that of their Body, soon renders

them Unfit for the use of Arms and gives a different Direction to their Ambition ... But the barbarous Highlanders, living chiefly by Pasturage, has Leisure to cultivate the Ideas of military Honour ... all this nourishes their martial spirit, & renders them, from their Cradle, compleat soldiers in everything but the knowledge of Discipline.

(Hume 1748: 9)

This contrast was recognized by the people of Edinburgh when they stopped the volunteer troops who were about to march out with Provost Stewart to confront the Jacobites and "represented to them the infinite Value of their Lives, in comparison of those Ruffians, the Highlanders" (Hume 1748: 22). But this contrast laid the basis of the paradox: without the intervention of the British army, "eight Millions of People" might "have been subdued and reduced to Slavery by five Thousand, the bravest, but still the most worthless amongst them" (Hume 1748: 11). Thus, *A True Account* posed a terrible paradox and problematic for Hume as he was writing *Political Discourses*. He shared them with the others of the social circle he was entering into during the early 1750s when he settled in Edinburgh, and took on the post of Keepership of the Advocates Library and that of joint secretary of the Philosophical Society of Edinburgh. Hume and his circle agreed that Culloden must have decisive social consequences: *the old Highland mode of life had to be terminated.* The question remained: How?

As William Ferguson put it:

Much more than Jacobitism died at Culloden. Thereafter the disintegration of the old Highland society, already advanced in some quarters, was accelerated. The patriarchal authority of the chiefs and great territorial magnates was gradually transformed into landlordism. The demilitarization of Highland life broke the bonds of mutual interest and idealized kinship which had bound chiefs and clansmen and paved the way for a new social relationship in which the landlords came to regard their people as tenants and cotters.

(Ferguson 1968: 154)

The Scottish Enlightenment figures felt the edge of the Highland knife at their collective throats for six months in the fall and winter of 1745–1746, while their fate hung in the political-military balance. All of them vowed that it would not happen again. But what was to be done?

The Homes, Elliots, Oswalds, the Clephanes, the Smiths and Hume's other correspondents were actively involved in finding a solution to the Highland problem. First, of course, was the phase of slaughter, extirpation, transport and exile.[19] Then came the legislation directed at destroying the fabric of the communalist-feudal-pastoral life, from the Act prohibiting Highland Dress to the abolition of Heritable Jurisdictions, a Parliamentary action that Hume informed Montesquieu was one of the most beneficent results of the 'Forty-Fiver (Mossner 1954: 181).[20] But slaughter and legislation followed the previous rebellions and nothing had essentially changed. Repressive violence and prohibition were not enough to transform the Highlands. Something more was required: civilization.

The task of civilizing the Highlands, that is, of transforming the Highland mode of life to a capitalism *fully* integrated with the rest of Britain and the world market would have to be "micro-managed," and that job fell to the juridical intellectuals of the Scottish Enlightenment. The Highlands became their special field of social experimentation in the half century after Culloden.[21] Hume's *Political Discourses* was one of many efforts to map out the strategy for such a program of transition. In this regard, it is worth noting the place and time of their publication: Edinburgh in [January] 1752. This was right in the midst of an intense but carefully negotiated period of legislation preparing the infrastructure of this International Monetary Fund-type planning effort and the selection of its personnel, which had its focus in the various legislative acts directed at first pacifying and then civilizing the Highlands. Youngson describes this period in the following words:

After the collapse of the Rebellion, a large number of estates, most of them in the Highlands, were forfeit to the Crown through the attainer for treason of their owners. The Vesting Act of June 1747 authorised the Scottish Court of Exchequer, as guardians of Crown revenues in Scotland, to survey and value these estates, appoint factors, determine claims and pay creditors. In all, fifty-three estates were surveyed, and forty-one of these forfeited estates were sold by public auction to pay creditors, but thirteen estates were inalienably annexed to the Crown by the Annexing Act of March 1752. This Act provided that the rent and profits arising from the estates where to be used solely "for the Purposes of civilizing the Inhabitants upon the said Estates, and other Parts of the Highlands and Islands of Scotland, and promoting amongst them the Protestant Religion, good Government Industry and Manufactures, and the Principles of Duty and Loyalty to his Majesty, his Heirs and Successors, and to no other Use or Purpose whatsoever." Unpaid Commissioners, of whom there were at various times between twenty-eight and thirty-five, were appointed; crown officials, noblemen, judges, substantial lairds.

(Youngson 1973: 27)[22]

Annette Smith, in her description of the preparations leading up to the drafting and passage of the Annexing Act, points out that "in the years preceding the successful passing of the Annexing Act, the ultimate aims of annexation, the methods of achieving these aims, and arrangements for administering the estates were widely discussed in Scotland" (Annette Smith 1982: 20). These discussions included the major figures across the Scottish political spectrum—from Lord Milton to Lord Desford—in agreement that something must be done to finally "civilize the Highlands." Indeed, General Bland, the Commander-in-Chief in Scotland, sent a paper titled "Proposals for Civilising the Highlands" to the *Caledonian Mercury* in June of 1747 (Annette Smith 1982: 20). The Annexing Act was an exemplary legal tool aimed at practically solving one of the major problems central to the *Political Discourses*, just as undoubtedly Hume's Edinburgh juridical circle helped set up the wording of the Act.

One way of establishing how close Hume was personally to the Annexing Act is to examine the number of members of the Board of Commissioners and Trustees for the Annexed Estates that met between 1755 and 1784 who were acquaintances, friends or colleagues of Hume. Of the fifty-five ordinary members of the Board, Hume was acquainted with at least twenty-three. Of the ten ex-officio members, Hume was in some communication with at least five.[23] Moreover, given Hume's identification with the legal profession via his position at the Advocates Library, the predominance of lawyers in the Commission would have also brought Hume directly in touch with the work of the Commission.[24] Finally, a number of Hume's closest intellectual peers like Lord Kames and friends like Gilbert Elliot became important players in the Commission.[25]

Thus, Hume's conception of civilization would have a ready audience among friends and colleagues who were legally charged in the text of the

Annexing Act with "civilizing the Highlands." This concept was at the center of their theorizing, and the *Political Discourses* analyzes the process of transforming a "barbarian" and "rude" people into a "refined" and "civilized" one, that is, a people which operate wholly within a legal system of property exchange relations.[26]

The very order of the essays in the 1752 *Political Discourses* (amplified 1753–1754 in the *Essays*) shows us Hume's intent:

I. Of Commerce
II. Of Luxury [later Of Refinement in the Arts]
III. Of Money
IV. Of Interest
V. Of Balance of Trade
VI. Of Taxes
VII. Of Public Credit
VIII. Of the Populousness of antient Nations
IX. Of the Protestant Succession
X. Of the Balance of Power
XI. Of Some Remarkable Customs
XII. Idea of a perfect Commonwealth[27]

Here we see the agenda of social reconstruction set out for the Commissioners in outline, from the material foundations to the demography to the political superstructure. The anti-Jacobite tenor is clearly determined by the inclusion of the essay on the Protestant succession that was ready for publication in 1748 but was withdrawn since it was still too "risky" then (Mossner 1954: 269). The first pages of the *Political Discourses* show us the way Hume envisioned the problematic of the Highlands:

As soon as men quit their savage state, where they live chiefly by hunting and fishing, they must fall into the classes [of husbandmen and manufacturers]; tho' the arts of agriculture employ *at first* the most numerous part of the society. Time and experience improve so much these arts, that the land may easily maintain a greater number of men, than those who are immediately employed in its cultivation, or who furnish the more necessary manufactures to such as are employed. If these superfluous hands apply themselves to the finer arts, which are commonly denominated the arts of *luxury*, they add to the happiness of the state; since they afford to many the opportunity of receiving enjoyments, which they would otherwise have been unacquainted. But may not another scheme be proposed for the employment of these superfluous hands?

(R 5–6)

The initial problem of the *Political Discourses* is posed by "superfluous hands" coming out of a transition from a "savage state" and being driven into the manufacturing labor market by increasing agricultural productivity. The question to be answered is: what is the best "scheme" for the employment of these "superfluous hands"? This indeed is the problem of "civilization," that is, how one transforms rural clans people into civilized beings. But this was exactly the problem that was posed by the Annexing Act of March 1752 and was on the minds of the hundreds of Scots who were simultaneously readers of the *Political Discourses* and prospective or actual Commissioners for the Annexed Estates.

Hume, of course, posed the problem of civilization in the form of "general principles" in the *Political Discourses*, as he warns us in the first paragraphs of that book (R 3). And, after all, in the world of the 1750s, there were many other barbarous people besides the Scottish Highlanders. But it would be unlikely that Hume, who was so deeply committed to "the application of experimental philosophy to moral subjects," would not be deeply interested in the fate of an experiment concerning one of the most important moral and political questions taking place in his own country, being run by his closest friends and involving his class' historical fate.[28] The civilizing of the Highlands clearly posed a paradigmatic test case for any theory of civilization. His work, therefore, was of immediate interest to those of his companions who were politicians involved with "the domestic government of the state, where the public good, which is, or ought to be their object, depends on the concurrence of a multitude of causes" (R 4).

MONEY AND CIVILIZATION

Now that one of the specific political projects of the *Political Discourses*, the civilization of the Highlands, has been established, the role of money in the project must be defined. It clearly is important in Hume's view by its placement in the series of topics in the *Political Discourses*, for the essay "Of

Money" follows immediately after "Of Commerce" and "Of Luxury." Hume's approach to the problematics of money, however, is rather different from the mercantile theorists who already had before them an ongoing, functioning world market. He was, of course, quite cognizant of the global aspect of money, since he was a citizen of the greatest power in this world market and his own immediate Scottish ruling group was beginning to share in it through the tobacco, sugar and slave trade:

> We know that by 1735 there were 47 square-rigged ships, mostly owned by Glasgow merchants, sailing out of Glasgow's harbours at Port Glasgow and of these 15 were trading to Virginia, 4 to Jamaica, 1 to Barbadoes, 1 to Antigua, 2 to St. Kitts, 5 to London, 3 to Boston, 5 to the Mediterranean, 2 to Holland, 7 to Stockholm and this in addition to many English and foreign-owned ships bringing cargoes.
>
> (Lenmen 1977: 91)

This trade expanded dramatically in the ensuing thirty years, so that:

> [in] 1738 the Scots accounted only for 10 per cent of the total British [tobacco] importation; but by 1765 this had risen to an astonishing 40 per cent of a UK trade which had itself expanded remarkably in the intervening years.
>
> (Devine 2000: 105)

But Hume had his eye not only on the slave plantations of Jamaica and the Carolinas or the sugar wharves of Amsterdam, his major immediate concern was nearer at hand. For the problem posed by the Highlands was the extension of commercial relations to an economy that had not been completely monetarized. Walter Scott, decades later, was deeply aware of this problem and chronicled the transition from a clannish to a capitalist attitude toward money in his *Waverley* series of novels. His works still have much to teach philosophers and historians of money. It would be worthwhile to reflect on the little exchange described in the epigraph of this chapter; it is classic Scott. First, money is not being exchanged between the Highlander Callum and the Englishman Waverly "productively" (i.e., for capital, labor or even commodities), but it is a quasi-gift to be spent on a "luxury." Second, the money itself is a golden object of "delight," it is a "treasure" and not necessarily an abstract mediator to a market world. Finally, the "spleuchan" represents the constrictions on the free flow of monetary exchanges embedded in Highland life. This small exchange illuminates the strength of archaic economic practices in the Highlands of the mid-eighteenth century.

What role, then, could money play in modernizing and civilizing the Highlanders, who were still in thrall to the "gift economy"?

With this problematic in mind, we see that Hume's continued references in the *Political Discourses* to "the ancient simplicity of manners" (R 44) and "the first and more uncultivated ages of any state" (R 42) are not only to some arbitrary anthropological construct, rather they also refer to the actual historical situation of the Highlands in the eighteenth century.[29] Further, his insistence on the primary standard of a policy's success or failure being a "change in the manners and customs of the people" is not just a generalized precept; it refers to the immediate political problem of his circle.

Money could be an important element in this change of manners, Hume argued, but not as the mercantilist logic supposed, for:

> The absolute quantity of the precious metals is a matter of great indifference. There are only two circumstances of any importance, viz., their gradual increase, and their thorough concoction and circulation thro' the state.
>
> (R 46)

The actual quantity of metals is not important, just as the relativity of motion makes the absolute constant velocity of a body unimportant, rather the dynamic differentials are crucial. The accelerative effects of an increase in the money supply and the extensive increase in the field of monetary impact are the crucial variables of change for Hume. This bit of Newtonianism in moral (here, "economic") subjects was typical of Hume. For he prided himself on bringing Newtonian "experimentalism" into "the science of MAN" (N 332–346), and the Newtonian "experimental method" was to go from the phenomena to the *forces* and hence back to the phenomena. *Real forces*, however, can only be seen at play when accelerative (or decelerative) effects are produced.[30]

Surely after Culloden, Hume's reflections on the real social force of money were quite useful in answering the question: What kind of monetary strategy had to be adopted to bring about a permanent change in the manners and customs of the Highlanders? First, there had to be an increase in the money supply, since "'tis only in this interval or intermediate situation, between the acquisition of money and rise of prices, that the increasing quantity of gold and silver is favourable to industry" (R 38). As the new money diffuses through the social field, thousands of surprising accelerative micro-effects arise: "manufacturers employ *more* workmen" but "workmen *become* scarce, the manufacturer pays *higher* wages, but at first requires an *increase* of labour" while the workman "returns from the market with *greater* quantity and *better* kinds" of goods, and the farmers who supply the market "apply themselves with alacrity to *raising more*." This increase in the absolute quantity of money "must first *quicken* the diligence of every individual" (R 38, my italics).

Similarly, what is important is not simply the ratio between the absolute quantity of money and the absolute quantity of commodities in a country. The real effect of money is measured in the increasing number of "collisions" between commodities and money. This number is determined by how much a society has moved from the "ancient simple manner" to a state of "industry and refinement." For as industry and refinement intensify, the number and area of money–commodity collisions increase, absorbing and digesting the money supply automatically.

These real effects are clearly not independent of each other. The first can support and amplify any movement of the second. This was important advice in 1752, for if the civilizing transformation from simple to refined manners is to be accomplished with alacrity in the Scottish Highlands, there needed to be an effort to "quicken the diligence of every individual." Thus, Hume's policy recommendation:

> The good policy of the magistrate consists only in keeping [the quantity of money], if possible, still increasing; because, by that means, he keeps alive a spirit of industry in the nation, and increases the stock of labour, in which consists all real power and riches.
>
> (R 39)

When one examines the banking industry in Scotland in the years immediately after the 'Forty-Fiver, we see that both London and Edinburgh seemed to be heeding the Humean message, or else Hume was considering the messages emanating from the Scottish bankers and financial advisors of

George II. Here is a list of financial actions taken in between 1746 and 1753 relevant to the money supply's relation to the Highland problem:

(a) In July 1746 the British Linen Company was chartered with an authorized capital of L100,000. As Neil Munro describes the operation, it quickly led to increasing the circulation of money throughout Scotland:

Its more obvious business was to foster the linen trade by the importation and distribution of flax, and the collection and sale of the manufactured product. This necessitated having agents all over the country with a certain amount of ready money at their command. In a very short time those agents were provided with British Linen Company promissory notes for L5, L10 and L20, payable on demand, and L100 bearing interest at 3.5 and 4 per cent. The agents used those notes in paying for goods received, and the Royal Bank [of Scotland], with whom the British Linen Company kept its account and had a substantial credit, retired them as a matter of course. This British Linen Company's network of agents throughout the country laid ... the foundation of the widespread system of branches which has given such an impulse to Scottish banking.

(Munro 1928: 110)

(b) New banks were begun in Glasgow and Aberdeen in 1749. The Banking Company of Aberdeen was the first private banking company to issue bank notes in Scotland.

(Munro 1928: 111)

(c) In 1751 the city fathers of Edinburgh asked for and received a loan for L5,000 from the Royal Bank of Scotland to launch a major "urban renewal" project that would make Edinburgh a "Modern Athens."

(d) In 1751 the two major Scottish Banks, the Bank of Scotland and the Royal Bank of Scotland, concluded a pact of cooperation and agreed upon a clearing house for financial paper.[31]

(e) "In March 1753 the Royal Bank introduced what was virtually the equivalent of the modern bank draft, to enable its customers to remit money by post without the necessity for sending bank notes" Munro (1928: 120).[32]

These actions set the basis of a system of paper-credit money that, within a short time, dominated Scottish economic life. For specie was incessantly "drained" into England. "To provide a currency for the payment of workmen's wages and the like, private companies and private individuals in many parts of the country issued notes for trivial sums" (Munro 1928: 120). Indeed, something of a small note mania exploded in post "'Forty-Five" Scotland making silver and gold a rarity in average transactions, to the point that Adam Smith in 1776 would note:

> An operation of this kind [the issue of paper money] has, within these five and twenty or thirty years, been performed in Scotland, by the erection of new banking companies in almost every considerable town, and even in some country villages ... The business of the country is almost entirely carried on by means of the paper of those different banking companies, and which purchases and payments of all kinds are commonly made. Silver very seldom appears except in the change of a twenty shillings bank note, and gold still seldomer.
>
> (Adam Smith 1991: 245)

Indeed, it would seem that this transition from a metallic to a paper-based monetary system was the practical answer to Hume's strategy of stimulating "the spirit of industry" in the Highlanders in order to help change their "customs and habits."

But Hume was extremely suspicious of this development, though he recognized that it could lead to the accelerative effects that he deemed crucial in the role money can play in the civilizing process. In recognition of this practical contradiction, he wrote as a footnote in "Of the Balance of Trade":

> We observed in Essay III [On Money], that money when increasing, gives encouragement to industry, during the interval between the increase of money and the rise of the prices. A good effect of this nature may follow too from paper credit; but 'tis dangerous to precipitate matters, at the risk of losing all by the failing of that credit, as must happen upon any violent shock in public affairs.
>
> (R 68)

Hume was not alone in his concern. Charles Munn quotes a passage the directors of the Bank of Scotland wrote in 1752:

> ... taking into consideration the circumstances of the country with regard to the great circulation of paper credits occasioned by private persons erecting themselves into Banking Companies without any public authority, particularly the two Banking Companies lately set up in Glasgow ... were of the opinion that some measure would be speedily taken for preventing the dangerous consequences that might arise not only to this company in particular but to the credit of the nation in general from too great a circulation of paper.
>
> (Munn 1981: 12)

After quoting the directors, Munn added, "Seemingly someone at the Old Bank had read the proofs of David Hume's *Essays, Moral, Political, etc.*, published in 1752" (Munn 1981: 12).[33] Hume continued his suspicion of paper credit throughout the 1750s, if his 6 April 1758 letter to Lord Elibank, his long-time Jacobite friend and critic of paper money, is any indication. Elibank had given Hume proofs of his *Thoughts on Money, Circulation, and Paper Currency* to comment upon, and in response Hume wrote:

> Banks are convenient by the safe Custody & quick Conveyance of Money; but as to the Multiplication of Money, I question whether it be any Advantage either to an industrious or idle Country. It seems to prevent the Importation of as much Bullion (which has a real intrinsic Value) as the Paper amount to. The Bank of Amsterdam does not multiply Money.
>
> (Mossner 1962: 441)[34]

Was Hume's hostility to paper credit based on theoretical metallism? Did he reject paper money because he argued that money had to be a commodity before it could become a meta-commodity (as he seems to do in his most mercantilist reference to bullion's "real intrinsic value")? Certainly his criticism is mainly directed at Scotland and the American colonies, where paper money was increasingly being used. What were his criticisms? They were four:

(i) paper money tends to drive precious metals from circulation, "paper credit or current paper was introduced in [our colonies], which caused all the silver to depart" (R 188);

(ii) paper money "gives too great facility to credit, which is dangerous" (R 72);

(iii) paper money is useless in international transactions, for "foreigners will not accept [it] in any payment" (R 35); and

(iv) paper money causes inflation "by increasing money beyond its natural proportion to labour and commodities, and thereby heightening their price to the merchant and manufacturer" (R 36).

Each of these reasons, however true they were for eighteenth-century Scotland, do not in themselves show us that Hume was a theoretical metallist, though it was undoubtedly Hume's hostility to "paper money," to "paper as money," to "paper-credit," that convinced Schumpeter that Hume was a theoretical metallist. Schumpeter concluded this in the face of some obvious counter evidence, especially the fact that Hume begins his essay "Of Money" with one of the classic formulations of functionalism in the philosophy of money:

> Money is not, properly speaking, one of the subjects of commerce; but only the instrument which men have agreed upon to facilitate the exchange of one commodity for another. It is none of the wheels of trade: It is the oil which renders the motion of the wheels more smooth and easy.
>
> (R 33)

But what was the source of Hume's critique of paper money? Did it arise from a deep sense of ontological violation evoked in him by paper money? Do the four problems with paper money listed above constitute such a thorough-going rejection?

The first of the four problems is an application of Gresham's law; the second is a sociological observation that was quite relevant for the Scottish situation in the immediate aftermath of the 'Forty-Fiver; the third is a simple recognition that Scottish paper shillings were not "world money"; but the fourth is the most telling on this account. For whenever a philosopher uses a word like "natural" in her/his critique, something basic is being signaled. What is the "natural proportion" that paper money upsets?

In order to answer this question we must recognize that Hume has a complex analysis of "nature" and the "natural." For he contrasts "natural" to "miraculous," to "unusual," to "artificial," to "civil" and to "moral" in *A Treatise of Human Nature* (N 474–475). The notion of "natural" he is using here is in immediate contrast to "artificial," that is, "performed with a certain design and intention" or "purposely contriv'd and directed to a certain end" (N 475 and 529). The natural/artificial contrast here is not so much one between the paper and precious metal *qua* money, but rather a contrast suggested by Hume's hydraulic model of international money flows that define a "usual" versus an "unusual" state. Hume asks us to suppose that, by a miracle, the "money of GREAT BRITAIN were multiplied fivefold in a night." This miracle, he ironically argued, would set off a process of equilibration that would bring the money of GREAT BRITAIN "to a level with foreigners." He then generalized:

> Now, it is evident, that the same causes, which would correct these exorbitant inequalities, were they to happen miraculously, must prevent their happening in the common course of nature, and must for ever, in all neighbouring nations, preserve money nearly proportionate to the art and industry of each nation. All water, wherever it communicates remains always at a level. Ask naturalists the reason; they tell you, that, were it to be raised in any one place, the superior gravity of that part not being balanced, must depress it, till it meet a counterpoise; and that the same cause, which redresses the inequality when it happens, must for ever prevent it, without some violent external operation.
>
> (R 63–64)

"Natural" here relates to this hydraulic model, which requires a communication and flow of the systemic fluid. But paper money does not flow throughout the *world system*, for example, foreigners would not accept the British Linen Company notes as payment for linen manufacturing equipment. Consequently, it cannot find its "natural" level. This characteristic of paper money does not necessarily make it "un-natural" on all dimensions. For, as Hume said of virtues and vices, paper and precious metals are *both* artificial *and* natural.

And here we should make a textual note. The following crucial passage for our argument was not to be found in the first five editions of the essays in *Political Discourses*, which were included in *Essays and Treatises on Several Subjects* in 1753–1754 (i.e., 1752, 1752 (2nd edn), 1753–1754, 1758, 1760), but it appeared in the 1764 edition and those after. Hume begins the vital paragraph in which the passage is placed a bit shamefacedly by noting "all these questions of trade and money are extremely complicated." Then, in a typically Humean turn of phrase, he continues:

> … there are certain lights, in which this subject may be placed, so as to represent the advantages of paper-credit and banks to be superior to their disadvantages. That they banish specie and bullion from a state is undoubtedly true; and whoever looks no farther than this circumstance does well to condemn them; but specie and bullion are not of so great consequence as not to admit of compensation, and even an overbalance from the encrease of industry and of credit, which may be promoted *by a right use of paper money.*
>
> (R 70, my italics)

Something had changed in the twelve years between 1752 and 1764 to bring about the new "light" on the matter of paper money. I suggest that it was the process that Smith described in the *Wealth of Nations*: the gradual dominance of paper in most transactions in Scotland and the tremendous growth of the Scottish economy based on the international tobacco boom, the increased prices for cattle, and the intensifying productivity of the linen trade (Lenman 1877: 86–100).

But at the same time, the effects of paper money that Hume warned of continued to intensify: (a) the outflow of specie from Scotland; and (b) the multiplication of small and branch banks and the uncontrolled issuance of notes by these banks and companies.

As Munn observes:

> The shortage of specie was particularly acute in the period 1761–5 but it was by no means a novel situation. Specie was never in abundant supply. The lack of coin forced many firms in trade and manufacturing to issue "Birmingham buttons" and notes of small denomination as substitutes for coins. Notes for 1 [shilling]—and 5 [shillings]—were the most common.

These notes often contained the option clause which was frequently invoked. In 1764 a writer in the *Scots Magazine* estimated that there were 14 note issuers in Scotland in addition to the public banks; the editor reckoned that there were twice that number.

(Munn 1981: 18)

This led to a "severe balance of payments crisis in 1762–63," which was the time of the sixth edition of the *Essays*. The two major banks of Scotland agitated for a bill that would deal "with the banking irregularities of those vexatious Scotsmen." It became Act 5 of George III. c. 49 (1766), which made it unlawful:

to issue any note, ticket, token, or other writing for money, of the nature of a bank note, circulated, or to be circulated as specie, but such as shall be payable on demand in lawful money of Great Britain, and without reserving any power or option of delaying payment thereof for any time or term whatever.

(Munro 1928: 129)

But let us not forget that Hume's 1764 additions include that telling little phrase "right use of paper-money." Was this evidence of a major conceptual fissure in Hume's thought? Had the ensuing twelve years of intense experience with the consequences of a paper-money economy in the context of a major piece of social engineering (the civilizing of the Highlands) revealed a contradiction lurking in Hume's philosophy of money from the beginning? That is, did this experience finally force him to recognize the mismatch between an earlier monetary metallism and his philosophical functionalist ontology?

In order to answer these questions we must examine what Hume meant by money from his earliest writings, that is, Hume's semantics of money.

MONEY AND REPRESENTATION

For Hume the basic semantic relation between money and commodities is that of "representation." Consider some typical passages in "Of Interest" dealing with this relation:

If a man borrows money to build a house, he then carries home a greater load; because the stone, timber, lead, glass, &c. with the labour of the masons and carpenters, are represented by a greater quantity of gold and silver. But as these metals are considered chiefly as *representations*, there can no alteration arise, from their bulk or quantity, their weight or colour, either upon their real value or their interest.

(R 48, my italics)

In all these transactions, it is necessary, and reasonable, that a considerable part of the commodities and labour should belong to the merchant, to whom, in a great measure, they are owing. And these commodities he will sometimes preserve in kind, or more commonly convert into money, which is their *common representation*.

(R 52, my italics)

But Hume develops two notions of "representation" in his general semantics that he presents in his *A Treatise of Human Nature* in the late 1730s. One such notion is based on the relations of ideas to impressions; the other is based on the formation of conventions and language.[35] Frequently, standard accounts of Humean semantics conflate both notions of "representation," but it is important to differentiate them carefully for our purposes.

The first notion of representation arises from the mechanics of impressions slowly fading away into ideas that then enter into a gravity-like associative force field of their own, which is continually being perturbed by new impacts of impressions. "Representation" is Hume's original word to describe that intimate binding between the two ontological domains of his system: ideas and impressions. For "when I shut my eyes and think of my chamber, the ideas I form are exact representations of the impressions I felt" (N 3). More generally, Hume's first major philosophical conclusion is stated in terms of "representation": "all our simple ideas in their first appearance are deriv'd from simple impressions, which are corespondent to them, and which they represent" (N 4). Thus, representation is an ur-relation in Humean philosophy that is presupposed by the field of associative attractions, "which to the mental world will be found to have as extraordinary effects as in the natural" (N 12–13). For an idea's representation of an impression is its original mark of identity before it gets carried off into the flux of association.

"Representation" plays another crucial role in Book I of the *Treatise* in the solution to the problem of abstract ideas. For "abstract ideas are therefore in themselves individual, however they may become general in their representation." Here, of course, representation loses the role of being the "birth mark" of ideas and leaps to infinity. For representation makes it possible for one idea to be connected not only to one, but to two, three or *n* other ideas as the forms of association, resemblance, contiguity and causation allow. From an ur-relation between ideas and impressions, representation becomes a meta-relation between ideas themselves. In Book I of the *Treatise*, therefore, representation is crucial to Hume's whole "ATTEMPT to introduce experimental reasoning into MORAL SUBJECTS" but it plays something of an extra-systemic role on the upper and lower bounds of his thought, for it mediates between ideas and impressions as well as ideas themselves.

Is money, then, an idea that represents commodities in the way that the idea of red represents red-impressions or the way the idea of triangle represents the infinite number of ideas of scalene, isosceles, equilateral triangles? Money would then be a vague, distant and abstract representation of the immediate impressions that the passions of mercantile affairs excite or an even vaguer, distant and abstract idea of mercantile ideas. But money is not an idea at all for Hume, for he explicitly connected the representative capacity of money with the functioning of conventions and language, the second notion of representation, not with the mechanics of impressions and ideas. Textually, we see this in the way that money is dealt with, cursorily, in Book III, while the presentation of impressions by ideas is discussed in Book I of the *Treatise*.

In Part II, Section II of Book III of the *Treatise*, Hume discussed "the Origin of justice and property" and mentioned money in passing. He argued that, before one can define the ideas of property, right and obligation, a certain framework of human coordination must be presupposed. This framework is rooted in convention:

> It is only a general sense of common interest; which sense all the members of the society express to one another, and which induces them to regulate their conduct by certain rules. I observe, that it will be for my interest to leave another in the possession of his goods, *provided* he will act in the same manner with regard to me.
>
> (N 490)

He then presented his famous example of the two men in a rowboat who, without any explicit agreement, regulate the rhythm of their strokes, as being the image of social coordination based upon convention. He continued:

> In like manner are languages gradually establish'd by human conventions without any promise. In like manner do gold and silver become the common measures of exchange, and are esteem'd sufficient payment for what is of a hundred times their value.
>
> (N 490)

So the great systems of representation—language and money—arise not out of the nexus of ideas–impressions–ideas, but on the mutual, reflexive expectations of human agents. Convention is also an ur-relation in the moral world just as idea–representation is an ur-relation in the mental world, but it arises out of *artifice*, that is, a response to the *instability* of possession and the *scarcity* of goods. Society is a human invention that solves the problems of instability and scarcity via linguistic and commodity exchanges. Just as in the world of ideas substances seem to be primary (because they seem to unify micro-differences), so too in the moral world it seems that the notions of property and justice ought to come first. But Hume argued that neither view looks carefully enough into the field of micro-relations that invest the largely fictional grand entities of these worlds.

Hume's moderately conventionalist conception of money is most explicitly stated in his July 10, 1769 letter to the author of *Dictionnaire du commerce*, M. Morellet (R 214–215). He takes Morellet to task for his view that "there enters nothing of human convention in the establishment of money" and dismisses the prejudices of metallism as simply confusing a method for preventing counterfeiting for a theory of money! "But, when I take a shilling, I consider it not as a useful metal, but as something which another will take from me; and the person who shall convert it into metal is, probably, several millions of removes distant" (R 214).

The rest of his argument against Morellet's metallism is strictly empirical, citing the fact that though average British shillings are 20–40 percent worn, "yet they pass," and pointing out the peculiarities of monetary units throughout history, including the "land money" of Pennsylvania. But then he mentioned, quite crucially for our work, "Our colonies in America, for want of specie, used to coin paper currency; which were not bank notes, because there was no place appointed to give money in exchange; yet this paper currency passed in all payments, by convention…" (R 214). In this case, Hume seems to have even gone beyond his more generous views of paper money advanced in the 1764 edition of the *Essay*. He seems to have endorsed, in Berkeleyan fashion, the possibility of a completely non-metallic, non-convertible currency and to have definitely dismissed "theoretical metallism." But he did add the following comment on the American use of paper money: "…and still might have gone on ['coining' paper money], had it not been abused by the several assemblies, who issued paper without end, and thereby discredited the currency" (R 214). Thus, the problem with paper-currency is not that it violates some deep ontological, representational relation with commodities. It simply arises from the greater possibilities of "abuse" due to its ease in iteration. This tendency to abuse paper-currency is not accidentally American and Scottish, that is, these were societies which are not completely in the orbit of civilization.

On reading this letter, one must conclude that Hume was certainly no "theoretical metallist" in 1769, but he still was a metallist. Why? Precisely because he argued that money is conventional! Since paper money was so deeply vulnerable to the quality of an infinity of mutual but dubious (Scottish) promises, Hume was a practical metallist. Ironically, previous metallists argued that because gold, silver, etc. were naturally money, any attempt to use paper in their stead would be "unnatural." Hume argued the converse: just because, by its nature, money is conventional and, so, artificial, the control of and restraint on its issue is directly dependent upon the refinement and civility of its issuers. A people just coming out of a rude and barbaric state (like the Scottish Highlanders) or a people merging into such a state (like the American colonists), would find it too tempting to abuse such a currency to deal with passing crises, even though its credit was essential to the general health of society.

One of Hume's last letters to Adam Smith on money referred to a "melancholy Situation" that seemed to answer his cautious ontology of money almost perfectly. The letter was dated June 27, 1772, in the midst of the Ayr Bank crisis, which not only engulfed Scotland but also initiated the first Scottish commercial crisis that threatened the English banking system, creating something like a monetary 'Forty-Fiver (Munn 1981: 33). The Ayr Bank began its meteoric career in Ayr in November 1769 with £150,000 initial capitalization and "branches at Dumfries and Edinburgh, agencies …

at Glasgow, Inverness, Kelso, Montrose, Campbeltown and other places so that there was an agency or branch in every region of the country" (Munn 1981: 31). Taking its motto "Pro Bono Publico" literally, it immediately began to issue notes in earnest, so that its paper soon constituted two-thirds of the Scottish notes issued, while it had a £600,000 debt to London banks by 1772. The results of the unrestrained (and uncivilized) overtrading quickly became evident. Hume described the calamity in staccato prose:

> Continual Bankruptcies, universal Loss of Credit, and endless Suspicions. There are but two standing Houses in this place ... The Case is little better in London. It is thought, that George Colbroke [head of a London bank and former director of the East India Company] must soon stop; and even the Bank of England is not entirely free from Suspicion.
>
> (Hume 1932: 476)

Figure 4.3 "A View of the Deluge of Scotch paper Currency for English Gold," an anonymous engraving from 1772. The artist satirizes the financial crisis of 1772 following the collapse of a speculative mania in Scotland, largely due to the Ayr Bank. A Scotsman rides off on a broom carrying off six large moneybags while scattering paper currency to men on the ground who sink into a bog. In the center, the reclining figure of Britannia says: "This Scotch paper diet has brought me to a consumption." In the background, three Scotsmen row out to sea in a boat loaded with moneybags, saying: "We'll over the Water to Charly."

He ended this breathless paragraph of financial horror by almost taunting Smith with queries: "Do Events any-wise affect your Theory? Or will it occasion the Revisal of any Chapters?" The only good Hume saw coming out of the catastrophe was a "Check given to our exorbitant and ill grounded Credit." Smith, who had developed a theoretical defense of paper money by the 1760s, did not take Hume's suggestion and refused any major revaluation of paper money in *The Wealth of Nations* on the basis of the crisis.[36] But for Hume it must have been a final verification of his monetary fears delivered to him on his deathbed.

CONCLUSION: HUME'S PRACTICAL METALLISM BY DEFAULT

Once the claim that Hume was a theoretical metallist is refuted, we can see that his philosophy of money was much more coherent than it initially appeared. Money and its representative function, for Hume, was not based on a "natural" and necessary representative relation between its precious substance and the glittering world of commodities. On the contrary, money operated on the basis of an ur-structure of mutual conventions that continually tested the reasoning and emotional capacity of the agents involved. There was nothing innately natural about any particular "proportion" between money and commodities. Putting this result in terms of his two immediate predecessors in the philosophy of money, Locke and Berkeley, Hume argued that money could "excite the industry of mankind" only if it *appeared* to measure and store value ... *but not too precisely.*

Now we see the practical paradox Hume faced: on the one side, the increase of the money supply of Scotland was essential in accomplishing the all-important task of civilizing the Highlands (and paper money seemed to be the way it was going to be done); but, on the other hand, if this increase in the money supply was to be managed on the basis of paper money without abuse, the "magistrate" must be civilized already! The Scots (especially those outside of Edinburgh) must be civilized in order to use the most effective method for their own civilization. *This was Hume's paradox: to put the control of money in the hands of the uncivilized in order to civilize them would defeat the very intent of his program.*

If one accepts this formulation of the problem, then Hume's solution was to argue that restraint in increasing the money supply could not be expected, if the power lay in the hands of uncivilized Scots. Certainly the task of issuing money could not be left to the new branch banks on the borders of the Highlands, the upstart companies and the Toms, Dicks and Harrys of the cattle trysts who were poised to let loose a swarm of "Wasp Notes" into the country.[37] *Hume advised against the paper route to civilization, not because of an ontological critique of paper-money, but rather from a moral critique of the character and motivations of the Scottish bankers and moneymen in the outlying areas who would abuse the currency at the first opportunity.*[38] Thus, Hume's support for practical metallism is conditional on the depth of the money users' civilization.

Gold and silver money would be the only way to bring restraint to Scotland because its level was determined by the powerful hydraulic system of international trade. Hume had good theoretical reasons to believe that this rejection of paper would not lead the post 'Forty-Five Scotland into a monetary depression further aggravating the Highlanders into yet another rebellion. For the opening of the Highlands would increase the area of monetary exchange, while the entrance of so many new "superfluous (Highland) hands" into the Lowlands would make Scottish manufacturers much more competitive than the English. Hence, world money in the form of silver and gold would flow north and guarantee the gradual increase in the money supply and stimulate the civilizing process.

Certainly, Hume's scenario—the avoidance of domestic issuing of non-convertible paper money in "under-developed" economies—has not lost its appeal in the halls of power. It is, after all, the reasoning the International Monetary Fund officers still use these arguments to justify their insistence on the adaptation of Structural Adjustment Programs in Africa and Latin America. This comes directly out of the pages of the *Political Discourses*.[39]

5

Did Hume Read Berkeley's *The Querist?* Notions and Conventions in their Philosophies of Money

Whether, if there was a wall of brass a thousand cubits high round this kingdom, our natives might not nevertheless live cleanly and comfortably, till the land, and reap the fruit of it.
—George Berkeley, *The Querist* (Johnston 1970: 136, SQ 134)

But as any body of water may be raised above the level of the surrounding element, if the former has no communication with the latter; so in money, if the communication be cut off, by any material or physical impediment, (for all laws alone are ineffectual) there may in such a case, be a very great inequality of money ... We need not have recourse to a physical attraction, in order to explain the necessity of this operation. There is a moral attraction, arising from the interest and passions of men, which is full as potent and infallible.
—David Hume, *Political Discourses* (Hume 1987: 312–313)

In this chapter, I shall introduce more directly with the role of philosophy in conducting political strategies to protect class rule in the transition from the period of primitive accumulation to fully articulated capitalism.

CANON CONSTRUCTION: PHILOSOPHY AND MONEY

Philosophers practice a form of ancestor worship (and denigration) that constitutes its own sub-discipline: the History of Philosophy. Philosophy is not unique in this worship; most disciplines have their own version of valuation of past performance that is often called in cultural studies "canon construction" or "the invention of tradition" or the creation of an "imagined community." The struggles around a discipline's canon construction, its

125

invention of tradition and its sense of imagined community—or its mythic metanarrative of origin and development, if you will—is a territory thick with the intersections of powers and knowledges that Marxists, sociologists of knowledge and post-structural theorists have studied intensely since the late 1960s. Inevitably, however, for philosophy this "sacred," hence bloodied, disciplinary territory is especially self-reflective and contested.

Certainly a major result of nineteenth- and early twentieth-century philosophical canon construction has been manufacture of the much refined and retold story of the "British Empiricists": Locke, Berkeley and Hume. According to this narrative, Locke begins philosophy's turn to Experience as the source of knowledge, Berkeley radicalizes the turn, and Hume leads the philosophy of Experience to a chilling skeptical dead end that awaits its transcendental transformation in Germany.

Like it or not, the trio and their tragicomic story appear together as implacably as the stone figures on Mount Rushmore. The structure of an untold number of introductions to philosophy, historical surveys, philosophy department curricula and final exams rely on the rubric, "British Empiricists," and texts from the three philosophers set in a row.

Such a long-lasting construction has attracted its share of skeptics anxious to deconstruct the unity of three figures who, historically and culturally, were quite distinct. After all, what made a seventeenth-century English imperial bureaucrat, an early eighteenth-century Anglo-Irish clergyman, and a mid-eighteenth-century Scottish man of letters all "British" and "empiricists" to boot? Many have taken both attributions to task when applied to one or another of the trio. We know that while Hume might accept being called a "North Briton," he was anxious to distinguish himself from the Scottophobic English. Who can forget Hume's letter to his close friend Gilbert Elliot in 1764 where he writes:

> I do not believe there is one Englishman in fifty, who, if he heard that I broke my Neck to night, would not be rejoic'd with it. Some hate me because I am not a Tory, some because I am not a Whig, some because I am not a Christian, and all because I am a Scotsman. Can you seriously talk of my continuing an Englishman? Am I, or are you, an Englishman? Will they allow us to be so?
>
> (Mossner 1954: 637)

Also, was Locke truly an empiricist? After all, he argued that moral and mathematical knowledge were rooted in definitions and reasonable deductions and he borrowed heavily from Descartes's *Meditations*. Similar objections and reservations can be easily multiplied.

In fact, as Michael Ayers pointed out more than twenty years ago, the "establishment" view of the relationship among the three philosophers (and especially that between Berkeley and Hume) is paradoxically contrary to the "traditional canon" (Ayers 1984: 304). There is

> a tendency on the part of some to see nothing good, "interesting," or even true in the old way of looking at things [concerning Berkeley's "influence" on Hume]. The anti-traditional stance has itself become a rather long-standing orthodoxy with a spurious air of innovation.
>
> (Ayers 1984: 304)

Indeed, for a period of time there was even a genuine debate as to whether Hume read Berkeley at all!

It began with Richard Popkin claiming that "It is highly questionable whether Hume ever read Berkeley, or derived any views from him" in a review of a history of modern philosophy written by George Boas (Popkin 1959: 71). Philip Wiener and Ernest Mossner responded to Popkin's provocative question in defense of the traditional view, though in a decidedly circumspect way (Wiener 1959; and Mossner 1959). Popkin's view seemed to be moving with the tide of non-conformity of the time until 1964 when he learned of a scholarly discovery in Cracow: a 1737 letter from the young David Hume to his friend Michael Ramsey where Hume urged his friend to read among other works, "the Principles of Human Knowledge by Dr. Berkeley" in preparation to examining his performance (Popkin 1964). But even this discovery did not settle the question, of course, since Popkin's admission, "So, Berkeley did read Hume," was mitigated by the supplement, "... but not much." The discussion as to how much evidence of Berkeley's views and words could be found in Hume's *Treatise* and *Inquiries* continued through the 1960s and early 1970s (cf. Conroy 1969 and Hall 1970). This debate was punctuated again by the discovery (this time unauthenticated) of an earlier letter of Hume's to Michael Ramsey stating—in 1734, long before the completion of the *Treatise*—that he was in Rheims where he had access to the Abbe Noel-Antoine Pluche library where "It is my Pleasure to read over again today Locke's Essays and the Principles of Human Knowledge by Dr. Berkeley" (Morrisroe Jr. 1973: 314–315; Mossner 1954: 97). But the debate continued, of course, on the matter.

Ayers, in an attempt to correct Popkin's overwrought perspective, argues that Berkeley's philosophy obviously "influenced" Hume's *Treatise*. He discusses just two areas of influence (among many other possibilities)— (1) in Hume's discussion of Space and Time; and (2) in Hume's discussion of substance (Ayers 1984: 306–323)—where Ayers finds Berkeley's work "influentially" present, even though there is no direct reference to Berkeley's texts. Ayers implies that there are many other areas in Hume's work where similar arguments can be made.

Indeed, there is no point in counting direct references in Hume's philosophical work to determine the source of an "influence." For example, in the *Treatise*, there are no *direct* references to Descartes, six to Spinoza, two to Hobbes, none to Leibniz, four to Locke, one to Malebranche and one to Berkeley (Hume 2000). But these references in a 400-page book hardly can give a fair assessment of a philosophic ancestor's influence on Hume's thought or of the intertextual transformations from other philosophical texts into (and out of) the *Treatise*, if we accept the now standard distinction between "influence" and "intertextuality" (Kristeva 1980: 15 and 37; cf. Orr 2003: 83–93, for a recent defense of "influence").

The process of canon formation in the Philosophy of Money, for good or ill, is in an early stage compared with Philosophy proper. In this chapter, I will deal with a small, but important sub-region of the territory. For a set of questions similar to the ones above concerning Philosophy can be posed for the "British Empiricists'" Philosophy of Money, in general, and for Berkeley's relationship to Hume in particular. For example, did Berkeley's philosophical views on money *influence* Hume's? What were the *intertextual relations* between *The Querist* and *Political Discourses*? Or, to paraphrase the earlier debate on whether Hume "read" Berkeley's major philosophical works (especially the *Principles*): did Hume read Berkeley's *The Querist*?

My first aim in this chapter is to answer these questions as best one can (since, of course, "reading" is such a subtly ambiguous word), and in so doing contribute to the discussion of canon formation of the Philosophy of Money.

To perform this task I will utilize terms that are in common use in literary theory: "influence" and "intertextuality." They are both problematic, of course. "Influence" is deployed in the history of philosophy in a rather offhanded way, while it carries with it an immense, untheorized historical baggage from astrology (the effluvia from the stars affecting human behavior) to medicine (e.g., "influenza") to physics (as an electromagnetic "action at a distance"). Therefore, its use in the history of philosophy is vague and indecisive, especially when we wish to answer the metric question: how much did philosophy X influence philosopher Y? "Intertextuality" was coined in the 1960s by Julia Kristeva. Hence it does not have a thick accretion of meanings due to centuries of use, but it has been at the center of a sophisticated, highly productive theoretical effort connected with poststructuralist literary criticism, social thought and philosophy (cf. Allen 2011; Orr 2003; Worton and Still 1990). Consequently, it has proliferated meanings just as it originally posited all words do, but to an even higher level of intensity, since its meaning production is self-reflexive (and, undoubtedly, a few more will be generated in this very text). For all their faults, however, "We cannot do without them," as Prospero said of Caliban.

I will use "influence" to demarcate a terrain of social causation, personal motivation and political strategy that will be anchored by David Hume *qua* author of the 1752 *Political Discourses*. I will use "intertextual" to demarcate a terrain of relations of the text of *Political Discourses* with other texts (including "social texts" like money) in terms of quotation, dialogue and exchange. In other words, "influence" will privilege the person, David Hume, and "intertextuality" will privilege the text, *Political Discourses*. Somewhere orbiting in the historical and intertextual cosmos, then, is the person, George Berkeley, and the text, *The Querist*, and the question, "Did Hume read the *The Querist*? The main conclusion of this paper is that indeed Hume did read *The Querist* and that there is a rich area of contextual, textual and intertextual relations between Hume's and Berkeley's philosophy of money. In order to make my case, I will examine the contextual evidence of "influence" first, and then the intertextual evidence.

My second aim relates to the question, "How much was Hume affected by *The Querist*?" I will argue that he was both indebted to it and radically critical of it. I trace the differences between Berkeley's and Hume's philosophies of money as well as between *The Querist*'s and *Political Discourse*'s rhetorical structure arising from: (1) these philosophers' different valuation of the notion and the convention; (2) their different estimation of what role money was to play in integrating (or "civilizing," in the parlance of the eighteenth century) the native Irish and the Scottish Highlanders respectively into the most advanced capitalist society of the day; and (3) the different relations between language and money that are implicit in *The Querist* and the *Political Discourses*. These differences were not incidental, for Berkeley and Hume did not just have philosophies of money, these philosophers were "had" by them.

Figure 5.1 The canonizing of Hume: David Hume's statue, sculpted by Alexander Stoddart ("Sculptor in Ordinary to the Queen in Scotland") in 1995. The statue is situated in front of the High Court Building on Edinburgh's Royal Mile.

EVIDENCE OF INFLUENCE

The first bit of evidence to note in determining whether the reading of Berkeley's *The Querist* influenced Hume in the writing of the *Political Discourses* is that Hume never directly refers to Berkeley or to *The Querist* in *Political Discourses*, Hume's main contribution to monetary theory and policy. Is this conclusive evidence that Hume never read *The Querist*? No, simply because the rules of scholarly reference in the eighteenth century did not require that an author publicly specify the text that s/he was consciously "influenced" by (for an extensive study of Adam Smith's unacknowledged "borrowing" or even "plagiarism" see [Rashid 1990]). The very legal concept of an author who owns a text was only beginning to be formed one or two generations before Hume's. He became the first (some might claim, last as well!) major philosopher writing in English at least who was able to support himself and grow rich on the basis of selling his writings to book publishers.

Aside from "Of the Populousness of Ancient Nations" and *History of England*, Hume made very few direct, named references in his writing. In the "economic" essays of *Political Discourses*, he made a number of references to participants in the French discourse on political economy (e.g., Melon, Dutot, Paris de Verney and Vauban), but Hume rarely mentions similar writers in English. I believe that only Mandeville, Swift, Gee, Hutcheson and Temple would qualify. Although they were important figures in the development of monetary theory in the English language, there are many eminent late seventeenth- and eighteenth-century names that are missing. Where are the references to Petty, Locke, Child, Davenant, Law, Barbon, North and Vanderlint as well as to Berkeley? Are we to believe that Hume, ever the bibliophile, did not peruse the work of these important figures, whose books and pamphlets were available in the bookshops and libraries of Edinburgh and London, in preparation for his mature work on money and commerce published in his forty-first year? Did not Hume, for example, peruse Locke's monetary writings when he made reference to the 1696 "recoinage" (Hume 1987: 288)?

In fact, we have good evidence that Hume did read many of the important authors in the literature that he did not openly refer to in *Political Discourses*. The evidence comes from the early memoranda that Hume made while reading during the period 1729–1740, a period when he was writing the *Treatise* and the first volume of the *Essays*. The bulk of the memoranda deal with readings from what we would today call the social sciences. Hume clearly read widely in the French literature on politics and commerce, but he also notes a number of English writers like Sir Josiah Child and Charles Davenant that he does not refer to in the *Political Discourses*. Even more important for the question of this paper, the young Hume studied John Law's *Money and Trade Considered, with a Proposal for Supplying the Nation* [i.e., Scotland] *with Money* and Arthur Dobbs' *An Essay on the Trade and Improvement of Ireland* (Mossner 1948), showing that he was already considering the particular problems of what we now might call "underdeveloped" economies (or "poor countries" then), including the two that were tied to the largest economy of the day (for Scotland and Ireland were a bit like Canada and Mexico today).

Moreover, we know that Hume self-consciously repressed the increasingly "modern" practice of using footnotes even in his historical works (much less his essays "moral, political and literary"). Seven years after he finished the *Political Discourses*, he regretted his past (mal)practice, at least with respect to his historical works. Horace Walpole chided Hume for his lack of notes in his *History of England*. In his reply to Walpole, Hume apologized for "my negligence in not quoting my authorities," and claimed that it would have "cost no trouble" for him to have added "the references on the margin" (quoted in Grafton 1997: 190).

Hume's excuse was stylistic. He claimed to follow the model of the Renaissance historians "Matchiavel, Fra paolo, Davila, Bentivoglio," who in turn mirrored the footnoteless classical tradition. But Hume conceded that the use of footnotes "was more modern than their time, and having been once introduc'd, ought to be follow'd by every writer" (quoted in Grafton 1997: 191). In fact, it was only with the formation of the initial "intellectual property regime" of the eighteenth century that the issue of quotation and attribution becomes increasingly vital as the author and work begin to have legal status. Indeed, a short time after receiving Walpole's nudge, Hume spent the winter months 1760 at a "very laborious, but not unentertaining Occupation ... adding the Authorities to the Volumes of the Stuarts" (quoted in Mossner 1954: 401).

Hume never revised the *Treatise* in a similar way of course, probably because it was never reprinted during his lifetime. However, the "economic" essays in the *Political Discourses* were reprinted and revised many times. They were originally almost footnoteless (with the sole exception of "Of the Populousness of Ancient Nations") and remained so throughout his life. Why is it that he never "added the Authorities" in the essays?

Perhaps it had to do with the nature of the essay that Hume described in his self-reflexive essay "Of Essay-Writing" (that was only included in the first 1742 edition of *Essays, Moral and Political* [Hume 1987: 533–544]). Hume, in an extended analogy, compared himself as an essay writer to:

> a Kind of Resident or Ambassador from the Dominions of Learning to
> those of Conversation; and shall think it my constant Duty to promote

a good Correspondence betwixt these two States, which have so great a
Dependence on each other.

(Hume 1987: 535)

Such an ambassador would hesitate to bring heavily freighted and lengthily
deferred internal commentary and textual evidence as part of his "traffic"
betwixt the learned and conversable. The footnote, which is introduced to
make explicit the commerce among texts, decenters the essay and adds a
weight that is antithetical to its goal of deriving its "Materials" from "Conversation and common Life" (Hume 1987: 535). In other words, a genuine
scrupulousness in footnoting might make the essay reader look upon
Hume's work as originating in the land of Learned alone, with harmful consequences to his income before the publication of the *History of England*.
This might especially be a source of concern since Hume, in continuing his
"allusion," calls "Women of Sense and Education" the "Sovereigns of the
Empire of Conversation" (Hume 1987: 535–536). These rulers might be
especially impatient with "the dull labors of Pedants and Commentators,"
who had made the footnote their weapon of choice.

Hume's anxiety to respect the essay genre might explain the lack of
reference to *The Querist*. But there is evidence that Hume *could* have read and
been influenced by *The Querist* as part of his preparation to write *Political
Discourses*. This possibility is due to *The Querist's* publication dates and
locales. It was published anonymously in three parts, one part each in 1735,
1736 and 1737 in both Dublin and London. Hume was living in London
from September 1737 until the end of 1738, correcting and preparing his
Treatise for publication. He might have seen it at that time. Then a revised
version of *The Querist* that carried Berkeley's name was published in 1750 in
four editions, three in Dublin and one in London. In 1751, *The Querist* was
published once again in London and then in Glasgow (Johnston 1970: vi–
vii). The publication of six editions of a book in two years means that it had
created quite a "buzz" in the not-so United Kingdom. If Hume missed *The
Querist* in its original 1735–1737 publication, he could hardly have missed
it in 1750 and 1751, the period he was composing and preparing *Political
Discourses* for publication. Moreover, in this second chance for *The Querist*,
with Berkeley plainly named as the author, Hume would hardly not have
been curious to know what "a great philosopher" who has "disputed the

receiv'd opinion" on abstract ideas had to say about exactly the issues he was writing about: money, commerce and public credit.

There is further support for this hypothesis in the Hume Library. *The Querist* was definitely in this collection (Norton and Norton 1996: 75). The book appears to have been the 1751 Glasgow edition and was, interestingly enough, bound together with *The Manual of Epictetus*. It was not identical to the 1735–1737 edition, because many of the detailed queries concerning the actual running of the National Bank that Berkeley suggested (to evade the fate of Law's Banque Royale) were redacted in this edition (for a book that presents both the original 1735–1737 edition and the later one, though in a somewhat confusing way, see Johnston [1970]). It definitely posed a subtle but strong anti-Lockean, anti-metallist, pro-paper money position and proposed a National Bank that would manage the new paper currency.

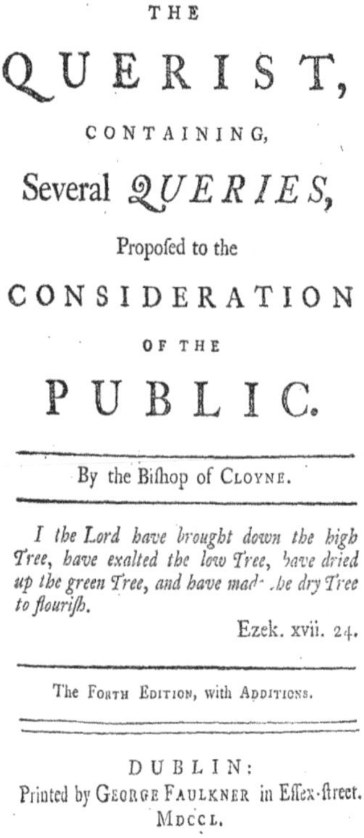

THE

QUERIST,

CONTAINING,

Several *QUERIES*,

Propofed to the

CONSIDERATION

OF THE

PUBLIC.

By the Bifhop of CLOYNE.

I the Lord have brought down the high Tree, have exalted the low Tree, have dried up the green Tree, and have mad .be dry Tree to flourifh.
Ezek. xvii. 24.

The FORTH EDITION, with ADDITIONS.

DUBLIN:
Printed by GEORGE FAULKNER in Effex-ftreet.
MDCCL.

Figure 5.2 *The Querist*: The fourth printing of the Dublin edition of Bishop Berkeley's *The Querist* from 1750. Image courtesy of Wikicommons.

We are not sure, of course, *when* Hume actually acquired this edition of *The Querist*, or, indeed, whether David Hume's nephew, Baron Hume, added it to the library after his uncle's death. Or *The Querist* could have been a very late arrival to the library, entirely inconsequential to Hume during the composition of *Political Discourses*. But this evidence certainly increases the probability that Hume took *The Querist* into account in writing his "economic" essays in the late 1740s and early 1750s.

Although we should remember that even if Berkeley's *The Querist* was not in Hume's library that would by no means have precluded his study of the quizzical text. After all, a review of the pre-1777 publications (that theoretically could have been acquired by David Hume) in the general field of political economy (as indicated by the authors appearing in the table of contents of Terence Hutchison's *Before Adam Smith* [Hutchison 1988]) reveal that Hume possessed books written by only fifteen of fifty-seven authors listed. The authors whose books he possessed included, beside Berkeley, Graunt, Davenant, Locke, Mandeville, Law, Cantillon, Montesquieu, Farbonnais, Galiani, Mirabeau, Beccaria, Morellet, Ferguson and, of course, Smith. But the authors missing are also important. They include Petty, Child, Barbon, North, Boisguilbert, Vanderlint, Franklin, Francis Hutcheson, Melon, Quesnay, Mercier, Verri, Turgot and Steuart, among others.

However, Hume definitely had access to other libraries besides his own in France, in London and in Scotland. This was especially true of the Advocates Library in Edinburgh. Long before he became its Keeper in 1752, he was able to borrow from the 30,000-volume library through the courtesy of lawyer friends. He most likely would have had ample opportunity to borrow *The Querist* from there, if he had not purchased his own copy before the publication of *Political Discourses*. The present National Library of Scotland (which received all the non-legal books of the Advocates Library in the early twentieth century) has four editions of *The Querist* published in 1750 (London), 1751 (Glasgow), 1751 (London again) and 1752 (Dublin). There is a good chance that at least one of these editions would have entered the library during Hume's preparation of the *Political Discourses*. But if Hume was acquainted with the original 1735–1737 edition of *The Querist*, it would not have been as a reader in the Advocates Library, since the library apparently has no record of it.

Now that we have established the possibility, or even the likelihood of Hume's reading *The Querist* on the basis of contextual evidence, let us look at the reasons *why* and *how* Hume might have read it. We need to take these motivations into account, since we are not in possession of evidence like Hume's decisive letters to Michael Ramsey that definitively answered the question "Did Hume read Berkeley at all?" affirmatively (Mossner 1954: 97 and 104). As far as I know, there is no comparable letter or memorandum that would make it possible to go from *whether* Hume read *The Querist* to *how* did Hume read *The Querist*. We must rely here on contextual evidence.

The textual evidence that Hume did read (and could have been influenced by) *The Querist* is strong, but it is not overwhelming. In this I take a position in opposition to Joseph Johnston who claimed that "Hume must have read *The Querist*, but it is impossible to say for certain whether he was consciously influenced by it or not" (Johnston 1970: 85). Johnston took this position because he believed that "essential elements in Berkeley's monetary philosophy failed to penetrate the mind of Hume" and that Hume was a "retrograde" monetary thinker whose "instinct, if not his reason" attached considerable importance of the precious metals (Johnston 1970: 85–87). What a barrage on Hume: thickheaded, passé and atavistic! This is not the Hume that we know. Somehow Johnston sees the subtle thinker of our contemporary studies as an arch reactionary in the monetary field because Hume is a "theoretical" metallist (in Schumpeter's terminology) whose influence on Smith "impoverished" monetary theory until the rise of Keynes.

However, Johnston's identification of Hume as a thoroughgoing metallist is mistaken, though Hume clearly argued for "the French road" from the 1720 bubble (Caffentzis 2001). For the French government, capitalists and aristocracy revalorized gold and silver coinage as their money vehicle of choice after their collective "fling" on the rue Quincampoix. Hume's reasons for this choice were not based upon an ontological preference for specie. Once that assumption is undermined, the effect of Johnston's barrage is blunted. Hume might not have been so thickheaded as to block the penetration of Berkeley's monetary philosophy in his mind; he might not have been so passé as to advocate for a totally metallic currency; and finally, he might not have been so atavistic as to deny the plain evidence that paper currency was "the wave of the future."

A more complex assessment than that provided by Johnston—Hume simply couldn't understand Berkeley—is necessary in order for us to understand the differences between Hume's and Berkeley's philosophies of money and their conflicting monetary policies.

The main contextual evidence for Berkeley's "influence" on the *Political Discourses* is rooted in the similarities between Hume and his circle's challenges in the Scotland of the early 1750s with the situation Berkeley and his circle faced in the Ireland of the 1730s. Berkeley had to both find ways to "excite the industry" of the native Irish (as he called the disenfranchised Catholic population) and to not provoke the mercantilist police of the London-dominated state (Caffentzis 2000). The Scottish Enlightenment circle had a similar problematic that they shared with their Anglo-Irish counterparts. For they had in the Scottish Highlands a recalcitrant, and at times rebellious, population that had not been integrated into the commercial society of the Lowlands and of England. This population was not, as in the case of the "Irish natives," politically catatonic at the time. The Highlanders were positively aggressive and had invaded England a number of times within memory. They had to be "civilized" (or exterminated or "cleared") in order for the Lowland Scots to have any claim to the power of being the citizens of a world empire (Caffentzis 1996; and 2005). In fact, the interest this similarity might generate among the reading public could have been the reason why the revised editions of *The Querist* published in the early 1750s were all accompanied with *A Word to the Wise*, a remarkable public statement addressed to the "Catholic clergy of Ireland" urging them to call on their laity to increase their work effort and to scrutinize their sanitary habits.

Money had an important role to play in this process of "civilizing" the Highlands according to Hume (Caffentzis 1996; 2001; and 2005). Consequently, the efforts of the Anglo-Irish "improving" intelligentsia to use money to motivate those outside of the money economy to come into it would have been important to understand. Since Berkeley and his circle made that their primary task and since this task was most forcefully expressed in *The Querist*, there is good reason to believe that Hume found it imperative to reflect on Berkeley's quizzical suggestions.

Others in the Scottish Enlightenment were definitely students of *The Querist*. A most prominent one for us was Robert Wallace, Hume's opponent in the "populousness of ancient nations" debate. He criticized Hume's strictures against "paper-credit" and directly referred to *The Querist* in his *Characteristics of the Present Political State of Great Britain* (1758) in suggesting that "a poor but growing country stood in need of paper money and credit to boost her economy" (Hont 1983: 290). In fact, Wallace urged that *The Querist* be "perused by every lover of this country and of mankind" (quoted in Hont 1983: 290).

In this regard, it should be remembered that Wallace was a member of the Rankenian Club, a group of faculty and students of divinity and law, who met in the 1720s and 1730s to discuss the "New Philosophy" with special reference to the work of George Berkeley. They carried on a correspondence with the then Dean of Derry concerning his philosophy and they earned his high regard. It was claimed that Berkeley had said, "no persons understood his system better than this set of young gentlemen in North Britain" (Mossner 1954: 48). Berkeley invited the Rankenians to join him on his venture to found a "utopian" college to educate together American Indians' and colonists' sons in the Bermudas. He was so persuasive that one of their number, John Smibert, did follow Berkeley "westward." The young Hume's teachers at the university included a number of Rankenians including, of course, the major expositor of Newton of the time, Colin Maclaurin. Hume, then, definitely imbibed some of Berkeley's thought (including his moral and political concerns) in Edinburgh, since there was likely no other place where his work was so well received (Davie 1965).

Hume in the *Treatise* had to confront the *Principles* or the *Three Dialogues* exactly *because* he learned so much from the "God-appointed Berkeley," as W.B. Yeats called him. But he had to take his distance with care. He could hardly have written, "I am Berkeley *without* God." In fact, he separated himself so slyly that 200 years later many of his readers could be wondering, "Did Hume read Berkeley?" Hume also had to confront the Berkeley of *The Querist*, again *because* though he shared so much of (or was influenced by) Berkeley's conception of money, he at the same time drew contrary conclusions, again for problematic reasons (both logical and political). Wallace clearly understood this ambivalence in and potential weakness of Hume's position. In pitting Berkeley against Hume, Wallace inevitably evoked the direct connection between Berkeley's *The Querist* and the bugbear of Scottish economics: John Law. Just as Hume does not refer to *The Querist*, he does not refer to Law's *Money and Trade Considered* (even though from the early memoranda we have definitive evidence that he did read that work, as noted above).

Let us consider what concepts of money Hume could have learned from or might have been confirmed by Berkeley's *The Querist*. Hume shared with

Berkeley the view that gold and silver do not function as money due to their "intrinsic value." This commonality is deeply rooted in the one affinity with Berkeley that Hume openly admitted to in the *Treatise*: the radical rejection of abstract ideas. This involved not only in the rejection of a contradictory, vague abstract idea that is supposed to subsume a set of contradictory predicates (a view that Berkeley attributes to Locke). But Berkeley, during his second conceptual revolution in the early 1730s, widened his rejection of abstract ideas to a rejection of ideas that "naturally" represented others, since there were no special ideas of X that "naturally" represent all X ideas because they have the "essential" properties of X, that is, they are self-reflexive. Thus, according to this view, a gold coin "naturally" represents monetary value because it is valuable, whereas paper notes cannot. Berkeley rejected such a view when he made algebra, not geometry, his model of signification in his mathematical writings (cf. Caffentzis 2000: 252–263). Just as the number can be represented by both "2" and the letter "x" in the equation:

$$7-x = 5$$

so too geometric lines need not be represented by geometric lines. This revolution had a profound effect on Hume who was a close student of Berkeley's critique of both abstract ideas and analysis. To the point that he paraphrases Berkeley's understanding of abstract or general ideas as "all general ideas are nothing but particular ones, annex'd to a certain term, which gives them a more extensive signification, and makes them recall upon occasion other individuals, which are similar to them" (Hume 2000: 17). The "annexing" process is, as the word implies, an arbitrary one, while the "recal" is "a kind of magical faculty in the soul … inexplicable by the utmost efforts of human understanding" (Hume 2000: 21). This combination of the magical and the arbitrary liberated Hume (with Berkeley's help) from a rigid similitude or homology between signifier and signified.

Once Berkeley leaped over this semantic hurdle, the path to a critique of theoretical metallism became evident. Hume shared not only his critique of abstract ideas but also the rejection of theoretical metallism. Both use rather similar but complex metaphors to express this shared functionalist notion of money. Berkeley, for example, queries:

Provided the wheels move, whether it is not the same thing, as to the effect
of the machine, be this done by the force of wind, or water, or animals?

(quoted in Johnston 1970: 127, SQ 34)

Berkeley clearly sees money's relation to force or power as crucial. Money
for Berkeley must both excite and regulate power, otherwise it is nothing.
That is why he follows SQ34 with SQ 35:

Whether power to command the industry of others be not real wealth?
And whether money be not in truth tickets or tokens for conveying and
recording such power, and whether it be of great consequence what
materials the tickets are made of?

(Johnston 1970: 127)

Berkeley's metaphor is complex, because there are three powers that must
be distinguished: (1) the power to "convey and regulate" a power y [P(y)];
(2) the power of command over x [M(x)]; and (3) the power of industry and
work (I)—and the third replaces the first in the metaphor. Money is, in this
symbolism, P[M(I)], and the point is that just as a machine will be moved
by a variety of natural forces (I)—wind, water, animals—so too the material
used for P might vary as well—paper, brass, gold, cowry shell, wampam.
Of course, there is an important lacuna in the set of forces Berkeley listed:
non-natural human labor power, but that is because it is that problematic
power that makes the metaphorical wheels of industry turn.

Hume takes a similar stance before the great metaphorical machine of
the economy as Berkeley does and his essays in the first sentences of "Of
Money"

Money is not, properly speaking, one of the subjects of commerce;
but only the instrument which men have agreed upon to facilitate the
exchange of one commodity for another. It is none of the wheels of trade:
It is the oil which renders the motion of the wheels more smooth and easy.

(Hume 1987: 281)

Hume makes the "same points" as Berkeley—(1) money is not the object of
commerce, but the "wheels"; and (2) there are alternative forms of money
whose consequences can only be judged by their results, "the motion of

the wheels"—but in a subtly different way. Hume sees money as a lubricant of economic motion, not a power that might drive it. Money facilitates movement; it does not originate or excite it. Moreover, not all oils are the same. Whale oil, olive oil and walnut oil have different lubricating properties and capacities. It might indeed be "of great consequence" to the machine what kind of oil is used "in" it, especially since a lubricant is not outside of the machine it lubricates (in the way that the motive power is outside of the machine it animates).

The subtle differences between Berkeley and Hume multiply in considering the two passages. Hume is insistent from the very beginning on the conventional aspects of money, whereas Berkeley does not tell us about how the "tickets or tokens" originate. In fact, they were usually "issued" by a company in a region to pay its workers or to facilitate in "making small change" for its customers. Returning to the money in *The Querist*, we do not find a set of men agreeing "to facilitate the *exchange* of one commodity for another," but a "wise" and "well-governed" State concerned "to encourage *industry* in its members," and therefore concerned about money, as the Querist asks:

> Whether money be not only so far useful, as it stirreth up industry, *enabling men mutually to participate the fruits of each other's labor?*
> (Hume 1987: 125, SQ 5. My italics)

These differences explode when we consider the conflicting monetary strategies Berkeley proposed for Ireland and Hume for Scotland. Indeed, it is *because* of these conflicts that Hume would have been driven to read and study *The Querist*. They are most clearly presented in two essays: "Of Money" and "Of the Balance of Trade." In "Of the Balance of Trade," Hume refutes *The Querist*'s suggestion that is vividly projected by the metaphor of "a wall of brass" in the first epigraph of this chapter. Indeed, the "wall of brass" referred to in Berkeley's query is directly answered by Hume's "hydraulic" model of money and trade. Hume questions the very possibility of creating such an impermeable barrier between, say, Ireland or Scotland from the English economy, for to do so would force the state to fight against the force of "moral attraction, arising from the interests and passions of men, which is full as potent and infallible," which was as subtle but as powerful as the force of gravity in the natural realm. The only way that such an economic and monetary delinking can take place is through physical distance and/or geological separation, that did not exist in this case. Moreover, such a "wall of brass" would attempt to block the main way a "poor country" can change its situation: the use of "cheap" wages to undercut the trade advantage of richer countries.

Interestingly enough, Hume's harshly criticizes Berkeley's mentor, Dean Jonathan Swift, and his *A Short View of the State of Ireland* (1727–28) in the original 1752 versions of "Of the Balance of Trade." He identifies Swift as "An author, who has more humour than knowledge, more taste than judgment, and more spleen, prejudice, and passion than any of these qualities" (Hume 1987: 633). Indeed, this characterization was so harsh that Hume left it out of all future editions of the *Essays*. Swift predicted in *A Short View* the dramatic decline of gold and silver coin in Ireland in a few years' time due to an imbalance of trade with England and was skeptical of any effort to have the country "trade" itself out of its predicament. In fact, it was in the late 1720s that Swift wrote *A Modest Proposal* suggesting that Irish parents exploit their "comparative advantage" in Irish children by offering them up to discerning British diners. Swift's favored approach out of this dilemma was one that we would now call "import substitution." It was an economic policy both Berkeley and Swift shared, although Berkeley chose what he thought to be a less confrontational strategy.

In the face of such "spleen, prejudice, and passion," Hume pointed out that if Swift was correct, then "in the course of 30 years [sic] the currency would be worth absolutely nothing" (Hume 1987: 311). However, by the early 1750s, Ireland had not become totally destitute. On the contrary, there was a noticeable "advance of riches" due, if contemporary research on Irish economic history is correct, to increased trade (Cullen 1968; and 1972). Consequently, Swift's (and Berkeley's) effort at "import substitution" was hardly the path to Ireland's (and Scotland's) transformation from poor to modestly rich countries.

In "Of the Balance of Trade," Hume also attacks the method Berkeley proposed to create the "brass wall": a paper currency issued by a National Bank. He uses his hydraulic model to argue that paper money literally "drives out" specie currency (in accordance to Gresham's law):

> I scarcely know any method of sinking money below its level, but those institutions of banks, funds, and paper-credit, which are so much

practiced in this kingdom. These render paper equivalent to money, circulate it throughout the whole state, make it supply the place of gold and silver, raise proportionably the price of labor and commodities, and by that means either banish a great part of those precious metals, or prevent their farther encrease. What can be more short-sighted than our reasoning on this head?

(Hume 1987: 316)

In the end, then, Berkeley's "reasoning" will inevitably make Ireland or Scotland, if either country took up *The Querist's* recommendations, unable to enter into world trade with dreaded consequences, according to Hume.

The other essay directly in conflict with Berkeley's policy recommendations is "Of Money," where Hume again invokes and attacks Berkeley's and Law's proposals for the founding of a National Bank (of Ireland and Scotland, respectively) that would regulate the issuing of "paper-credit" money that is "so generally esteemed advantageous to every nation" (Hume 1987: 284). Hume rejects this "paper" path to increasing the amount of money in a nation, since it will lead to set of "inconveniences": (1) it will "encreas[e] money beyond its natural proportion to labour and commodities" leading to higher prices of labor and provisions; and (2) foreigners will not accept the "counterfeit money" whose value "any great disorder in the state will reduce to nothing." Hume recognizes the advantages of paper money for the rich who find it dangerous to transport large quantities of specie. He specifically mentions the private bankers of Dublin who provide such a service, and who perhaps, along with Law's Banque Royale, were practical models for Berkeley's suggestions. But Hume finds any Bank that did not "lock up all the money it received" (like the one that Berkeley suggested) dangerous to the nation, since it tended to create "counterfeit money."

Hume's critique of Berkeley's monetary strategy was not based on Berkeley's ontological rejection of "intrinsic value" (or "theoretical metallism"), but on semantic and practical considerations. He argued in a utilitarian fashion that in fact "paper-credit" money, when one examines its actual and potential use, just like public credit in general, one "will find no comparison between the ill and the good which result from them" (Hume 1987: 354).

I conclude that Hume's decision not to directly refer to Berkeley's *The Querist* was a sign of its influence on *Political Discourses*, not of its lack. His critical reference to Swift's *A Short View* (and his positive reference Swift's maxim: "in the arithmetic of the customs, two and two make not four, but often make only one" [Hume 1987: 324]) as well as the description of the Dublin private bankers made it clear to the philosophical politician, the ideal reader of *Political Discourses*, that he was cognizant of and had taken into account the theoretical and practical monetary situation in Ireland. And, to be so in 1752 required familiarity with the suggestions of *The Querist*.

CONCEPTUAL PERSONNA AND GENRES

A key to understanding these differences of Berkeley's and Hume's concepts of the linguistic genre appropriate to money that each text projects:

Money in *The Querist* is nothing if it does not excite action and industry. Therefore, its appropriate linguistic analogue is the question: an incomplete utterance in itself that is only completed by the action of another (Caffentzis 2000). Money demands, necessitates and requires nothing, since the other may never be excited enough to respond to the question, hence reducing it to a useless sign. It eschews all "musts."

Money projected by *The Querist* is a sign of a future step to take, like every other sign. That is why, of all the interrogative terms—"who," "what," "why," "when," "where"—"whether" is the most appropriate. For "whether" is used to indicate alternatives of action and/decision. It puts the questioned "on the spot" and provokes a response concerning explicit alternatives: "whether A or B?" This too is the role of money as well. It too provokes a response, otherwise it is not functioning as money.

Money in *The Querist* is, in the terminology of Berkeley's post-1734 "second conceptual revolution," a notion, since it is neither a sensory idea with fixed "objective" qualities nor an indescribably active spirit with a life of its own (as some novelists in the eighteenth century humorously depicted). Berkeley had defended a mutually exclusive and exhaustive dichotomy between ideas and spirits in his philosophy until he began to draft a flurry of works in the early 1730s (inspired, perhaps, by his American voyage) including *Alciphron*, the revisions of the *Principles*, *Dialogues*, the *Analyst*, *A Defense of Free Thinking in Mathematics*, as well as *The Querist*. In this period, he realized that he needed to have a concept that would describe the acts of the spirit (a task he deemed impossible before) (cf. [Caffentzis 2000] for Berkeley's "second conceptual revolution"). This was especially true in the description of money. Once the view that money was an objective thing with intrinsic properties and values is rejected, as it was in *The Querist*, then a description of money required reference to acts and characteristics of the spirit like excitement, desire, aspiration, wants, fancy, effort, etc. Money had to be designed so that it would actually excite the spirit into action. A pure sensationist physics of money would not be enough for *The Querist*, money *queries* the spirit and the response is *an act* of the spirit.

Hume, although he was profoundly influenced by Berkeley's philosophy, had no need for his notions. Hume drew a seamless connection between impressions and ideas of sensation and reflection. The red impression and the flash of anger were not distinguished as in Berkeley's ontology where the first is a thing in itself while the latter is an act of the spirit. Indeed, there was no indescribable active "spirit" in Hume's universe. Consequently, there was no need to hypothesize a realm of special entities or modalities of the spirit. That is also why there could be something of a "science of human nature," since the same forms of reasoning and experiment are to be found in both natural philosophy and this science. That is why, after writing the *Treatise*, Hume recognized that the ideal literary form of his science would be the essay, since it meant in his day (as Samuel Johnson would have it) "a trial; an experiment."

Money, on the plane of linguistics genres in the *Political Discourses*, is not a query series, it is the essay, that is, an experiment (often mental) confirming (or disconfirming) a general law. The money form arises out of a "moral attraction" as necessary in human nature as gravitation is in physical nature. For it is rooted in convention, not contract nor state decree.

The essayist is a very different conceptual persona than the querist and the essayist's questions are of a different order than the querist's (on the notion of conceptual personae, see Deleuze and Guattari [1994: 61–83]). The essayist's questions are meant to provoke an experimental state of mind and in the "Of the Balance of Trade" especially, they are dramatically integrated in thought experiments. They are not meant to keep thought indefinitely suspended until there is action. The essayist continually intrudes in the text, unlike the querist who remains forever at an infinite ironic distance from the reader, and presents an answer. For example, the essayist launches a thought experiment: "Suppose that there are 12 millions of paper ... and suppose the real cash of the kingdom to be 18 millions" (Hume 1987: 317). It hypothesizes that if there had not been 12 millions of paper, there would have been 30 million of real cash. The dialogue continues:

Here is a state which is found by experience to be able to hold a stock of 30 millions. I say, if it be able to hold it, it must of necessity have acquired it in gold and silver, had we not obstructed the entrance of these metals by this new invention of paper. *Whence would it have acquired that sum?* From all the kingdoms of the world. *But why?* Because, if you remove these 12 millions, money in this state is below its level, compared with our neighbors: and we must immediately draw from all of them, till we be full and saturate, so to speak, and can hold no more.

(Hume 1987: 317)

6
Fiction or Counterfeit?
Specie or Paper?

People of Baetica, do you want to be rich? Imagine to yourselves that I am very rich and that you are too. Each morning put it into your head that your fortune has doubled during the night. Then arise, and if you have creditors, go pay them with what you have imagined and tell them to do some imagining of their own.

—Montesquieu, *The Persian Letters* (Montesquieu 1961: 259)

This Office was not Constituted for Impossibilitys, nor to gratify wild imagination.

—William Chetwynd, Master of the Tower Mint, to the British Treasury in 1745 (quoted in Dyer and Gaspar 1992: 411)

HUME AGAINST THE MONETARY GRAIN

The publication of newspapers and the work of journalists in London and Amsterdam resulting in up-to-date stock price lists and foreign exchange rates were crucial to the financial and monetary revolutions of the eighteenth century (Neal 1990). These revolutions, however, not only required the development of new information networks, but they also called for the creation of suitable ways to conceptualize these bits of information and effective self-definitions of the agents who used them. Many of the major philosophers of the period invested a considerable intellectual effort in creating categories and self-definitions in response to these revolutions. Some philosophers like George Berkeley did so enthusiastically. For the Anglo-Irish Bishop Berkeley saw in the increasing role of paper money—a central feature of the monetary revolution—a chance for Ireland to escape the cycle of poverty it was trapped in (Caffentzis 2000). David Hume, from his vantage point in Scotland, was much more nuanced and cautious in his interpretation of these "revolutions."

147

Hume certainly witnessed a dramatic expansion of the use of non-metallic forms of money in his lifetime. Between 1744 and 1772, the circulation of bank notes in Scotland increased fifteen-fold, thirteen provincial banking companies opened and the total bank assets rose from £329,000 to £3,100,000 (Whatley 2000: 67). But the banks were not the only sources of paper money in Hume's time. In order to circumvent the "shortage of specie" problem, manufacturers and merchants created paper money notes that served as substitutes for metallic coin. By 1764, there were at least fourteen note issuers in Scotland in addition to the banks (Munn 1981: 18).

Another major source of paper-credit instruments was the public debt. In the course of Hume's life, the British national debt increased from approximately £20 million to £140 million (Brewer 1988: 115). This national debt became the basis of a market in governmental securities that functioned as a means of exchange in large business transactions.

Hume was fully apprised of how public debt instruments functioned, as illustrated in the following passage:

> Public securities are with us become a kind of money, and pass as readily at the current price of gold or silver ... our national debts furnish merchants with a species of money, that is continually multiplying in their hands, and produces sure gain, beside the profits of commerce.
>
> (E 353)

He also was well informed as to growing use of bank notes as well as checking credit (or "bank-credit") in Scotland, as the following passage indicates:

> A man goes to the bank and find surety to the amount, we shall suppose, of a thousand pounds. This money, or any part of it, he has the liberty of drawing out whenever he pleases, and he pays only the ordinary interest for it, while it is in his hands ... As a man may find surety nearly to the amount of his substance, and his bank-credit is equivalent to ready money, a merchant does hereby in a manner coin his houses, his household furniture, the goods in his warehouse, the foreign debts due to him, his ships at sea...
>
> (E 319)

Hence, Hume establishes the apt metaphor of "coining" the commodities one owns. For Hume realized that a modern commercial economy gives rise to numerous money substitutes that constitute an elastic currency with the capacity to accommodate the demand for additional means of exchange as the economy expands. However, even though he had a sophisticated understanding of paper money, he was critical of its government debt and private bank sources. For paper money, he argued, inevitably tended to "banish gold and silver from the considerable commerce of the state" and "render all provisions and labour dearer than otherwise they would be" (E 355).

Hume cautioned his readers about the expansion of paper money and paper-credit with these words:

> to endeavour artificially to increase [paper-credit], can never be the interest of any trading nation; but must lay them under disadvantages, by encreasing money beyond its natural proportion to labour and commodities, and thereby heightening their price to the merchant and manufacturer.
>
> (E 284)

Indeed, the kind of bank that he deemed most "advantageous" was one, like the Bank of Amsterdam, that "locked up all the money it received and never augmented the circulating coin, as is usual, by returning part of its treasure into commerce." The advantage of such a bank is that it would result in the "low price of labor and the destruction of paper-credit" (E 284–285). Thus, Hume only countenanced the most disciplined paper money regime, that is, one that "destroys" other undisciplined uses of paper money and paper-credit.

Hume's suspicion of "paper money," "paper-credit" and the institutions of banks and public debt that supported them, though often qualified, was a lifelong disposition.[1] For example, one of his early criticisms in 1752 of public debt and its allied paper instruments is that they, "being a kind of paper-credit, have all the disadvantages attending that species of money" (E 355). Toward the end of his life, in 1776 to be precise, Hume delivered an apocalyptic critique of public debt and, by implication, the paper instruments monetarizing the debt in his *The History of England*:

Our late delusions have much exceeded any thing known in history, not even excepting those of the crusades. For I suppose there is no mathematical, still less an arithmetical demonstration, that the road to the Holy Land was not the road to paradise, as there is, that the endless increase of national debts is the direct road to national ruin. But having now completely reached that goal, it is needless at present to reflect on the past. It will be found in the present year, 1776, that all the revenues of this island north of Trent and west of Reading, are mortgaged or anticipated forever … So egregious indeed has been our folly, that we have even lost all title to compassion in the numberless calamities that are awaiting us.

(HEiv: 363)

Similar critical, though qualified, passages concerning the use of bank notes and other forms of paper-credit can be found throughout his work.[2]

Hume clearly had a complex, ambivalent attitude to paper money. He recognized it both as a product of "commercial modernization" and as its nemesis. As he wrote, after two pages of harsh criticism of paper money,

It must, however, be confessed that, as all these questions of trade and money are extremely complicated, there are certain lights, in which this subject may be placed, so as to represent the advantages of paper-credit and banks to be superior to their disadvantages (E318) … But whatever advantages result from these inventions [like Bank-credit], it must still be allowed that, besides giving too great facility to credit, which is dangerous, they banish precious metals …

(E320)

In a telling, but paradoxical formulation of this attitude, he claimed in the *Political Discourses* (1752) that though gold and silver money has "merely a fictitious value, arising from the agreement and convention of men," (E 297) paper money is "counterfeit" (E 284).[3] This was not a passing insight. Hume certainly emphasized the conventional or what he called the "fictional" character of metallic money throughout his life. For example, in his first published comments on money in Book III of the *Treatise* (1740), he claimed that both languages and metallic money developed as conventionally coordinated practices:

In a like manner are languages gradually establish'd by human conventions without any promise. In like manner do gold and silver become the common measures of exchange, and are esteem'd sufficient payment for what is of a hundred times their value.

(T 315)[4]

Nearly thirty years later, toward the end of his life, in his 1769 letter to Abbé Morellet, he gently disagrees with his correspondent's anti-conventionalist view of "the establishment of [metallic] money" and argues that the conventionalist or fictional view of metallic money has "some foundation" (R 214; Caffentzis 2001: 326–327).

Why then did Hume choose to defend "fictions" (metallic money) over "counterfeits" (paper money), which, after all, are fictions as well? This was certainly a provocatively idiosyncratic way to make his point. It was in contrast, for example, to the way a "theoretical metallist" like Richard Cantillon depicted the difference between metal and paper money in his *Essai sur la nature du commerce en général* (completed in 1734 and published in London in 1755) (Schumpeter 1954: 288–289). For Cantillon, paper money is "fictitious and imaginary" while silver money is "real." He writes:

An abundance of fictitious and imaginary money causes the same disadvantages as an increase of real money in circulation, by raising the price of land and labour, or by making works and manufactures more expensive at the risk of subsequent loss. But this furtive abundance vanishes at the first gust of discredit and precipitates disorder.

(Cantillon 1964: 311)

Hume, however, was cautious of binary contrasts like fictitious/real, for his philosophy reveals that there is much of the fictional in the "real" (and vice versa). Hence, Hume's "fiduciary theory of money" was a nuanced one.

In this chapter, I examine Hume's distinction between fiction and counterfeit in his pre-1752 writings, especially in *The Treatise on Human Nature*, in order to explore the philosophical motivation for his provocative formulation of the distinction between metallic and paper money. It is a contribution to a lively research program in recent Hume scholarship whose core hypothesis is that Hume's philosophical work (especially his *Treatise*) played a crucial role in the formulation of his "economics."[5] In particular, I locate the philosophical basis of the fiction/counterfeit contrast in Hume's distinction between natural fictions that are arrived at unconsciously and universally through conventions and artificial fictions that are arrived at consciously and particularly and are expressed as promises. I argue that Hume applied his philosophical analysis of natural and artificial fictions in the formulation of his monetary policy recommendations, including his "scandalous" support for the debasement of the coinage as a legitimate tool of statecraft.

COUNTERFEIT AND FICTION IN HUME'S PHILOSOPHY

A typology of the false, the fictitious, the fallacious, and the widely believed, but unproved and, perhaps, unprovable permeates Hume's thought. This play with and revaluation of the many variations of falsehood gives his work a certain freedom and charm that is absent from most systems of Truth piously announced in the history of philosophy.[6] Hume's interest in the varieties of falsehood arose immediately out of one of his central philosophical tenets: truth is not explanatory, that is, simply because a proposition like "The Himalayan Mountains have existed for millions of years" is true does not explain how creatures like ourselves come to accept this proposition. The ironic Hume found that fiction, fallacy and illusion, not truth, provided a better explanatory road to comprehend human understanding.

Hume distinguished at least two kinds of fictions that, for want of better terms, can be called "natural" fictions and "artificial" fictions (in parallel to Hume's distinctions among virtues) (Norton and Norton 2000: 576). He was eager to legitimate natural fictions that include such central ideas like time, enduring sensible objects, ideal standards, substances and the self. These fictions are anxious cruxes for his thought since they seem both to be indispensable for everyday common life and to violate his crucial epistemological axiom: all ideas are ultimately "deriv'd" from impressions. Of course, Hume recognized an "exception" to the axiom from the start of the *Treatise*, with his famous and heavily commented on "shade of blue" counter-example (T 10).[7] But this fictional creation of a previously unexperienced pseudo-impression, which Hume first treats as an oddity, becomes his model of a general process of the human mind that creates vivid ideas verging on impressions in order to respond to moral and epistemological crises.

I can only briefly sketch out this philosophical territory with full recognition that all of the separate fictions in Hume's *Treatise* I discuss here have been commented upon and debated about in a rich, ever-growing philosophical literature especially stimulated by the publication of Annette Baier's *A Progress of Sentiments* (Baier 1991).

The first use of such a fictional analysis in the *Treatise* is the discussion of the origin of the idea of time. Hume argues that the idea of time or duration "is deriv'd from a succession of changeable objects" (T 30), but this idea is also applied to objects that are unchanged or unchangeable. How is this possible? "Ideas always represent the objects or impressions, from which they are deriv'd, and can never without a fiction represent or be apply'd to any other" (T 30). Thus, the idea of duration can only be applied to unchanging or unchangeable objects with "a fiction." What is the source of that fiction? Hume locates it in a variety of universal experiences, the most prominent one being the "continual succession of perceptions in your mind" that gives us a sense of change even when observing unchanged objects. The idea of duration "deriv'd" from this internal machine of fancy is "by a fiction" applied to unchanged objects, without our noticing it. The timeless unchanged object is thus fictitiously, but naturally, drawn into time by our own inner agitation.

Another type of natural fiction is encountered in the process of constructing ideas of ideal (or fictional) standards. For example, we have rough-and-ready ideas of greater, lesser and equal distances between objects that are often refined and corrected by the use of measuring instruments. This process of correction seems to have an ideal limit: the idea of "some imaginary standard of equality, by which the appearances and measuring are exactly corrected, and the figures reduc'd entirely to that proportion" (T 36). This "standard is plainly imaginary," since it goes beyond any distinction an instrument or art can make. But such a "fiction however is very natural" (T 36–37). Hume finds such an idealization process taking place in those involved in ever-more exact measurements of time, in musicians who claim to have the idea of perfect pitch, in painters who claim to have an idea of a perfect color, and in the "mechanic with regard to motion." In other words, artists and artisans naturally tend to create ideal fictions by taking the everyday refinements they practice in their craft to the limit.

Hume's most prominent use of the notion of natural fiction is in his solution of Berkeley's conundrum concerning the continued existence of sensible objects. Surely, books, chairs, trees and mountains are not sensed continually. On the contrary, the perception of such objects is often interrupted. But what gives "the unthinking and unphilosophical part of mankind (that is, all of us, at one time or another)" the belief that these objects continue to exist even though they do not continue to sense them? Hume appeals to a natural fiction to solve the puzzle:

> Here then we have a propensity to feign the continu'd existence of all sensible objects; and as this propensity arises from some lively impression of the memory, it bestows a vivacity on that fiction; or in other words, makes us believe the continu'd existence of body.
>
> (T 138)

A similar operation takes place in the creation of the fiction of substance. For when we notice a unity of the qualities in objects, the imagination is obliged "to feign an unknown something, or original substance and matter," that might give the compounded object "a title to be call'd one thing, notwithstanding its diversity and composition" (T 146). The ancient philosophers, of course, developed this natural fiction to unnatural levels. The peripatetic philosophers, for example, created a whole system of occult qualities and unintelligible chimeras of substance that "yet is deriv'd from principles as natural as any of those above explain'd" (T 147).

Finally, and most radically, personal identity is based on a fiction as well, according to Hume:

> The identity, which we ascribe to the mind of man, is only a fictitious one, and of a like kind with that which we ascribe to vegetables and animal bodies. It cannot, therefore, have a different origin, but must proceed from a like operation of the imagination upon like objects.
>
> (T 169)

Hume's argument for the fictionality of personal identity is more extreme than the one he produced for the continued existence of objects of perception, simply because the fictitious object in question must be a most intimate one to the reader. But Hume manages to "alienate" the self by using the tools of his proto-phenomenological impression/idea analysis, so that the self's very existence is brought into question. Once that is done, the procedure he uses to prove fictionality is applied and the self itself is shown to be a fiction. But it is a fiction that is arrived at by "feigning" the existence of an entity that unifies acts and perceptions. This "feigning" is not a conscious mental act, of course, though it is done by everyone, everywhere and at all times.

Time, continued existence of objects, the self, substance and ideal standards: all fictions! Hume's notion of natural fiction must bear a remarkable weight. Therefore, it is important to determine what status Hume ascribes to it and its products. Does Hume mean that they do not exist in the same way that a fictional character (e.g., Robinson Crusoe) does not exist? Or, is he claiming that the existence of these entities cannot be adequately proven (i.e., their existence is not verifiable)? Or, is he claiming that the beliefs in their existence are not falsifiable? Annette Baier's characterization of these "non-truths" is more faithful to Hume's intentions:

> Hume calls them "fictions," and this is quite different from calling them false. What is provably false is to deny that they are fictions, and Hume does think that we are prone to such falsehoods. Fictions are plausible stories we tell ourselves to organize our experience.
>
> (Baier 1991: 103)

Baier's "plausible stories" are convincing, according to Hume, because they arise when the mind is tempted to apply a variety of useful mental mechanisms beyond their justifiable limits. Although these mechanisms in the case of time, self, body, substance and standard are different, I will call their fallacious, but effective, result the "confounding of identity with relation" (T 166).

The texts of the *Treatise*, the *Enquiries* and *Essays* constitute an autobiography of individual and collective "unconscious" mental tricks, displacements and oblique transitions-without-reflection that conflate relations with identity.

Hume's quest, then, is for a set of criteria differentiating natural, involuntary fictions and artificial, consciously orchestrated ones. This quest is important to my argument, for it is exactly along this divide, I claim, we will find the differentia of metallic and paper money and the philosophical motivation for Hume's monetary conclusions.

Natural fictions have an aura of dignity (or at least necessity about them), since they are the "feigned" though "natural" products of essential mental mechanisms. But what are artificial fictions? Are they just plain fantasies, manufactured illusions or Machiavellian lies? To answer this question let us consider a small census of passages in the *Treatise* that deal with such fictions.

An early, but major reference to such fictions is in Hume's contrast between belief and fiction: "an idea assented to feels different from a fictitious idea, that the fancy alone presents to us" (T 68). The passage that includes this sentence is, of course, one of Hume's most important, for he distinguishes belief not on the basis of an internal feature of any idea or set of ideas, but upon the manner the idea is being conceived. Fictions of the fancy differ from beliefs assented to because the latter "are more strong, firm, and vivid, than the loose reveries of a castle-builder" (T 68). In such discussions, ("idle," "loose") fictions (of the imagination and fancy) are evoked for contrast to beliefs, that is, ideas that surprisingly transform themselves back into semi-impressions due to the force and vivacity with which they are experienced.

This contrast between belief and artificial fiction, however, is not absolute, since almost any such fiction can become a belief (in someone, somewhere, sometime) given the powers of passion and artifice. For example, among the vulgar,

> quacks and projectors meet with a more easy faith upon account of their magnificent pretensions, than if they kept themselves with the bounds of moderation. The first astonishment, which naturally attends their miraculous relations, spreads itself over the whole soul, and so vivifies and enlivens the idea, that it resembles the inferences we draw from experience.
>
> (T 82–83)

This permeable, but at first glance mysterious, barrier between belief and artificial fiction is the basis of some of Hume's most entertaining philosophical exercises. For example, he observes that poets, "tho' liars by profession," always try to "give an air of truth to their fictions," otherwise their performances will not be entertaining. Similarly, he observes that those who always lie can never give satisfaction to the mind, since what they say is immediately dismissed and cannot have a hold on one's mind.

Hence, according to Hume's philosophy of falsehood, artificial fictions must be presented in the context of "truth and reality" in order to be emotively effective. Poets often use historical settings and the names of real personages to make a deeper impression "on the fancy and affections" (T 84). But even this is not always necessary, since such a context of "truth and reality" can be manufactured by the repetition of images and names (as in the case of propaganda). So there is a continual traffic between the judgment and fancy in literature. Inevitably, when the permeability between judgment and fancy increases sufficiently, poetical fiction ends and madness begins. For madness is a state where "every loose fiction or idea, having the same influence as the impressions of the memory, or the conclusions of the judgment, is receiv'd on the same footing, and operates with equal force on the passions" (T 84). Poetical fiction, however, can hardly create genuine madness because it never generates a level of feeling beyond that of the lowest "species of probability."

Of course, many more artificial fictions, beyond the rather innocent literary ones I mentioned, inhabit Hume's human cosmos, from philosophical ones (e.g., "the state of nature") to political and economic ones. Hume (in)famously located many examples of artificial fiction in religious belief as well. He found that:

> the conviction of the religionists, in all ages, is more affected than real, and scarce ever approaches, in any degree, to that solid belief and persuasion, which governs us in the common affairs of life … They make a merit of implicit faith; and disguise to themselves their real infidelity, by the strongest asseverations and positive bigotry.
>
> (quoted in Bernard 1995: 231)

Conviction is often lacking because, according to Hume, there is no innate religious faculty. Consequently:

> a habit of dissimulation is by degrees contracted: And fraud and falsehood become the predominant principle. Hence the reason of that vulgar observation, the highest zeal in religion and the deepest hypocrisy, so far from being inconsistent, are often or commonly united in the same individual character.
>
> (quoted in Bernard 1995: 233)

Hence, the field of artificial fiction is much broader than that of natural fictions. The artificial fictions of religion, myth, art and literature have an infinity of possible linkages since they play with the inevitable surplus energy of the imagination while the natural fictions of the understanding are much more limited, since they depend upon specific mechanisms of thought (especially the unconscious ability of confounding "identity with relation" through projection, inertia, or "feigning").

What, indeed, are the general differences between these "artificial" fictions and the "natural" ones that are at the foundation of our conceptions of space, time, body, standards, substance and self? David and Mary Norton, in their edition of Hume's *Treatise on Human Nature*, sum up the distinction in the following passage:

> In general terms, such natural fictions are ideas that, although they take us beyond experience, are none the less the involuntary result of experience and the usual processes of the mind. In contrast, the fictions of the poet or the dramatist might be called artificial fictions, these arise voluntarily or, to use Hume's language, as the result of contrivance and design.
>
> (T 440)

Table 6.1 displays some of their specific differences:

Table 6.1 Table summarizing Hume's conception of "natural" and "artificial" fictions

Natural Fictions	Artificial Fictions
universally believed	not universally believed
unconscious mechanisms of belief	belief involves conscious deception
difficult to doubt	overuse can lead to lack of conviction
without this belief, a life of "melancholy and delirium" (T 175)	if not controlled, they lead to "philosophical madness"
formed by mental mechanisms that turn "relations to identities"	formed by the attachment of belief to a fancy
a precondition of a common life	a consequence of and parasitic upon a common life

Artificial fictions can be transformed into beliefs by being "counterfeited" as ideas of memory or impressions through artful repetition or through being placed in "truth-like" contexts or environments of excitement and interest. As Hume pointed out:

> an idea of the imagination may acquire such a force and vivacity, as to pass for an idea of the memory, and counterfeit its effects on belief and judgement. This is noted in the case of liars; who by the frequent repetition of the lies, came at last to believe and remember them as realities.
>
> (T 60–61)

Natural fictions, on the contrary, become established in the mind through normal mental mechanisms operating beyond their standard range through a principle of ideational inertia. For example, the development of perfect standards brings the procedures of correction and comparison "beyond what we have instruments and art to make" for there is not "any thing more usual, than for the mind to proceed after this manner with any action, even after the reason has ceas'd, which first determin'd it to begin" (T 36–37).

The "speculative politicians," therefore, had two paths to follow, not one, in preparing the minds of their people for a fiction like money.

MONEY, FICTION AND COUNTERFEIT

Given the importance of the distinction between natural and artificial fictions for Hume's philosophy, it should not be surprising that it would be useful in the explication of his explicit but controversial contrast between "fictitious" metallic money and "counterfeit" paper money. For this apparent dichotomy is problematic simply because Hume recognizes that in commerce metallic money and paper money are often substituted for each other and that banks often issue paper money "backed" by precious metals. Is Hume simply trying to steer his readers away from paper money *tout court* or is he calling for a more sophisticated understanding of the relation between the two?

Clearly, Hume does not denounce the directors of the Bank of Scotland or the officials of the British government as counterfeiters in the standard sense of the word "counterfeiter" at the time, that is, those who make false resemblances of coin to fool the public and enrich themselves. For counterfeiters are the quacks and "professional liars" of the monetary world, who voluntarily and deviously use the existence of a common metallic monetary system to make less valuable metallic copies that sensibly resemble real coins enough to confuse the average person into accepting them (cf. Wennerlind 2002).

Indeed, eighteenth-century bankers who issued paper-credit money (in contrast to those who issued stocks, bonds and other speculative instruments) promised that their paper truly represented a certain amount of metallic coin and that this coin would be returned on presentation of the paper to the appropriate person. But the frequent experiences of bank failures and credit crises showed that bankers systematically broke this promise. Indeed, it was widely known that the amount of metallic money in the banks' vaults was usually only a fraction of the total paper money they issued. National government officials also falsely claimed that they could entirely pay off the national debt in specie even though they recognized that this was neither possible nor even desirable (Brewer 1988: 123). Hence, the counterfeit aspect of paper money does not lie in the sensory resemblance of the paper to the metal, of course, but in its claim to symbolize (while actually falsifying) a higher-order feature of the monetary system: the monetary promise.

Still, Hume also claims that metallic money is a fiction as well. Of course, metallic money does not have the same status as natural fictions like time, enduring sensible objects, ideal standards, substances and the self, but for the social realm it attained a status similar to language and justice. It is true that justice is an artificial not a natural virtue in Hume's philosophy, but with a typical Humean qualification:

> as no principle of the human mind is more natural than a sense of virtue; so no virtue is more natural than justice. Mankind is an inventive species; and where an invention is obvious and absolutely necessary, it may as properly be said to be natural as anything that proceeds immediately from original principles, without the intervention of thought or reflection.
>
> (T 311)

Similarly, the slow development of a monetary system (which presupposes justice and language systems, of course) has the same character as the property system: "it arises gradually, and acquires force by a slow progression, and by our repeated experience of the inconveniences of transgressing it" (T 315).

To test this view of the correspondence of the natural fiction/artificial fiction distinction with metal/paper money distinction in Hume's philosophy, it would be worthwhile to apply the oppositions in Table 6.1 to the monetary realm. Metallic coinage has a claim to a universal belief based upon unconscious conventions that are difficult to forego. Once one is in a monetary economy, any attempt to reject money makes it impossible to lead a common life and ends in "melancholy and delirium." With exposure to the world of exchange, coins are inevitably worn, clipped and bagged; they gradually come to have a very different "intrinsic value" from what they had when they were originally coined; but these facts do not block the confounding of "identity with relation" during usage. On the contrary, the difference between judging coins by weight or by tale (i.e., by the stamped official value) is an excellent example of how this confounding of "identity with relation" takes place. For in the eighteenth century, as previously, there was a continual exchange of coins that were not full weight (because of clipping and wear) as if they were. This shifting from the material location of value (the weight and purity of the coin's metal) to the representation of value and back again is a conventional aspect of coinage that paper money (which represented, at best, an absent and abstract mass of metal) could not mimic.

Hume was conscious of the millions of unconscious acts in commercial exchange when underweight coins are treated "as if" they were up to the standard stamped on their sides. This confounding of "identity with relation" certainly had to make a huge leap in the face of a dramatic deterioration of the British silver currency in Hume's lifetime. For example, by 1777, government officials found that "L300 in silver, which ought to have weighted 1,200 ounces, weighed 624 ounces" (Thompson 1996: 135). This was similar to "[a]n experiment … made [in the preparation of the 1696 re-coinage] which showed that L57,2000 sterling in silver coin, which should have contained 220,000 ounces of pure silver, contained only 141,000 ounces" (Caffentzis 1989: 20).[8] That is, the average deterioration of the silver coinage in 1777 was 48 percent in contrast to the 1690s when the deterioration rate was "only" 36 percent. The margin of "fiction" in the British silver coinage of Hume's time was very wide indeed, but coined money still retained universal conviction because it was based on social conventions and mental mechanisms that created all natural fictions.[9]

Paper money did not generate a similar universal conviction. Certainly Hume was far from being the only paper money skeptic of his time. On the contrary, he shared his suspicions with commentators from Massachusetts (William Douglass) to Naples (Ferdinando Galiani) because it was widely recognized that the issuing of paper money required conscious deception and its overuse could easily lead to a sudden loss of conviction in the monetary promises that gave paper its credit. But, even worse, if its audience did not quickly lose conviction in these promises, the continued issuing of paper money would lead to monetary bubbles, hyper-inflations and other social catastrophes (as in Law's "System's" and the South Sea Company's crises). The essence of paper money is that its attractiveness requires a specific but potentially fanciful belief that some bank, company or government is, respectively, growing, profitable or triumphant.

These were well-known objections to paper money. Hume, however, showed that the problem with paper money was not that it was paper and not specie. The crucial difference between the two kinds of money was in the differential effects on their users and originators. Though the paper signifier is brazenly circulating in public, its signified is hidden either behind physical vaults or behind the even more mysterious vault of the future. Its referent is both "absent and general" and its functioning depends upon an explicit promise from its issuers that it will be exchanged for specie at some specified time and place.

The functioning of metallic money does not depend on promises, since its referent, the coin in one's hand, is both "present and individual." Metallic money is rooted in a deeper, conventional layer of social life which arises from "a general sense of common interest; which sense all the members of the society express to one another, and which induces them to regulate their conduct by certain rules" (T 315). Just as "even promises themselves ... arise from human conventions" (T314), so too paper money (which depends on promises) arises from the ur-world of conventions supporting specie. Paper money is thus based on and is parasitic upon a common monetary life; it cannot be the basis of such a life in the way that coinage can.

This is not to say, however, that for Hume paper money (like art, religion and literature) does not have an important role to play in the development of commerce and civilization. This Humean theme was familiar to the many poets and writers of the eighteenth century who appreciated, criticized and marveled over the connection between literature and paper money brought about by the so-called financial revolution. The many ironies, puns and metaphors implicating the realm of paper money with writing in the work of Pope, Swift, Johnson, among others, make Hume's use of the trope "coun-terfeit" in characterizing paper money almost trite.[10] For example, Patrick Brantlinger quotes the famous lines from Pope's *Epistles*:

> Blessed paper-credit! last and best supply!
> That lends Corruption lighter wings to fly!
> Gold imp'd by thee, can compass hardest things,
> Can pocket States, can fetch or carry Kings…

and then Brantlinger comments:

> Even more impressively (and impishly and impiously), Pope under-scores the analogy between such "paper credit" and literature (or perhaps literacy—reading and writing in general—and therefore civilization in general). His own poetry is a sort of "paper-credit," imp'd, impowered or "empired" only by individual fantasy or genius to be, like Sibylline prophesy, scattering fates, fortunes, kings, queens, and nations to the winds (just as Britain was an island "Debtor to the Wind").
>
> (Brantlinger 1996: 63–64)

Hume also recognized that the imagination creates artificial fictions in liter-ature as well as in the monetary sphere that are crucial for the development of a polite culture. However, unless the surplus energy of the symbolic realm in literature and money is restrained, it can become the basis of destructive passions and madness. The problem with paper money from Hume's per-spective is that the "present and individual" restraint internal to coinage (the weight-versus-tale dialectic) does not exist for paper notes. Their referent is "absent and general" and any restraint on their iteration must be external, hence "political" (in a pejorative sense of that word).

Inevitably then, the divergent structures of use and verification presup-posed by "natural" metallic and "artificial" paper money create a tremendous tension in a monetary system. It is no surprise that Hume would concern himself with this tension, for he lived on the cusp between two great and simultaneous monetary transformations in Britain. First, Britain was shifting from a dominant use of silver to that of gold coinage and, second, Britain was moving away from specie to paper currency (Feavearyear 1963: 150–173). Paper money, as an artificial fiction or counterfeit, requires the dynamics of belief to function. The continued acceptability of its issuers' promises depends on artful repetition and on being placed in 'truth-like' contexts or environments of excitement and interest. On the other hand, the conventions sustaining metallic money operate on the basis of the mind's inertial tendency to try, as much as possible, to feign the correspondence of a given perception with a standard (to confound "identity with relation"), even if it is known that the standard is never perfectly attained. Surely, both kinds of money operate as fictions, but the coin's acceptance is based on mental mechanisms that are essential to the construction of nature and

Figure 6.1   This engraving and Figure 6.2 indicate something of the contentious public debate surrounding the use of paper currency. Here, a laudatory broadside from 1775 celebrates William Pit the Younger, and London merchants and traders who continued to accept paper money at a time of financial crisis caused by the Jacobite Rising and other events in 1745. Figure 6.2, from two decades later, ridicules the same William Pit for ruining the nation by an ingestion of gold and defecation of paper currency. Image courtesy of Wikicommons.

society while the paper note must continually depend on external reinforcements to keep up its force and vivacity so that it can counterfeit (literally, "to make in opposition") its face value. Thus, in the moment of greatest tension between these two radically different, but interdependent systems of money in the mid-eighteenth century, Hume sided with William Chetwynd, the Master of the Mint and author of the second of this chapter's epigraphs, in eschewing "wild imagination" as the arbiter of Britain's monetary life.

Figure 6.2 "Midas, Transmuting all into Gold Paper": a satirical print by James Gillray from 1797. William Pitt the Younger, is shown as a grotesque king Midas in reverse, by the process of digestion, turning gold into paper currency. He straddles a Bank of England latrine into which he defecates a shower of paper currency. The opposition is depicted as a group of Jacobite rebels crouching in the reeds. Collection of the British Museum.

THE NATURAL LIMITS OF MONETARY MANIPULATION

This investigation throws new light, I believe, on Hume's rejection of an absolute quantity theory of money in his essay, "Of Money." He argues that "the alterations in the quantity of money ... are not immediately attended with portionable alterations in the prices of commodities." In the course of this discussion, Hume gives his remarkable blessing to the debasement of the currency in France and recommends a similar one in Britain (the first since 1559, in Hume's later estimation) (HEiv: 364). In order to understand this support for debasement we must put it in the context of the monetary discourse of Britain and France after the bubbles of 1720.

The man who set the terms of the discourse was the infamous Scotsman, John Law, the object of Montesquieu's satire in this paper's first epigraph. This child of Aeolus, the god of winds, and a Caledonian nymph, called on French investors "to leave the country of base metals. Come to the Empire of the Imagination..." (Montesquieu 1961: 258). In this Empire, of course, they were promised ever-increasing riches. According to Sir James Steuart, when the Law System (or Mississippi Scheme) collapsed, the French collectively decided "to bid a long farewell to credit and confidence; and to return to the old system of rent upon the town-house of Paris; and of coming at money in the best way they could" (Steuart 1966: 557). Antoin Murphy's late twentieth-century assessment echoes Steuart's, namely, that "The collapse of the System left a legacy of animosity towards financial innovation, which restrained and strait-jacketed the French economy under its control until the Revolution" (Murphy 1997: 333).

The British experienced the bursting of the South Sea Company's Bubble almost simultaneously with the crash of the Law's System in 1720, but the results were radically different. In France, the Compagnie des Indes and the Banque Royale (the organizational vehicles of Law's System) were dissolved and most of the holders of bank paper lost everything. In Britain, the Bank of England and the South Sea Company were preserved and investors came off with "tolerable losses" (Ferguson 2001: 114). As a result, the British and French monetary systems dramatically diverged after their 1720 bubbles. The British, especially the Scottish, approach was to intensify the opening of private banks and the issuing of paper money notes. The French approach was to eschew paper instruments as much as possible and re-establish the reliability of and trust in metallic currency.[11]

Hume generally supported the post-1720 French monetary model:

> It is not to be doubted, but the great plenty of bullion in France is, in a measure, owning to the want of paper credit. The French have no banks: Merchants bills do not there circulate as with us: Usury or lending on interest is not directly permitted; so that many have large sums in their coffers: Great quantities of plate are used in their private houses; and all the churches are full of it. By this means, provisions and labour still remain cheaper among them, than in nations that are not half so rich in gold and silver. The advantages of this situation, in point of trade as well as in great public emergencies, are too evident to be disputed.
>
> (E 317)

He also had a cosmopolitan admiration for many features of the French absolute monarchy, especially its ability to escape enslavement to the national debt (E 96), which was a continual source of anxiety for Hume. The French king, according to him, can "make a bankruptcy when he pleases" (Forbes 1975: 173–174).[12] Moreover, Hume was certainly not convinced as to the general reliability of the monetary managers, private and public, in both England and Scotland (Caffentzis 2001 and 1995).

Hume's support of the post-1720 French preference of coin over paper money included a suggestion that the oft-decried but more oft-practiced art of debasement should be revived in Britain. After all, debasement was no stranger to the English Mint from the seventh to the sixteenth centuries (Challis 1992). The practice ended in Britain due to the crisis ignited by the Great Debasement of 1544–1551, when minting activity was stimulated by "a substantial monetarization of plate and ornament from the suppressed religious houses" (Gould 1970: 33). The ambitious Henry VIII apparently was not content with the seigniorage from this monetarization of the "Great Plunder." He embarked on a reckless debasement that dramatically reduced the silver content of English coins.[13]

After Henry VIII's death, Elizabeth I tried to reverse its effects in the first years of her reign. Moreover, a large critical literature on the Great Debasement sprang up to excoriate it. Just as the crash of Law's System put paper money instruments in retreat in France, the Great Debasement banished the strategy of debasement from the region of polite monetary conversation in Britain.

Hume's controversial support for debasement in Britain, approximately two centuries after the Great one, is a clear sign of the importance of the distinction between metal and paper in his monetary politics. For Hume recognized the stimulating effects of an expanding monetary area and supply and, at the same time, he was suspicious of the most available instrument of expansion, paper money, since he claimed that "I scarcely know any method of sinking money below its level, but those institutions of banks, funds, and paper-credit, which are so much practised in this kingdom" (E 316).

He saw that debasement might answer the conundrum posed by this tension between the need for monetary expansion and paper money skepticism, if it were practiced in a way that recognized the natural fictionality of coin. Debasement, according to Hume, could be acceptable just so long as the operation is done "to preserve the illusion, and make [the new coins] be taken for the same [as the old coins]" (E 288). We have here the exact formula for the natural fiction in Hume's terminology: the confounding of identity with relation. In effect, reasonable debasement only applies (and does not strain) the standard mental mechanisms required for the normal functioning of the conventions underlying the coinage. Hume's support for debasement, in effect, is his answer to any of his critics (like Smith) who might have charged him with monetary passivity. Hume approves of the right of monetary authorities to manipulate gold and silver money in a way that private bankers do with the issuing of paper bank notes, though with more limitations. The public authorities can deploy the natural fiction of money in order to excite industry, just so long as they do not disturb the conventions based on "the illusion" of identity between old and new coinage. But it is exactly this illusion that guarantees the expansionary process has its own internal limit. The monetary authorities should have the right to use the self-reflexive dialectic between the "intrinsic" and "official" value of coins to "excite the industry of mankind," to use George Berkeley's phrase, for the nation's well-being, just as the private bankers can turn the semantic distance between paper money and the gold and silver in their vaults into a personal profit.

Hume wanted to eliminate an economic hobgoblin, the Great Debasement, from the minds of his readers and to join in the lively debate on the effects of debasement taking place in France and Italy, that was initiated by Jean-François Melon's positive assessment of debasement in his *Essai Politique sur le Commerce* (1734) (Monroe 1966: 236–240). To do so, Hume refers the reader to "the frequent operation of the French king on the money" and he points out that "augmenting of the numerary value [of the coinage] did not produce a proportional rise of the prices, at least for some time" (E 287). His clinching example is the price of corn, which "is now sold at the same price, or for the same number of livres, it was in 1683; though silver was then at 30 livres the mark, and is now at 50" (E 287).

Hume presents, in an infamous footnote to this passage, a case for debasement in Britain by first referring to the work of Melon, Dutot and Paris-Duverney on the issue. He then goes on to argue:

> Were all our money, for instance, recoined, and a penny's worth of silver taken from every shilling, the new shilling would probably purchase every thing that could have been bought by the old; the prices of every-thing would thereby be insensibly diminished; foreign trade enlivened; and domestic industry, but the circulation of a greater number of pounds and shillings, would receive some encrease and encouragement. In executing such a project, it would be better to make the new shilling for 24 halfpence, in order to preserve the illusion, and make it be taken for the same.
>
> (E288)[14]

Stealthy terms abound in this passage: "probably purchase," "insensibly diminished," "some encrease," "preserve the illusion" and "make it taken for the same." The perfect Machiavellian political economist is at work here, simultaneously preserving the conventional fiction of the coinage while secretly exciting the industry of mankind. Hume slyly suggests in this footnote that if the French can do it, so can the British.

FROM PLATE TO CHINA-WARE:
TRANSCENDING THE METALLIC STAGE?

Loren Gatch has argued that Hume's view of money could support an "entirely fiduciary circulation" system similar to our present one (Gatch 1996: 185). Hume's defense of "the French solution," debasements and all, as a response to the crisis generated by the 1720 collapse, however, suggests a different interpretation. One might have thought, along with Gatch, that the most Deleuzean of eighteenth-century philosophers should have seen and even embraced the possibility of a monetary economy not founded on specie (Deleuze 1991). If all society was based on opinion, convention and unconscious fictions, then why should money be eternally stuck in a metallic stage? Hume certainly had philosophical predecessors who pointed to the new monetary horizon. He was familiar, for example, with George Berkeley's *The Querist* that was published fifteen years before the *Political Discourses*. Berkeley there suggested the complete substitution of a total paper money economy for gold and silver coinage (Caffentzis 2000). The historic Hume, however, seems to have been ambivalent at best to the direction the money form actually took in the previous two and a half centuries.

Why then, did Hume not hypothesize the elimination of specie and the institution of a completely paper money system in Britain as Berkeley proposed for Ireland, if gold and silver money was a fiction? After all, if, according to Hume, the Dutch (among others) had completely substituted china-ware, a "brittle commodity," for silver plate in their dining rooms (E 318), why could the British not rid their markets and pockets of specie with equal ease?

Some might claim that this limitation arose from a purely technical fact: paper money could be infinitely iterated without a corresponding increase in work while the iteration of coinage required a proportional productive effort. But Hume recognized that this technical fact is not central to the operation of metallic money. As he wrote to Morellet:

> It is true, money must always be made of some materials, which have intrinsic value, otherwise it would be multiplied without end, and would sink to nothing. But, when I take a shilling, I consider it not as a useful metal, but as something which another will take from me; and the person who shall convert it into metal is, probably, several millions of removes distant.
>
> (R 214)

For Hume, the difference between paper and specie is based on the different structure of relations the two monetary regimes impose on issuers and users and on the users with themselves. Coinage shares with time, ideal standards, substances, endurance of sensed objects and the self a fundamental "pathos of identity," that is, every coin reflexively says of itself to both buyer and seller that it has a certain intrinsic value. But this pathos is based on a false but reflexive elision of perceptual fact and intrinsic value that is indispensable for the creation of the conventions at the base of commercial life. For the "use value" of the coin to the buyer is that the seller accepts it. This acceptance is based on the condition that the seller is convinced that sellers will accept the coin when s/he becomes a buyer as equal or greater in value to the commodity they are selling. Indeed, the magistrate in charge of debasing the currency recognizes and depends upon this eternally productive mistake, just as the wise philosophical ruler recognizes that it is essential to develop and strengthen unsupported confoundings of identity with relation in order to guarantee individual and social stability. For the key question of money is whether it is "something another will take from me" in exchange for a commodity, but Hume holds that there ultimately has to be a sensible external something there to be taken as the object of a convention, not just a promise of something.

Can there be a specie-less monetary system? If the parallel between natural/artificial fictions and metallic money/paper money is at all convincing, then the Humean answer is: it is possible to have such a system, but only if its inhabitants are willing to live in a state of continual monetary "melancholy and delirium." Hume, I argue, would conclude that a complete anti-foundationalism is ultimately unlivable in both the intellectual and commercial spheres, even though foundationalism is false in both.

CONCLUSION

My answer to the question, "Why does Hume call metallic money 'fictitious' and paper money 'counterfeit'?" is complex, since it requires that one apply both Hume's discussion of natural and artificial fictions and his thoughts on the differences between conventions and promises to the problem. From this perspective, paper money is not based on collective, "natural" conventions (like language), but it is an artificial product of the promises of specific institutions: private banks, companies and governments. Hence, it is prone to the secular superstitions of trust in individual institutions that can degenerate to epidemical madness's (panics and bubbles). Metallic money is also a fiction but it is a natural fiction that is based on resemblances eliding into identities. After long habituation to the coordinating conventions, coins give a sense of equal exchange even though this equality is "really" not there. This "natural fiction," however, puts equally "natural" limits on its possible abuse, whereas there are no such natural limits to warn the magistrates with paper-credit money.

According to Hume then, a monetary economy is "fiduciary," that is, it is based on "opinion" (Wennerlind 2001). But there is opinion and opinion. When the fate of a monetary economy is based upon an "artificial" fiction—a fancy barely bound to a belief—then the bonding opinions, trust and credit are open to being rapidly discredited, distrusted and debunked. Therefore, Hume looked to France to see a monetary system based on "natural" fictions, after it thoroughly repudiated John Law's attempt to systematically defetishize gold and silver and eliminate metals from its circulatory system. Hume definitely had more confidence in the French system and he showed why it was even open to a limited monetary activism through careful debasements.

Hume was committed to a philosophical distinction between metallic and paper money and not merely a technical one. This commitment is best reflected perhaps in the depth of the passion behind his dying apocalyptic footnote about the national debt and the implicit monetary use of public credit instruments in *The History of England* (Pocock 1985: 125–141; Hont 1993). But his prophecy was apparently mistaken. After all, "metallic" France had its Revolution barely a decade and a half after his death, whereas "paper" Britain has been able to defer it indefinitely.

7
Wages and Money
Pegasus' Mirror

That most metaphysical of articles, labor power.
        —Karl Marx, *Capital*, Vol. I. (1867)

It takes centuries ere the "free labourer," thanks to the development of capitalist production, agrees, i.e., is compelled by social conditions, to sell the whole of his active life, his very capacity for work, for the price of the necessaries of life, his birthright for a mess of pottage.
        —Karl Marx, *Capital*, Vol. I (1867)

Unlike the historian of class relations in the 19th and 20th centuries, whose subject matter is studied through the glass of money, the 18th century historian needs sources of information that are as particular as the things of the 18th century and as concrete as the labouring history of 18th century persons.
        —Peter Linebaugh, *The London Hanged* (1992)

INTRODUCTION: THE CONCEPTUAL EMERGENCE OF THE WAGE-RELATION

The wage is such a commonplace relation that we often do not think about it, except in its absence. But there is nothing common about it, since the wage links two of the most metaphysical of articles in capitalist society: labor power (or the capacity to labor) and money. These "articles" are not easily understood jointly, either historically or logically, even though labor power is apparently fated to be alienated for money, if capitalism is to exist.

There is nothing natural about such a destiny either. One of the most important contributions of historians of eighteenth-century Britain like Peter Linebaugh, Christopher Hill and Edward Thompson and feminist thinkers like Silvia Federici has been their accumulation of evidence to show that wage labor did not appear fully-grown out of the head of capital. The nineteenth-century ideology of "free labor" was exactly that, both nineteenth century and an ideology. Eighteenth-century Britain (and by "Britain" I include the colonies, as well as Ireland and Scotland) was the conceptual forcing house of a notion of wage labor that would later appear to be in opposition to slavery, though it was not quite that. The work of Hill, Thompson, Linebaugh and Federici has shown that there was no straight and narrow path to the wage. Marx's account of its role as the hegemonic relationship between the classes is a powerfully logical one, but as he himself suggests (see epigraph), one that is historically inaccurate for the past, and, I might add, for the present and future. In other words, the exchange, theft and extortion transpiring between classes in capitalism under the rubric of the wage were not easily engendered and the wage relation itself has never been total, especially since it hid an enormous amount of unwaged labor.

Whether we look at the wage-relation in the eighteenth century from the point of view of the working class (where the customary "takings" were an essential part of the exchange-relation with the boss) (Linebaugh 1992) or of the capitalists (among whom there was a continuity between chattel slavery, conscription, coverture, indenture, imprisonment, transport, servitude, housework, artisan work, work-house labor, prison labor, etc.) all was in flux on both sides of the relation. Empirically, money wages were not the dominant character of the wage in two senses: (1) "perquisites" (wages-in-kind) were quite common; and (2) "alternative" and "near" forms of money (e.g., tokens and tickets) were often used in wage payments. As Elizabeth Gilboy pointed out long ago: "Especially in the eighteenth century, money wages were only a part, and often a small part (particularly in the country districts) of what the laborer earned" (Gilboy 1934). Throughout Britain, the lack of "small change" also created an "other" economy of proletarian buying and selling involving token coinage. It became a significant monetary form of what Marx called "small-scale circulation," that is, the realm where the workers' wages purchase the "approvisionnement" and the wage's historical and moral element is realized (Marx 1973: 672–677).

Conceptually, the two major poles of the wage-relation—labor power and money—were also rapidly metamorphosing in this period. Money was being transformed both in body and in soul. After all, the gravitational tie between money and specie was snapped in a number of historical moments and locales (from Rhode Island in the 1730s to Paris in the 1790s) in the eighteenth century. At the other pole, it was only beginning to be understood that labor power was a valuable "thing" and that the being embodying and "possessing" it, should and could negotiate its price.

The key problem of studies in the genealogy of the wage is often taken to be the unraveling of the different conceptions of labor and labor power that appeared before the nineteenth century. A good example of such studies is Richard Biernacki's methodologically sophisticated book, *The Fabrication of Labor* (1995). He takes the following as his problematic in attempting to explain the "enigmatic transaction whose original strangeness now eludes us: the sale of human labor as a commodity":

> I try to show that during the fateful transition to the new commercial order [capitalism, CGC], a different apparition of labor as a commodity took hold in each of the leading economies of Western Europe. In each country a different solution prevailed for determining just how the precious but subtle thing called labor could be calibrated and transferred from hired hands to the employer in the workshop.
>
> (Biernacki 1995: 1)

I argue that, if we are to properly understand the genealogy of the wage in the eighteenth century, one must look not only to the "labor face" of the wage relation; the "money face" is equally important, for labor power begins to recognize itself and its qualities—abstraction, potentiality, immateriality—in its monetary reflection. Once labor power is so transformed, its surplus-value creating capacity can be more efficiently captured. Labor power is like Medusa in the ancient tale, Perseus could safely approach her, decapitate her and put her head in his wallet only by seeing her image in a divine mirror. Indeed, the importance of the monetary image is not only true of the origin of wage labor, it is also true of slavery and other forms of alienation of the person in capitalist society (including housework and sexwork). In other words, the full account of this "great (though partial) transformation" from servitude to wage labor requires not only an understanding of the "fictional" commodity of Labor, but also that other fictional commodity, Money, as Polanyi (following Hume) would put it. The former path has been well trod in the history of philosophy: not as an analysis of the commodification of labor power, *aka* the wage, of course, but rather as the history of the development of the self, of the autonomy of the ego and of individualism. The latter, monetary path has been less taken (or, more precisely, it is only beginning to be researched by historians and philosophers of money), since it deals with money not as the product of capitalist-to-capitalist or capitalist-to-state exchange but as an inter-class phenomenon. The question dealt with being: *How is it possible to have such a creative power with an infinity of possible qualitative manifestations, Labor, be reflected by a fixed measure, Money?* Indeed, it is exactly *because* money is in flux during this period that it is so central to historical reflection on the wage.

In this chapter, I will show how David Hume's philosophy of money played a role in the formation of the notion of the wage through the covariant concepts of the self and money. In so doing, it laid the foundation of the "high wage" strategy of Scottish capital in the eighteenth century.

Hume's effort was profoundly influenced by Locke's and Berkeley's writings on the wage. I will also show how John Locke's and George Berkeley's interpretations of the monetary practices of the period had a profound impact on their philosophical theories of the self and, through their writings on the conception of money and self, on their contemporaries, including Hume. I will use their writings to survey this terrain between the self and money, not with the pretense of exhaustiveness or typicality but with the thought that though literary texts are an important source of insight on the relation between money and the self in the eighteenth century, philosophical texts can also serve as convenient nodes of orientation in the complex and conflicted field of the wage, since they are already strategic documents that mirrored, reflected *and* acted on that very field. They are especially useful guides for the long eighteenth century when the final construction of "economics" was still a project for the future.

I write this chapter not claiming that Locke, Berkeley and Hume presented full-blown, self-consciously derived "theories of the wage," but that these philosophers definitely did have philosophies of the Self and Money as well as some strategy to link them through the Wage. They also argued for high- or low-wage strategies by using their philosophical tools.

I agree with Antoin E. Murphy's chronological judgment that "despite the strong claims for the view that macroeconomics was founded in the 1930s … it is [his] contention that macroeconomics had effectively been founded many centuries before [in the late seventeenth and eighteenth centuries]."

(Murphy 1997: 2) This was a time before "economics" got its autonomy and still mixed easily with "moral philosophy" and "political economy."

In the course of this discussion, I will comment and elaborate on Table 7.1 to see how Hume and his predecessors were able to use their philosophical tools to devise strategies for the control of their respective working classes:

Table 7.1   Chart showing the relation between the self, money and the wage in Locke, Berkeley and Hume

	Self	*Money*	*Wage*
Locke	A thinking remembering substance	A specie-backed substance	Low-wage
Berkeley	A spirit	Paper currency and "small change" tokens	High-wage
Hume	A bundle of impressions	Not easily counterfeited currency, most likely backed by specie	High-wage

JOHN LOCKE AND THE WAGE: ENGLISH SUBSTANCES

It is hardly surprising that the discourse on the wage in the eighteenth-century is so confused and confusing. Consider the exemplary "long eighteenth-century" philosopher, John Locke. His conception of the distinction between wage labor and slavery is far from the logical consistency that the abolitionist movement later demanded of him. He was not alone. For in the seventeenth century the confusion between slavery and servitude was rampant even in the writings of that most "hard nosed" of philosophers, Thomas Hobbes. He saw the issue of slavery as a matter of physical restriction. So, for example, for Hobbes those who are technically servants, such as conscripted sailors on the high seas, are the equivalent of slaves (even though they are expected to be paid at the end of their voyage). As Prof. Lott pointed out to me in conversation, "Hobbes was prone to view slavery as an extreme form of servitude." This confusion was to later become clarified in the nineteenth century, once the ubiquity of contractuality becomes hegemonic; but before then, especially in the period when the abolitionist movement and slave revolts were hardly rippling the social waters of Britain, the relation between field hands on plantations and the sailors that brought them there was to remain vague.

Similarly, Locke's thinking about money was also caught in a moment of extreme fluidity. Money was about to be defetishized and to lose its metallic body and gain a paper soul in the late seventeenth century. The simultaneous arrival of the coinage crisis and the origin of the Bank of England indicated that a great monetary transformation was imminent. Locke was concerned about this transformation from the point of view of empire (he was, after all, a member and for a period the secretary of the Board of Trade and Plantations for a total of a decade (Armitage 2004: 603). For he saw that the parochial interests of local British capitalists could easily create a monetary regime that was inflationist and vulnerable to inter- and intra-class pressure. He tried to represent what he saw as the larger imperial interest that took the world market as its point of reference, and that is why he insisted on the substantial aspect of the monetary form. Consequently, his view of money as a pole in what was later to be called the wage relation was antagonistic to the developments in the monetary domain in the eighteenth century (he saw the future shade of John Law in the shadow of Lowndes, his opponent during the recoinage debate).

I will review briefly the key elements of Locke's conception of money in order to show how it not only was homologous to his idea of the self and person but it also provides an explanation of his notion of the wage (and the justification of coercion in the management of non-wage labor in his *Representation Containing a Scheme of Methods for the Employment of the Poor* (Locke 1997). Let me proceed schematically in presenting Locke's views.

Historically, money's origin must be placed before the origin of civil government, since the class conflicts that made civil government necessary arose from the widespread deployment of money. Locke's conjectural history depends upon some simple inferences. Before money, there would be no reason why anyone would transform through one's labor the common into private property beyond one's own immediate subsistence. Indeed, to have anything that was taken from the common spoil was a sin against natural law. Money changed all that, since it is something "lasting and scarce, and so valuable to be hoarded up." "And as different degrees of industry were apt to give men possessions in different proportions, so this invention of money gave them the opportunity to continue and enlarge them" (Locke 1980: Ch. 5, para. 48). Labor might give title to property; but it is an empty right, until money made having and accumulating property without limit both reasonable and desirable. Civil society was then devised in order to "preserve property."

Ontologically, money is a complex, dual idea: a substance idea attached to a mixed-mode one. The substance of money is intrinsically durable and scarce that can vary from, say, gold to silver. Corporeal substances that become money arise in nature while the mixed-mode aspects of money are created by human thought. As Locke notes, "[t]he mind often exercises an *active* power in making these [mixed-modes]" (Locke: 1959, 382). Being so, it is abstract, since the same mixed-mode element can be attached to different substances. Moreover, it is universal and potentially ubiquitous. This universality is important for Locke since it is a condition for the existence of "world money." Each society produces different mixed-mode monetary ideas that might not be translatable from one language and legal system to another, but Chinese, Aztecs and Londoners can agree as to what is gold.

Epistemologically, money is self-reflexive in establishing its value. Its own substantial value makes it possible for one to know every other value. Monetary value is like the truth in another mixed-mode field: geometry.

Semantically, money refers to *past* value that has already been created and stored by the monetary substance.

Practically, the possession of money immediately differentiates the operation of an "industrious and rational" person from a "quarrelsome and contentious" one. The discipline of money accumulation makes this differentiation inevitable (as a corollary) in Locke's framework because labor gives the title to and makes "in great part, the measure" of the value of money and through money, the value of every other commodity.

Locke noted a deepening mutual implication between money, labor and the self. As we have seen, his notion of money is of an entity that is abstract, universalizing, self-reflexive, metamorphosing from substance to substance, defined by past labor and only of use to the industrious and rational. Thus, it could play the role of "Perseus' mirror" to the world of values created by labor. As Locke writes,

if we will rightly estimate things as they come to our use, and cast up the several expenses about them, what in them is purely owing to nature and what to labour, we shall find, that in most of them ninety-nine hundredths are wholly to be put on the account of labor.

(Locke 1980: Ch. 5 para. 40)

This applies universally. Even the much-maligned Indigenous Americans had a right to the deer he hunted and killed: "the deer [is] that Indian's who hath killed it; it is allowed to be his goods, who hath bestowed his labour upon it, though before it was the common right of every one." Moreover, labor gives one a title to property because "every man has a property in his own person: this no body has any right to but himself. The labour of his body, and the work of his hands, we may say, are properly his" (Locke 1980: Ch. 5 para. 27).

Labor and work are not inalienable parts of the person, however, for one can make one's self a servant:

to another, by selling him, for a certain time, the service he undertakes to do, in exchange for wages he is to receive: and though this commonly puts him into the family of his master, and under the ordinary discipline thereof; yet it gives the master but a temporary power over him; and no greater than what is contained in the contract between them.

(Locke 1980: Ch. 5 para. 85)

If the labor of the servant is done during the temporary period s/he is under contract, then the results are the master's as well.

Thus the grass my horse has bit; the turfs my servant has cut; and the ore I have digged in any place, where I have a right to them in common with others, become my property without the assignation or consent of any body.

(Locke 1980: Ch. 5 para. 28)

Here we have a remarkable converging series of *my's*—my animal's, *my* servant's and *my* self's actions—transforming common into private property.

At the center of this ever-extending circle of possession (from my self to my labor, from my labor to my commodities, from my commodities to my money, from my money to my servant's labor) is the primal possession: self-possession. What is it to possess a self? How can it (or at least a part of it) be alienated? What must the self be in order to be exchangeable for money? Must it take on the characteristics of money, that is, be a dual idea, abstract, detachable from its substance, self-reflexive, defined by the past, reified, objectified and requiring an internal discipline? A study of Locke's writings on the self (and its equivalents, person and personality) would show that, in fact, these are its characteristics and comprise an early conceptualization of a waged self.

Let us begin with self-possession. The reason why the self can be possessed, according to Locke, is that it, like the paradigmatic gathered acorns, is a result of labor. In this case, the labor is of internal consciousness and not the external labor of bodies, but the result is the same, possession. Conscious labor creates a set of memories of past actions that one literally "owns up to." Locke writes:

> Person, as I take it, is the name for the self ... It is a forensic term, appropriating actions and merit; and so belongs only to intelligent agents, capable of a law and happiness, and misery. This personality extends itself beyond the present existence to what is past, only by consciousness—whereby it becomes concerned and accountable; owns and imputes to itself past actions, just upon the same ground and for the same reason as it does the present.
>
> (Locke 1959: 466–467)

This self-creation process, of course, is part of the grand narrative of the bourgeoisie from "up from the bottom" success stories to Hegel's Absolute Spirit; but it is also central to the genealogy of the wage. For this process involves both a detachment of the self from any particular substance and context as well as the reification and objectification of the self.

The reflexive detachment of the self is crucial training for the creation of a waged worker since s/he requires the ability to alienate essential aspects of his/her life. Thus, the self created in this process of consciousness picking and choosing of memories of past actions—did I do it or did my brother? did I do it on the boss' time or mine?—makes it possible to *delete* memories as parts of one's self as well as *appropriate* them. This detachment, Locke argues, is also one from the substances that might be united with consciousness. Locke refuses any such identification of consciousness and substance, for he argues with a variety of examples (verging on cannibalism) that continuity of substance is no evidence for personal identity. The self, like money, is not identifiable with any particular substance or locale. It has within it a great abstraction and universality that is open potentially to uniting with many different substances. As Charles Taylor notes of Locke's concept of the self:

> The disengagement from the activities of thought and from our unreflecting desires and tastes allows us to see ourselves as objects of far-reaching reformation. Rational control can extend to the re-creation of our habits and hence of ourselves.
>
> (Taylor 1989: 171)

Hence, it is open to being constructed and deconstructed for greater success in the process of becoming a better "servant." The huge collections of ideas that Locke invokes in the *Essay* are structured in a variety of dimensions and genres, but most clearly they have an atomic-molecular structure that invites the reader to see that there is much freedom in linking and delinking (associating and dissociating) ideas. The self is not a microcosm structured to imitate the macrocosm, it is a field of moveable elements ready for numeration and experimentation in order to increase pleasure or, at the least, avoid unease. The possibilities of self-creation (and alienation) are combinatorially infinite.

This self—abstract, universal, quantitative and self-alienating—is exactly the kind of entity required to match the money pole of the wage-relation. Locke proposed both a memory theory of the self and a matching memory theory of property and money (Caffentzis 1989: 54). For the servant's self must understand what is the "service" for what "certain time" that s/he is alienating by "contract" for what money "wages." Each of these is a component of the construction of the self that existed, according to Locke, before the formation of the state. Money organizes the path for the creation of the waged self, since money measures the self objectively and compares it to universal standards.

The ability to discipline one's self into becoming compatible to a universal equivalent in value is not a given, however. There are many possible ways to fail. Indeed, for Locke there is a circle of connections—the self–labor–property–money–wages–self—that assures the self-reinforcing character of the self's mirroring of money. One can see its disciplinary force when Locke deals with those outside the circle in his *Draft of a Representation Containing a Scheme of Methods for the Employment of the Poor* (1697) (Locke 1997 [1697]) also known as *An Essay on the Poor Law*. For him, the wageless poor exemplify an existential condition: they neither suffer a misfortune nor are the victims of a statistical anomaly. When Locke looks on the wageless beggars on the streets of London, he sees a failure in the construction of the self and not a failure in the construction of civil society, since these poor beggars have not created a necessary connection between money and themselves. He diagnoses the problem in the following terms:

> If the causes of this evil be looked into, we humbly conceive it will be found to have proceeded neither from scarcity of provisions, nor from want of employment for the poor, since the goodness of God has blessed these times with plenty ... The growth of the poor must therefore have some other cause; and it can be nothing else but the relaxation of discipline and corruption of manners ... The first step, therefore, towards the setting the poor on work ... ought to be a restraint of their debauchery...
>
> (Locke 1997 [1697]: 184)

The second step is the seizing of adult beggars and sending them to his Majesty's ships or to houses of correction, there to be kept at hard labor for three years (Locke 1997 [1697]: 449). The third step is to take any boy or girl under fourteen years of age found "begging outside of the parish where they dwell ... they shall be sent to the next working-school, there to be soundly whipped."

The whippings, the hard labor and the British equivalent of the galleys are meant to cause unease on the "lazy, contentious and quarrelsome" and are standard fare of Poor Law ideology. But the most interesting aspect of *Representation* for us is Locke's emphasis on work and wages. If a poor person complains that s/he wants but lacks waged work, then the parish's guardian of the poor (in Locke's proposal) would be obliged to ask "whether anyone is willing to employ him, at a lower rate than is usually given, which rate it shall be in the power of the said guardian to set..." (Locke 1997). If no one is willing to hire the poor person making the request, the guardian of the poor will oblige the inhabitants of the parish to hire him "according to the proportion of every one's tax in the parish" and "if any person refuse to set the poor at work in his turn as thus directed, that such person shall be bound to pay them their appointed wages, whether he employ them or no." In other words, the cure of poverty is a matter of training the recalcitrants in the construction of a self in a capitalist society and if any capitalist is lax in supporting such a project, he too should be punished! This is so because when one enters into wage labor (instead of begging and stealing) one enters into a human cosmos that is universal, abstract, objectively measurable and responsible, thus crowned by money. Indeed, being waged, for Locke, is the mark of entrance to humanity for workers.

As I mentioned in Part I, Hume shared with Locke a commitment to a specie-backed currency that would keep the connection to the world market intact. For the "Scottish Empire" was built on the English navy's crews (who were not only English, in some vessels, for example, black sailors consti- tuted 25 percent of the crew) and who were essential for the creation and retention of the colonies and the trade routes. But there was a major differ- ence between Locke's and Hume's wage strategies. Locke's whips and work houses of *Representation* pointed to a low-wage future for waged workers, whereas Hume advocates a high-wage strategy. As Margaret Schabas and Carl Winnerlind state:

> Hume championed higher wages, arguing that a healthy remuneration was the best incentive for diligence and ingenuity and that higher levels of consumption tend toward greater happiness, at least up to a point. While conservative in temperament, he discerned that at the margin, higher incomes brought more happiness to the poor than to the rich.
>
> (Schabas and Wennerlind 2011: 221)

Or in Hume's words: "Every person, if possible, ought to enjoy the fruits of his labor, in full possession of all the necessaries, and many of the conve- niences of life" (Hume 1752 [1955]: 265).

GEORGE BERKELEY AND THE WAGE: IRISH SPIRITS

A key to understanding George Berkeley's role in the eighteenth-century story of the wage also lies in his conception of money. Berkeley's view of money is famously similar to his general philosophical turn toward a form of philosophy that has been variously called "idealism" or "immaterialism," and equally famously at odds with Locke's "primary quality"-"mixed mode" conception of money. Marx took to mocking the parallel between Berkeley's refutation of materialism and his rejection of specie as the hegemonic substance of money:

> Very fittingly it was Bishop Berkeley, the advocate of mystical idealism in English philosophy, who gave the doctrine of the nominal standard of money a theoretical twist ... Because tokens can be substituted for precious metals in the sphere of circulation, Berkeley concludes that these tokens in their turn represent *nothing*, i.e., the abstract concept of value.
>
> (Marx 1970: 78)

Marx in his philosophical joking, however, did not notice that Berkeley's conception of money was responding to a very important class reality. The "native Irish" posed a deep problem for Berkeley's class, the Anglo-Irish Ascendancy elite of Ireland. The "native" Irish refused to work with vigor, consistency and earnestly for their Anglo-Irish "betters." They were armed with what Berkeley called "cynical content," *the* anathema of a mercantile age. In the face of this resistance, at times the dominant strategy of the Ascendancy ruling class was to attempt to reduce the "natural Irish" to slavery and/or extermination (see Cromwell's transporting of thousands of prisoners in the wake of his Irish campaign and Petty's plans for the transport of the Irish population to England and the Americas). But Berkeley clearly rejected this approach, since he saw a self-debilitating *will* in Irish poverty that could not be conquered simply by repression. The planned subversion of the "Anglo-Irish other" through the self-subversion of the "native Irish" self, embedded in this will, in its ever-active inactivity, was at the center of Berkeley's problematic.

Berkeley recognized that cynical content was a matter of the will and spirit, which were neither imaginable nor imaged things, according to his philosophy. Indeed, the self in whole or in part could not be exchanged for a thing, since there was no set of ideas (things), however large and complex, that could be equated with a spirit. In effect, such equations are a form of idolatry, that is, the identification of ideas with spirits. As the youthful Berkeley conjectured,

> Did men but consider that the sun, moon, and stars and every other object of the senses are only so many sensations in their minds, which

have no other existence but barely being perceived, doubtless they would never fall down, and worship their own ideas.

(Berkeley 1957: 26)

Thus, if money (a complex idea, according to Locke) was to be equivalent to an aspect of the self, it must not be reducible to a set of fixed ideas.

Money too had to be "spiritual" and transcend the realm of ideas, if it were to be equated to spirit. It could not be a thing like a silver or gold object that is defined by a set of ideas (e.g., of weight and of chemical composition). For Berkeley (as the Querist, the quizzical voice of *The Querist* [1735–1737]) money was a "ticket, a counter, a token, a tally, or a mark." All these terms slightly differed in meaning, but they all had a similar ontological and rhetorical effect: they were scandalously notional and therefore, as Marx ridiculed, "nothing." Indeed, they were the medium of the wage for many workers in this period throughout Britain. Whereas for Locke the crucial question was whether money truly represented a given quantity of a thing or substance, Berkeley substituted another query: does money efficiently signify and excite future activity? The decisive point of the Querist's analysis was not only the rejection of the "mercantile" identification of money with gold and silver. He was just as anxious to insinuate an "excitation" model of money, for the object of money was activity, not things. Monetary signs signified by stimulating the spiritual actions and powers of one's self and others' selves. Therefore, these signs required their interpreters to have notions of these actions and powers. These were units of monetary signification.

Money was not to be the universal substantial measure of value. Its main purpose was to excite and activate the recalcitrant, passive-aggressive, catalectic workers (in his case, the "Irish natives") into action and guide them once they get into motion to a greater good. The legislature, suggests *The Querist*, must deploy an excitation of the wants of the "native Irish" to make them "accustomed to eat beef and wear shoes" and experience a "general habit of living well" in order to unleash their labor potential. These quizzical reflections of money were not only political, however. They had a profound effect on his philosophy by igniting a "second conceptual revolution" in his thought.

Historically, Berkeley had a rather Aristotelian view of the origin of money. Thus, he queries about a classical Robinsonian scenario: "Whether in order to understand the true Nature of Wealth and Commerce, it would not be right to consider a Ship's Crew cast upon a desert island" (Berkeley 1970: 128). After a period of exchange of "superfluities" among these ship-wrecked people, Berkeley suggested that credit would arise and then they would soon "agree on certain Tallies, Tokens, Tickets or Counters" made out of any material as "conveyances" of this credit. Thus, money comes into being out of exchange. However, with the origin of the state, a new possibility and concern arises: the momentum of the state, which he defines as "the sum of the Faculties put into Act, or in other Words, the united Action of a whole people" (Berkeley 1970: 129). This momentum could be weak or strong, coordinated or chaotic and it is the duty of the state officials to find a monetary system that would strengthen and coordinate the powers of the people.

Ontologically, money by being a sign system has no "intrinsic value" in itself or "resemblance" to what it refers to any more than the "round" visual idea resembles the "round" tactile idea. Moreover, Berkeley's appropriate temporal dimension is the *future*—aspiration, hope, desire—while Locke saw the main temporal dimension of money to be the *past* (as "a store of value," in the language of the nineteenth-century political economy).

Semantically, monetary signs are "tickets entitling to Power" and as Berkeley has repeatedly pointed out, Power like Force is not an idea any more than is the Trinity or grace. That is, the whole point of signs, including monetary ones, is

they have other uses besides barely standing for and exhibiting ideas, such as raising proper emotions, producing certain dispositions or habits of mind, and directing our actions in pursuit of that happiness which is the ultimate end and design, the primary spring and motive, that sets rational agents at work; that signs may imply or suggest the relations of things; which relations, habitudes, or proportions, as they cannot be by us understood but by the help of signs, so being thereby expressed and confuted, they direct and enable us to act with regard to things: that the true end of speech, reason, science, faith, assent in all its different degrees, is not merely, or principally, or always the imparting or acquiring of ideas, but rather something of an active operative nature, tending to a conceived good: ... for instance, the algebraic mark, which denotes the root of a negative square, hath its use in logistic operation, although it be impossible to form an idea of any such quantity, and what is true of algebraic signs is also true of words or language, modern algebra being in fact a more short, apposite, and artificial sort of language.

(Berkeley: 1957: 32)

Epistemologically, one can only know the truth and meaning of a monetary sign through action, since they are more like questions rather than declarative sentences. There are various criteria that must be satisfied in order for one to say of a declarative sentence P, "I know that P"—for example, I believe that P, I have good reasons to believe that P, and P is true—but for the question, such criteria are irrelevant. The most important question about a question is whether it stimulates our curiosity, whether it sets us in the right direction, and whether it suggests important connections with other questions, etc. Those are the criteria for a good monetary system, not whether it measures the value of a commodity accurately or not.

Practically, Berkeley argued for a National Bank that would manage a new paper currency and a Mint that would manufacture small change tokens. These institutions, if run properly, would solve a number of chronic problems of the Irish body politic. On the one side, they would make it possible for native Irish workers to begin to enter into the world of trade and commerce through the wage labor market. On the other side, the fact that the rents of the Anglo-Irish gentry would not be paid in internationally recognized gold and silver coins but rather in currency that was only recognized in Ireland would immediately curtail their absentee jaunts to the continent and their luxurious import bills. Thus, the new monetary system would be able to square the Irish political circle (Caffentzis 2001).

This view of money that he developed after a three-year stay in Rhode Island (the center of monetary experimentation in the North American continent) between 1729 and 1731 was very important since it was part of an important transformation in Berkeley's own philosophy (which I call his "second conceptual revolution.") At the heart of this transformation is his rejection of the simple ontology of his early works that recognized ideas (that can be imaged and described) and spirits like the self and god (that can not be imaged or described). Berkeley's most powerful arguments in his early work were dependent on this stark dichotomy, but it made the investigation of how humans actually learn to make connections among ideas in order to create a social and moral world impossible. The abandonment of his earlier dichotomy was especially important for his understanding of labor and labor power as well as notions like self-possession that, inevitably, were not ideas, since they were rooted in spiritual substance.

The problematic of Irish labor is that many workers suffered from a sick level of excitation of their spirits. It is not enough to say, as Locke did, that self-possession gives a right to property to a class of selves whose right to own land had been severely restricted. Nor is it enough to point out, as Berkeley did in the company of the chorus of those who reflected on these themes in the eighteenth-century Britain, that labor is the source of all wealth and value, if the selves in questions are hostile to and in rebellion against their own situation in society. Locke's solution to such a circumstance is, on the one hand, whipping, hard labor and the galleys and, on the other, an offer of a (below subsistence) wage (or servant's) labor which, if refused, would unleash more whippings, hard labor and galleys.

Berkeley's solution was quite different, for he saw that the key fulcrum of the problem of Irish labor was the will. He introduced into his analysis of the problem a series of intermediary notions of the will—appetite, want and aspiration—that a notional conception of money can mediate. That is, money is analogous to the animal spirit of the body that excites and guides the will in the mind's interactions with the world. To do this, money should lead to the satisfaction of wants of the native Irish so that they would be "accustomed to eat beef and wear shoes" and experience a "general habit of living well." This creation of wants requires a redistributive policy and a small change coinage that would give the native Irish the experience of eating beef and wearing shoes, since one can not want what one has not sensed. These wants and their satisfaction subtly lead to aspirations that would point the native Irish beyond the immediate horizon of subsistence to a new status of being. For aspirations have spirits as their objects, while the object of a want is an idea. One may want to eat beef, but one cannot aspire to it (at best, one can aspire to be a beef-eater). One may aspire to be Einstein, but one cannot not fully imagine Einstein's spirit. Berkeley suggests that there is a relation between wants and aspirations: "Whether there be any instance of a State wherein the people, leaving neatly and plentifully did not aspire to wealth?" (Berkeley [1735], quoted in Johnston [1970: 130]).

The devil in this analysis is the appetite, since it has an aspect of infinity that wants do not. For one can have an appetite for something that one has not experienced but has heard that another has. One can have an appetite that is not finitely satisfiable, that is, an addiction. Finally, one can have an appetite for something that has never been experienced. The abstract negativity, the susceptibility to emulation, the potential infinity of appetite makes it freer, more fanciful, and harder to control and direct.

Given this "mechanics of the soul," the legislature could use the monetary system to suggest, goad, entice and restrict the wants, appetites and aspirations of the native Irish and the Anglo-Irish elite. On the one side, the appetite of the Anglo-Irish elite was to be restrained by forcing them to "buy Irish," since their rents would be paid in non-convertible currency or coin; on the other, the native Irish laborers were to be given increased employment, money wages and commodities for the satisfaction of wants. The result would be a Berkeleyean utopia, not for a select few in Bermuda, but for a whole nation. This utopia depended upon a careful calibration of the type of money appropriate for each social class; in effect, paper bills for the elite's consumption and token coins as wages for the native Irish laborers. It also required an ever-vigilant corps of national bankers whose main role would be to keep the money supply in a proportion that would ensure that the results of newly stimulated economic action are proportional to the "just pretensions and industry" of each of the social members.

Money would thus become the basis of the symbolic interaction of two spirits—the state and the inhabitant—an algebraic language of ciphers referring to an unimaginable spiritual "roots of negative squares" that would, all the same, be of inestimable value for this would become the basis of the concept of the wage. Berkeley in his philosophy of money has ironically transformed the use of tokens "entitling the bearer to future power" in wage payments into the model of how money in general is to be understood. It is the power to command the Industry of others and to promote, transfer and secure "this Property in human Labour."

DAVID HUME AND THE WAGE: SCOTTISH FICTIONS

The formation of the wage in Berkeley's Ireland had to confront the "native" Irish workers' passive-aggressive recalcitrance in the "native Irish." The understanding of money as a sign in a world of spirits called for the development of the notion of the human spirit. This was a call that Berkeley answered. In David Hume's Scotland of the 1740s and early 1750s, the key issue was not the lack of excitation of a defeated population. The Edinburgh-centered Scottish Enlightenment elite had to determine what to do with the rebellious "wild" Highlanders, who had recently driven their 1745 rebellion against George II to the gates of London. The choice seemed to be either extirpation or integration. The problem the Highlanders posed is how to transform a people that had continued a life outside the wage (using extended kinship networks and common land to create their subsistence). Hume's conception of money was deeply influenced by this problematic: how was money to be of use in order to "civilize" the Scots (especially the Highlanders)?

The first thing to note about Hume's notion of money is his insistence on its fictional and conventional character. In his main "economic" text, *Political Discourses* (1752), Hume spares no effort to present the reader with his conviction in passages replete with dismissive gestures:

> Money having chiefly a fictitious value, arising from the agreement and convention of men, the greater or less plenty of it is of no consequence...
>
> ... money is nothing but the representation of labour and commodities and serves only as a method of rating or estimating them. Where coin is in greater plenty; as a greater quantity of it is required to represent the same quantity of goods; it can have no effect, either good or bad, taking a nation within itself; any more than it would make an alternation on a merchant's books, if, instead of the Arabian method of notation, which requires few characters, he should make use of the Roman, which requires a great many.
>
> (Hume 1752 [1987]: 285)

This was not a passing insight in 1752. Hume certainly emphasized the conventional or what he called the "fictional" character of metallic money throughout his life. For example, in his first published comments on money in Book III of the *Treatise* (1740), he claimed that both languages and metallic money developed as conventionally coordinated practices. Nearly thirty years later, toward the end of his life, in his 1769 letter to Abbé Morellet, he gently disagrees with his correspondent's anti-conventionalist view of "the establishment of [metallic] money" and argues that the conventionalist or fictional view of metallic money has "some foundation," since "when I take a shilling, I consider it not as a useful metal, but as something which another will take from me; and the person who shall convert it into metal is, probably, several millions of removes distant" (R 214–215).

What does the "fictionality" of money come down to? Marx noted that Hume's skeptical attitude to money was strategically designed to subvert the "Monetary and Mercantile systems," by, in effect, deflating the worth of their God on earth, specie, to *nothing*. While appreciating this rhetorical move, Marx satirized Hume's contention in these words (perhaps thinking of the huge, painful and deadly labor of thousands of miners in Potosi and other such gold and silver hell-holes):

> The fact that gold and silver are money only as the result of the function they perform in the social process of exchange is thus taken to mean that their specific value and hence the magnitude of their value is due to their social function. Gold and silver are thus things without value, except in the process of circulation, in which they *represent commodities*, they acquire a fictitious value.

> (Marx 1970: 164)

But Marx was a bit too quick with his sarcasm. For Hume did attribute a real effect to money (and not merely a capacity to mechanically adjust to the quantity of commodities available). That effect could only be detected when the supply of money was changing in the same way that Newtonians claimed that one could isolate real forces only where they were producing acceleration (or deceleration). In the case of money, a sudden increase in the money supply has thousands of surprising accelerative micro-effects: "manufacturers employ *more* workmen" but "workmen *become* scarce, and the manufacturer gives *higher* wages, but at first requires an *increase* of labour," while the workman "returns from the market with *greater* quantity and *better* kinds" of goods, and the farmers who supply the market "apply themselves with alacrity to raising *more*." Thus, the apparently transparent veil of money in these circumstances reaches into the minds of the populace and "quicken[s] the diligence of every individual, before it encrease the price of labour" (Hume 1987: 287).

This slight correction of Marx brings us to a sketch of Hume's view of money:

Historically, money arises as part of the gradual development of a system of property based on convention, that is,

> a general sense of common interest; which sense all members express to one another and which induces them to regulate their conduct by certain rules. I observe, that it will be for my interest to leave another in possession of his goods, provided he will act in the same manner with regard to me.
>
> (T 314-315)

Money does not arise from some state fiat or a spontaneous social contract, it is similar to language in this regard:

> In a like manner are languages gradually establish'd by human conventions without any promise. In like manner do gold and silver become the common measures of exchange, and are esteem'd sufficient payment for what is of a hundred times their value.
>
> (Hume 1987: 315)

Ontologically, money has no privileged substance, since it is conventional. Its function is to *represent* "labour and commodities" and *not to be equivalent* in value to them. Hume concludes that Locke's idea that money has a substance whose intrinsic value makes it equal in value to other signs and other commodities expresses a pathos of identity that leads to error. But there are some substances that serve this representation function more amenably than others. After all, some possible substances like paper are so easily produced that the money supply can grow overnight to a dimension that would make the currency worthless. The decision to use one or another substance is purely pragmatic.

Epistemologically, one can only know the meaning of a particular monetary sign in the context of the whole system. There is no reflexive certainty as to what an individual monetary unit refers to. Hence, Hume's position can be seen as one verging on monetary nihilism.

Semantically, money's representative functioning is not to be found in an intrinsic relationship between sign and signified; individual monetary units do not have any intrinsic measure. Such a measure only arises globally. As Hume writes: "Where coin is in greater plenty; as a greater quantity of it is required to represent the same quantity of goods." Consequently, the reference of a particular coin or paper bill is dependent upon both the other coins or bills in circulation and the extent of commodities being offered for sale on the market. Thus,

> if the coin be locked up in chests, it is the same thing with regard to prices, as if it were annihilated while in the first and more uncultivated ages of any state, ere fancy has confounded her wants with those of nature, men, content with the produce of their fields, or with those rude improve-ments which they themselves can work upon them, have little occasion for exchange, at for money, which, by agreement, is the common measure of exchange.
>
> (Hume 1987: 290–291)

Thus, monetary reference arises between *systems* of monetary signs and *forms of life* producing commodities.

Practically, the best monetary substance is one that resists easy iteration and can be carried on outside of some state regulation. As Hume wrote to Morellet: "It is true, money must always be made of some materials which have intrinsic value, otherwise it would be multiplied without end, and would sink to nothing" (R 214–215). This is especially true of societies that are in transition from a state characterized by an "ancient simplicity of manners." Hume definitely applied this maxim to Scotland, even in the face of a dramatic (and successful) increase in branch banking and expansion of "paper-credit" in the post-1745 era. He called for a return to specie and the social discipline it would impose on the Scots (both Highlanders and Low-landers). Hume's philosophy of money ends so typically: the most radical, even nihilistic, theory becomes a justification for the most conservative of practices!

Hume developed a concept of self which was appropriate to such an economy of monetary signs, for the self, like money, is a fiction: "The identity, which we ascribe to the mind of man, is only a fictitious one, and of the kind with that which we ascribe to vegetables and animal bodies" (T 169). There is neither an idea of the self nor a self-substance that can unite all perceptions into one. As he writes decisively in the *Treatise*:

I may venture to affirm of … mankind, that they are nothing but a bundle or collection of different perceptions, which succeed each other with an inconceivable rapidity, and are in perpetual flux and movement and it must be our several particular perceptions, that compose the mind. I say *compose* the mind, not *belong* to it.

(T 165)

The self is, therefore, created (it is "bundled," "composed" and "invented"). Although clearly the self is the object of the passions and the foundation of a system of justice and property, it is not a given.

An important consequence of its fictionality is the self's capacity to un-bundle, de-compose and dis-solve all or part of itself. It explains Hume's enthusiasm for both waged labor (often referred to as "industry") and suicide. Indeed, suicide is the supreme example of our capacity to "edit" ourselves out of existence and ironically claim self-ownership. Hume defiantly (though prudently) supported suicide to the hilt as he did waged labor. This support for both waged labor and suicide arises from the plasticity of the self that was discovered in eighteen-century philosophy, and emphasized by Hume. Suicide involved the "all"-aspect of our capacity for self-editing, but the ability to sell a temporal "part" of one's self is not an easily conceivable act in an era when the discourse on the self and on the soul (in philosophy and religion) was still so intimately connected. Even though, of course, waged labor had been going on for thousands of years.

Just as money was not intrinsically valuable in Hume's thought, he also casts a cold eye on the property- and value-creating character of labor. He responds by pointing out that property is an artificial virtue created out of human conventions, especially concerning the rule of division of property, having multiple sources. In reviewing Locke's labor theory of property creation, which he paraphrases as "everyone has a property in his own labour; and when he joins that labour to any thing, it gives him the property of the whole," Hume clearly does not approve of Locke's naturalistic metaphor of "joining" labor to a thing: "We cannot be said to join our labour to any thing but in a figurative sense. Properly speaking, we only make an alteration on it by our labour." In his labor theory, Locke was engaging, Hume implies, in a bit of philosophical superstition here just as "the Roman Catholics represent the inconceivable mysteries of the Christian religion, and render them more present to the mind, by a taper, or habit, or grimace, whish is suppos'd to

resemble them." There is nothing "natural" about property, and consequently these efforts to naturalize it simply encourage "false light" (T 331).

Hume, in his refusal to attribute intrinsic value to money, also did not
isolate an intrinsic value to commodities. It is only in the "collision" of commodities and money that value is created. As Hume argues:

> If the coin be locked in chests, it is the same thing with regard to prices,
> as if it were annihilated; if the commodities be hoarded in magazines and
> granaries, a like effect follows. *As the money and commodities, in these
> cases, never meet, they cannot affect each other.*
>
> (Hume 1987: 290)

After noting that a farmer's subsistence consumption of his crops should
not be considered in the estimation of the total mass of commodities
to be compared with the money supply, Hume concludes that "It is only
the overplus [production meant for sale on the market], compared to the
demand, that determines the value" (Hume 1987: 290). Hence, value is a
global property of the coordination of all the "meetings" of commodities
and money throughout the society; it does not exist hidden in them before
it is revealed/created in their mutual affect. This radical rejection of "the
signature of all things" conception of exchange—so dramatically presented
by Foucault's use of a passage from Davanzati's writings in *The Order of
Things*—is part of Hume's "attempt to introduce the experimental method
of reasoning into moral subjects." Like the idealized Newton, he refused to
countenance the "occult" in any form he could detect.

This is true of labor as a commodity as well, since its value is determined
not by an intrinsic quality or property but by the amount of the labor that
its owners intend to place on the market. It is true, of course, that Hume is
as enthusiastic about labor, activity and industry as his mercantile predecessors. He writes, for example, "Everything in the world is purchased by
labour," but he adds, "and our passions are the only causes of labour." Indeed,
he places "action" as one of the three ingredients of human happiness. But
again, he is concerned with the effect labor, activity and industry has on the
agent rather than on the product. The latter is something that is, like money,
a cipher. Just as money *per se* "is not, properly speaking, one of the subjects
of commerce," nor is labor *per se*, for Hume, it is only in their meeting that
they count. This is what annoyed Marx, of course.

The imperative for Hume in facing the crisis posed by the wage-earning class was to bring about this "meeting." In doing so, a "civilization" of wage-workers, especially south of Scottish border, could begin.

CONCLUSION: THE MEDUSA'S REVENGE

These three different models of the wage relation are incomplete, of course, and do not show a dialectical teleological process leading to the triumph of the wage contract, as Marx put it, "a very Eden of the innate rights of man" since "[i]t is the exclusive realm of Freedom, Equality, Property and Bentham" (Marx 1967: 176). This imperfection arises for two reasons: (1) the means: the class dynamics of England of the 1690s, the Ireland of the 1730s and the Scotland of 1740s that proved decisive in the thought of Locke, Berkeley and Hume were not comparable; (2) the end: the wage relation itself, under any model, is fundamentally conflictual and contradictory. In other words, the lack of a royal road to the labor market is not surprising; the opposite would be.

And we can see this instability in what I call "the Medusa's revenge." For the ancient myth did not end with the decapitation of Medusa. Such a powerful force could not be destroyed without consequences. Medusa's gaze remained just as dangerous in death as in life. For example, as Perseus flew over the Sahara desert on Pegasus, some drops of Medusa's blood fell from his wallet and they turned into venomous snakes. In our case, "Medusa's revenge" lies in workers' continual efforts to reject the wage relation in fact and in theory, often with success.

This lacuna can be seen in the writings of all three philosophers who noted in the activities of their opponents an anti-wage counter-philosophy, whether it be the London coin-clippers, the cynically content Irish natives or the Scottish Highlanders. It is this "other" philosophical tradition of the Medusas that needs to be studied as deeply as the canonical texts of the philosophical Perseuses.

Conclusion
Locke, Berkeley and Hume as Philosophers of Money

Not accidentally, Locke, Berkeley and Hume fit the definition of philosophers of money outlined in my Introduction. In conclusion, I will sketch out answers to the main question of this book: "How does each of these philosophers satisfy this definition?" In so doing I will provide a synopsis of the entire trilogy with the help of Table 8.1:

Table 8.1   A chart showing the relative positions of Locke, Berkeley and Hume as regards their key monetary policy texts, the political crises of their immediate concern, their social milieu, their theories of money, the genre of their primary writings on money and the role that they envisioned for money in society

	Locke	*Berkeley*	*Hume*
Texts	Some Considerations... (1692); Further Considerations... (1696)	The Querist (1735–1737)	Political Discourses (1752)
Crisis	The recoinage crisis of 1696	The "tithe agistment crisis" of 1734	The "45er"
Circle	The Shaftsbury Whigs and the "Junto"	The Dublin Society and Anglican Church of Ireland	The "Enlightenment" intelligentsia of Scotland
Opposition	Clippers, "Coiners," Baggers and the "inflationists"	Irish "natives" and the Anglo-Irish gentry	The Highland rebels, the mercantile protectionists and the urban English Proletariat
Concept of Money	Substance and Mixed Mode	Notion	Convention
Genre	Pamphlet	Query Series	Essay
Impact of money	The Mother of Civil Society	Part of B's "second conceptual revolution"	The philosophy of commercial society

LOCKE AS A MONETARY PHILOSOPHER: SUBSTANCE AND MIXED MODE IDEAS ARE THE FOUNDATION OF HIS CONCEPT OF MONEY AND MONETARY PHENOMENA ARE CRUCIAL TO HIS THEORY OF SOCIETY

John Locke was a philosopher who was definitely committed to a monetary program precipitated by the so-called "Recoinage Crisis" of 1696. He, along with a number of other experts (including his friend, the Master of the Mint, Isaac Newton), was asked by Sir John Somers to present his recommendation to deal with the fact that the English nation's silver coinage had experienced a dramatic decline in silver content during the previous three years. Something had to be done with the coinage since its deterioration was affecting the government's power to borrow money in the midst of a war. William Lowndes, the Secretary of the Treasury, called for a recoinage that would make the *de facto* devaluation of the currency in terms of silver content *de jure* (Locke 1991: 412).

Locke entered this contested territory with a clear program directed against Lowndes' proposal: the clipped coins in circulation should be returned to the mint and be exchanged (by weight) with the newly minted full value coins ("full weight recoinage"). He argued that Lowndes' devaluation or "inflationist" solution would in effect reward the coin clippers, baggers and counterfeiters and put them in a position of dictating the monetary policy of the most powerful nation on the planet. Such a resolution was an anathema for Locke, but he also recognized that his policy recommendation posed the threat of dramatic deflation in the midst of a war.

He used his philosophical apparatus to defend his recommendation and resolve this dilemma by defining money in such a way that the consequences of not going through with a "full weight recoinage" were evidently much more dangerous than the threats of deflation and economic crisis posed by going through with it. For Locke points out that in exchanges "[silver] is the thing bargain'd for, as well as the measure of the bargain" (Locke 1991: 15). It operates partially as a desired substance, but when silver is coined, a new ontological element is added, what Locke called a mixed mode: "The Coining of Silver, or making Money of it, is the ascertaining of the quantity by a public mark, the better to fit it for Commerce" (Locke 1991: 412).

The idea of money then has a twofold ontological character: a substance idea and what Locke called a "mixed mode" idea.[1] Together they form a very subtle (and ever potentially duplicitous) idea that spans nature and culture and synthesizes physical primary qualities with language-based unions of ephemeral acts, thoughts and events. Locke was clear as to the contrast between the two ontological categories: "Besides the greatest part of mixed modes, being actions which perish in their birth, are not capable of lasting duration, as substances which are the actors" (Locke 1959: II, 90). Is it any wonder then that money has a mysterious character?

Figure 8.1 The "clipping" of coins: Two examples of clipped silver shillings: a 1652 "Pine-Tree Shilling" from Massachusetts and a Shilling from the reign of Charles XII in Sweden (1697–1718). (Right) A collection of a hoard of clippings from England in the seventeen and eighteenth centuries of coins from the reigns of Elizabeth I, James I and Charles I. Images courtesy of Wikicommons. (Left) A whole and a "clipped" Shilling. The larger coin is an English silver shilling from the reign of James I, 1621–1623 and the smaller "clipped" coin from the reign of Elizabeth I, 1558–1603. In the British Museum. Images courtesy of Wikicommons.

For Locke, however, since the study of money involves mixed modes that define real essences, it allows for a form of demonstrable reasoning as strict as that found in mathematics (even though the ideas are less orderly). Indeed, monetary reasoning operates in the disjunctive realm that includes both the moral (*practica*) and the physical (*physica*). That can explain why his monetary writings are rife with moral conclusions—"robbing the Honest Man," "defraud the King," "totally destroy the publick Faith," "Clipping and false Coining heightens the Robbery into Treason"—derived with demonstrative reasoning (Locke 1991: 417, 417, 417, 415 respectively). For moral reasoning, being about humanly defined ideas, can have deductive consequences. For example, he writes:

"Where there is no property, there is no injustice," is a proposition as certain as any demonstration in Euclid: for, the idea of property being a right to anything, and the idea to which the name "injustice" is given being the invasion or violation of that right.

(Locke 1991: 18)

Indeed, the reason why money can be studied deductively is not due to its substantial physical aspect; it is due to its being a mixed mode.

Once one understands the metaphysical complexity of money, one understands the vital importance (and difficulty) of coordinating its substance and mixed mode aspects carefully. Indeed, Locke's defense of his monetary program—full weight recoinage—was based on this kind of reasoning; he argued that the threat of monetary deflation was less problematic than the possibility of undermining of the entire monetary system. Both the criminal clippers and the legal devaluationists (or "inflationists") undermine the mutual trust between citizen and state required for the functioning of a modern monetary system: "Altering the Standard, by raising the money ... will weaken, if not totally destroy the publick Faith, when all that had trusted the Publick ... shall be defrauded by 20 per Cent" (Locke 1991: 417), that is, a monetary crisis (like deflation) is infinitely less dangerous than a crisis of the money form itself.

Locke's program and the impact of his philosophy on the concept of money was definitely powerful, but what of the impact of money on Locke's philosophy? Is there evidence of this affect? I argue that there is and that it is best seen in Locke's *Second Treatise on Government*, where he literally defines both a period of human history as well as a social stratum that is always already in existence with the realm of money. Historically, money drove the transition from the period of subsistence to the emergence of a fully developed system of accumulation. Moreover, the contemporary world of international trade that operates in a pre-civil society manner is based on money (especially its substantial element).

Money, for Locke, is the mediator between nature and culture in history as well as metaphysically. This mediation arises from an unintended consequence to the tacit agreement to accept gold and/or silver as the universal equivalent taken by an overwhelming majority: the end of the moral obligation to share the surplus and to provide a "potlatch," if one can. This sets the stage for the development of the accumulation process, the privatization of land and eventually the whole system of civil government. So, for Locke, money is "The Mother of Civil Government" (Caffentzis 1989: 70).

Thus, we see that Locke is, according to my definition, a philosopher of money in that he proposes a monetary program, he uses his philosophical apparatus as a tool for the formation and defense of his proposal and his philosophical work is deeply affected by his money environment.

BERKELEY AS A MONETARY THEORIST: THE CRITIQUE OF SUBSTANCE, PRIMARY QUALITIES AND OBJECTIVITY AND THE ROLE OF MONEY IN HIS "SECOND CONCEPTUAL REVOLUTION"

It should not come as a surprise that John Locke was a philosopher of money. Marx, for example, characterized Locke's role in the recoinage crisis in the following words: "John Locke, who championed the new bourgeoisie in every way ... even demonstrated in a separate work that the bourgeois way of thinking is the normal human way of thinking—took up Lowndes' challenge" (Marx 1970: 77). But it may come as a surprise that Berkeley was also a philosopher of money.

Berkeley certainly had a monetary program that he proposed and actively supported. It called for the creation of a National Bank and a National Mint for Ireland. However, the Bank would issue paper money while the Mint will coin "small change" tokens with no trace of specie content in them. He proposed this plan with the help of members of the "improving" Dublin Society and in defense of the tithes and rents of the Church of Ireland (that alliance indicates Bishop Berkeley's complex socio-political position).

Berkeley was also clear as to his opposition: the poor, but cynical Irish "natives" who refused to work and the wealthy, libertine-influenced rural gentry who refused to pay their tithes and the British mercantile class that refused to let Ireland be. The whole point of his monetary program was to excite the Irish natives into productive labor, to force the wealthy gentry to spend their income (derived from rents and profits) "at home" and to liberate the Irish economy from the control of the Parliament in London.

Berkeley deployed his philosophy in the development and defense of the form of paper money he was advocating barely fifteen years after the crash of the great experiment with specieless money: the Law System. This was not an easy task and he definitely needed to attack the notion of money that his predecessor, John Locke, presented. Key to Locke's concept was the necessity for the substantial aspect of money. Berkeley suggested in the voice of the Querist that there was no such necessity. On the contrary, Locke's prejudice for a metallic substance element in the idea of money was an invitation to intellectual and political catastrophe for Ireland.

Berkeley criticized the view that material substances had a level of objectivity that notions (the self, its powers and activities) lack. Moreover, he questioned the necessity for a material basis of the monetary system. For the essential function of money is not to represent a valuable thing or substance, but it is to excite productive action. The presence of gold or silver substances in a coin was no "guarantee" as to its objective value and worth *qua* money. For money is fundamentally notional and has no attachment to material substance ideas that are intellectually incoherent anyway. For gold and silver's primary quality character (that supposedly gives them the virtue of an enhanced objectivity) is open to decisive mental relativity arguments by which Berkeley shows that "primary" qualities are as relative to the mental agent as are "secondary" ones.

This critique of Locke's concept of money and Berkeley's subsequent defense of a specieless currency called on all aspects of his philosophical system. Did money also affect Berkeley's philosophy as well? I believe that it did. For Berkeley's philosophy until the 1730s was divided by a dichotomy between ideas and selves. Ideas were dependent on selves, but selves and their faculties and actions were undescribable by ideas.

This dichotomy made for a powerful critical machine when aimed at materialist doctrines, however it left Berkeley unable to describe or plan for a world of selves. Berkeley went through a "second conceptual revolution" in the 1730s through the introduction of the notion (and its cognates) that allowed him to do exactly that. As I wrote in *Exciting the Industry of Mankind*:

> For Locke, money was a complex idea bringing together material substance ideas with mixed-mode notions, whereas for Berkeley money was a mixed-mode notion stripped of any essential dependence on material substances. Its purpose was to stimulate and regulate action, not to measure and store a quantity or specie.
>
> (Caffentzis 2000: 274)

The Querist was a vital part of Berkeley's larger intellectual revolution, for in differentiating between his and Locke's view of money, Berkeley was able to apply his thought onto collectivities of selves, describe their momentum and plan their future trajectories.

The inspiration for this effort, I believe, arose from his experience in the American colonies, especially his two and a half years of life in Rhode Island, the epicenter of a great monetary experiment in defetishizing specie that was taking place (Caffentzis 2000: 80–100). As I wrote: "[Berkeley] saw in Newport a society which had transcended the metallic gravity of coinage to survive and even flourish" (Caffentzis 2000: 82).

In this American context, there was also another factor, for the Rhode Island colony was:

> surrounded by a sea of gift-exchange relations among the native Americans … the colonists' wampum transactions with the native Americans liberated their monetary imagination just as the masterless character of the North American Indian peoples liberated the colonists' political imagination (Brandon 1980).
>
> (Caffentzis 2000: 418)

Thus, George Berkeley was a philosopher of money. He proposed and fought for a monetary program (that, though it failed in the short run, it eventually triumphed two centuries later); he deployed his philosophical thought in its defense and development, and finally his philosophy was deeply affected by monetary experiences.

HUME AS A MONETARY THEORIST: A REACTION TO THE
'45; THE IMPORTANCE OF CONVENTION AS THE BASIS OF
MONETARY EXCHANGE; MONEY AND MONETARY PHENOMENA
MAKE THE CREATION OF HISTORY POSSIBLE (I.E., HUME'S
RECOGNITION THAT THE FUTURE WILL NOT BE DETERMINED
BY THE PAST)

Berkeley was dealing with the problem of having the finances of the Church of Ireland depending on an Irish Catholic working class that was passive and resistant to work. His conception of money was dependent upon this problematic. Hume published his *Political Discourses* in Scotland seven years after one of the most momentous events in his country's history: the almost successful Jacobite rebellion against King William called the '45er. The enlistment of thousands of Highlanders (and many Lowlanders) from both the elite and the "common people" of Scotland into the army of the rebellion showed that the 1707 Act of Union between Scotland and Britain had not succeeded in convincing Scots that it marked a path to their economic betterment. Scotland could no longer remain a poor country and Hume, a leader in the growing circle of Scottish Enlightenment thinkers, had to show the path out of poverty. Hume's 1752 *Political Discourses* was his "What is to be done?!" text, where he proposes a monetary program (as well as a critique of other monetary strategies). His key idea was rooted in a response to the so-called "rich country–poor country" debates that had their origin in the post-Glorious Revolution era: if a poor country (with low wages and cost of living) was inserted in the midst of world trade flows and was hindered neither by geographical barriers nor tariff walls, it would inevitably be able to successfully compete with the rich countries, due to the low price of the commodities it produces (Hont 1993: 243–327).

The proper monetary policy to promote this "natural" advantage that a poor country has is one that opens it up to the flows of money that participation in world trade invites. The introduction of surplus money due to the positive balance of trade induced by the competitive edge of the poor country's low wages will stimulate the industry of workers and capitalists and thus further drive them on the path of commercial development. Hume was hostile to any program like George Berkeley's that called for withdrawing from world trade into autarky and for substituting local paper money created by a national bank for world money (which at that time was specie-based coinage). Autarky and paper money, Hume argued, would doom a country to an eternal sentence of poverty and misery. In the case of Scotland, it would also inflame the passions igniting futile rebellion again and again.

Hume's answer to Scotland's plight required that he promote world money (gold and silver coinage) and criticize the invention of new paper financial instruments, especially those based on credit and debt. This position was surprisingly reactionary and might appear a bit paradoxical given his other philosophical commitments. Hume, however, used his philosophy to support his monetary program and criticize his opponents. One of the most salient examples of this effort is to be found in his differential approach to metallic versus paper money.[2] Hume argued that the use of paper money issued by a National Bank is a catastrophe waiting to happen and in a society like Scotland, where the refinement and discipline required to preserve trust in a commercial world were lacking, the wait would not be long. Why this hostility to paper money? Hume, after all, was as clear as Berkeley about the conventionality and "fictionality" of money in general, so why did he accuse paper money in particular to be "counterfeit"?

The answers to these questions lie in Hume's philosophical analysis of fictions and conventions. For Hume distinguished between natural and artificial fictions and between conventions and promises. Natural fictions are those that arise in the construction of concepts like duration through time, continued existence of objects, self, substance and ideal standards. They operate through a universal mental propensity of confounding "identity with relation." Though strictly they are not arrived at either by deductive or even inductive methods they provide, as Annette Baier characterizes them, "plausible stories we tell ourselves to organize our experience" (Baier 1991: 103).

Artificial fictions, however, are not universally believed. They are the equivalent of constructed illusions whose success is dependent upon the idiosyncratic gullibility of individuals. They can be found in art, literature, myth and religion and not only in circuses and magic shows.

Hume also distinguishes between conventions and promises. Both are products of human exchanges, but the former is much more basic and reliable than the latter. A convention arises from the interlinked activities of at least two persons whose logic is: "Whatever is advantageous to two or more persons if all perform their part, but what loses all advantage if only one person performs…" (Hume 1983: 95) Conventions are the ur-relations that form society, promises and contracts come later. Hume includes the collective activities (like rowing), money and language under rubric of convention:

> Thus two men pull the oars of a boat by common convention, for common interest, without promise or contract; thus gold and silver are made the measures of exchange; thus speech, and words, and language are fixed by human convention and agreement.
>
> (Hume 1983: 95)

Consequently, we can see some basic philosophical distinctions arising between metallic and paper money. For metallic money "shares with time, ideal standards, substances, endurance of sensed objects, and the self a fundamental 'pathos of identity,' that is, every coin reflexively says of itself to both buyer and seller that it has a certain intrinsic value," while paper money clearly does not have the character of a "natural fiction" (Caffentzis 2008: 164). Also, coinage has the original character of conventional exchange—I give you this coin, if you give me this apple/I give you this apple, if you give me that coin—while paper money has the quality of a promise that requires a threatening deferral in time. Thus, paper money is an artificial fiction based on a promise while metallic money is a natural fiction based on a convention.

This philosophical distinction between metallic and paper money gave Hume the intellectual support to challenge Berkeley's autarky and paper money solution to the rich country–poor country problematic. But was Hume's philosophy affected by the monetary forces of his day? From his earliest works to his final efforts, there is a constant emphasis on the importance of money not as a thing but as a set of social relations in his philosophy. Hume saw in the increasing intensity of monetary exchange not just a sign of increasing wealth but also of industry, art and refinement, that is, civilization. His philosophy was therefore a reflection on money and its multiple shadows. As Carl Wennerlind, a scholar of Hume's work, concludes in a recent study of Hume's theory of money:

> Money also plays a central role in Hume's political philosophy. As one of the three foundational conventions of the modern social form [along side property and markets], Hume suggests that money is a necessary

condition for the establishment of a civilized, prosperous, and liberal society.

(Wennerlind and Schabas 2008 124)

Hume, therefore, satisfies the final criterion, clearly making him a philosopher of money.

CONCLUSION: AN APOLOGY VINDICATED?

The defense of my definition of what it is to be a philosopher of money and its application in the cases of Locke, Berkeley and Hume are now complete. I recognize, however, that there is a remaining but additional question that could only be asked at the conclusion of this book and trilogy: what is the value of such an effort? Clearly, the ultimate answer to this question is not mine to give. But I can make one observation as to why this work has been valuable politically to me (besides the pleasure of researching and writing it).

I also have found that working on this trilogy has made it possible for me to more adequately understand the great monetary transformation that was taking place (with much struggle and confusion) in the latter part of the seventeenth and throughout the eighteenth centuries in Europe by fits and starts (and that "ends" in August 1971): the development of a specie-less world money system. This transformation required not only a change in the concept of money; a change in the self-understanding of money users was also required. This happened neither automatically nor irenically. But philosophers of money played an important role in the creation of this new self-understanding. I have no doubt that when, or if, the Grand Narrative of this process is ever written, the conflicting and conflicted work of Locke, Berkeley and Hume will be central to telling the tale.

Coda
A Critique of Marx's Thesis 11 on Feuerbach

What does this trilogy show concerning philosophy and philosophers? It definitely makes clear that philosophers like Locke, Berkeley and Hume in the early period of capitalist history were deeply involved in arguing for particular forms of money and of monetary institutions by using concepts from their broader philosophic efforts. These philosophers were not personally detached from the outcome of their philosophies of money, for they and the circle they operated with would face serious concrete consequences if they failed. For example, consider the case of John Locke: on the one side, he faced execution for treason if the Settlement State of William and Mary he supported collapsed due to monetary mistakes and the Jacobites re-took state power; on the other side, if his work and advice helped the William and Mary state to survive its monetary crises, he would have his economic future guaranteed and his claim to "immortality" secured.

We should remember that understanding how a modern monetarized capitalist state operates requires not only a substantial ideological cover to mediate the often sharp class struggle, it also requires an immense amount of knowledge, both empirical and theoretical. The mixture of the false (ideology) and true (science) varies throughout capitalist history and makes the always-shifting dividing line between them difficult to determine. Marx, for example, confronted this challenge many times in his review of the intellectual production of the previous 200 years concerning surplus value—in his *Theories of Surplus Value*—made a distinction between classical theorists like Ricardo and apologists like the Comte du Buat. What separated Ricardo from Buat was the class struggle they faced. Marx acutely wrote: "Political Economy can remain a science only so long as the class struggle is latent or manifests itself only in isolated phenomena" (Marx 1970: 122). Once the class struggle takes on "more outspoken and threatening forms … In place of disinterested inquiries, there were hired prize-fighters; in place of genuine scientific research, the bad conscience and the evil intent of apologetic" (Marx 1970: 122).

Similar comments have been made about Philosophy's relation to the class struggle. But Marx had even sharper critical comments to make about Philosophy compared to his comments on Political Economy. This can be seen on examining the young Marx's eleventh Thesis on Feuerbach: *The Philosophers have Only Interpreted the World in Various Ways; The Point is to Change It.* Logically speaking, the aphorism is a conjunction and the first conjunct—The Philosophers have only interpreted the world in various ways—is a universal affirmative statement. If there exists at least one philosopher who has changed the world, then Thesis 11 is falsified.

One can read this philosophy of money trilogy as a long critique of Marx's very short aphorism, for on the basis of the evidence I provide, Locke, Berkeley and Hume are examples of philosophers who have tried to change the world using their philosophical tools. This trio would constitute counter-examples to a straightforward reading of Thesis 11. After all, Locke tried to control the form of England's (and the trading world's) (in the guise of "the gold standard") money supply for centuries (and he succeeded); Berkeley tried and failed to create a paper currency controlled by a national bank in Ireland that would regulate the flow of money for the purposes of stimulating "cynically content" Irish workers to enter into the waged working class and blocking the Anglo-Irish landed elite from squandering their rents in luxury consumption; and Hume used his writings on money to block the spread of "free banking," to thwart the introduction of paper currency in Scotland and to civilize the rebellious Highlanders through monetary transformations.

There are, however, non-literal readings of Marx's aphorism that preserve its truth that are worth confronting. One is by Ernst Bloch, a prominent twentieth-century German Marxist philosopher. He anxiously read the 11th Thesis in a way that would confirm it by interpreting its key terms in what I think is a strained manner. Let us hear Bloch's defense of Thesis 11:

> Thus the first part of the proposition in Thesis 11 is directed against philosophers who have only interpreted the world—and nothing else. Then, as the second part shows, the Thesis embarks on a thoroughly planned journey in quest of a new activistic philosophy, indispensible for changing the world and of use to it.
>
> (Bloch 1971: 94)

Bloch's reading of Thesis 11 remains anchored firmly in the world of philosophy: both bad philosophy produced by the third-rate Hegelians of his day, and good activist philosophy that has real-world consequences, but still is philosophy. This sets the stage that Bloch chose for his climax, the exuberant passage Marx wrote to criticize and ridicule his contemporary "philosophic" rivals in Germany like Max Stirner,

> One has to "leave philosophy aside," to leap out of it and devote oneself like an ordinary man to the study of actuality, for which there is an enormous amount of literary material, unknown, of course, to philosophers ... Philosophy and the study of the actual world have the same relation to one another as masturbation and sexual love.
>
> (Marx and Engels 1970: 103)

Masturbation (like Philosophy in this metaphor) can bring monadic pleasures and have other mental effects, but it does not, like sexual love, change the world of the sexual partners and relations, most obviously, it does not bring new living beings into the actual world. Thus, the objects of self-excitement in masturbation are fantasy objects with "barren" results while the objects of excitement of sexual love are actual bodies that can result in new beings and new relations. So too the objects of philosophy are fantasies that should be replaced by "the study of actuality" that would *actually* be liberating.

Bloch's valiant attempt to save Thesis 11 from falsification is not successful simply because it asks us to read the word "philosophers" in the aphorism in a way that is not consistent with the reference of the word he used in the period he was composing the Theses. Bloch would have us believe that "[Marx's] attack was directed against a *particular* type of contemplative philosophy, produced by the third-rate Hegelians of is day, which was, rather a non-philosophy" (Bloch 1971: 94). But Marx's other *Theses on Feuerbach* have a perfectly standard reference for a philosophic doctrine he is most concerned with in the text, materialism, both ancient and modern. There is no reason to take writers like Stirner as the special referents of "philosophers" in Thesis 11 when the philosophers Marx was referring to in *Theses on Feuerbach* were either materialists in general or Feuerbach in particular.

If this argument nullifies Bloch's effort to "save" Thesis 11 (and, by the way, Philosophy), we now can see that the trilogy offers Locke, Berkeley and Hume as counter-examples to the truth claims of Thesis 11 even if one agrees with the second conjunct of the Thesis: "the point is to *change it*." Marx was clearly seeing his and Engels' work as the transcending of philosophy (mechanical materialism included), but philosophers have been changing the world (or at least trying to) since philosophy's beginning. Locke, Berkeley and Hume are simply the most obvious counter-examples to Thesis 11 among many others from Heraklitus to Newton to Derrida who have tried to change the world with the help of philosophic tools. In fact, since the origin of philosophy, there has been an activist aspect to philosophers' work, especially in periods of social crisis.

A consequence of this reading of the aphorism, however, is the recognition that, though some philosophers have been active in changing the world, they were, for the most part, changing the world in the interest of the ruling class. What I have done with respect to Locke's, Berkeley's and Hume's philosophies of money could be replicated from the pre-Socratics to the postmodernists and with issues that are not just monetary. This recognition of philosophy's preferential option for the ruling and oppressive class runs counter to the claims that philosophy is liberating.

After all, lovers of philosophy (however widely the net is cast) have always claimed that it liberates humanity from pointless fears of death in particular and mental slavery in general. From Plato's Cave to Bacon's Idols to Wittgenstein's Bottle, philosophers have congratulated themselves on providing concepts and methods that were liberating. Indeed, the most typical philosophical "ideas" (Truth, the Good, the Beautiful, History, Freedom, Reason, Being, etc.) are infinite, universal and self-reflexive. Hence, by definition, they provided models of liberation and escape from intellectual enclosures. One cannot think of a genuine philosophical idea without experiencing a dizzying freedom of thought that has so often been a model of social and political liberation as well. The temptation at this juncture is to quote a relevant passage from Hegel ... for example,

> To think is in fact *ipso facto* to be free, for thought as the action of the universal is an abstract relating of self to self, where, being at home with ourselves, and as regards our subjectivity, utterly blank, our consciousness is, in the matter of its contents, only in the fact and its characteristics.
> (Hegel 1892: 45)

among many others, but this is not the place for corroborating this claim with a string of quotations stretching from the time of the Eurasian warring states to the present. I need simply ask you, in the spirit of the empiricists of old, to imagine and verify the claim for your self. After all, it is the experience of this kind of freedom that has been the primary attraction (if not seduction) of philosophy.

Similarly, the activity of philosophizing is also immediately an experience of conceptual creativity. As countless philosophers have pointed out, philosophical activity is unpredictable and unprecedented (even when it takes on the genre of a commentary). In this respect, I agree with Deleuze and Guattari that "philosophy is this continuous creation of concepts" (Deleuze and Guattari 1994: 8).

[For] the concept is not given, it is created; it is to be created ... What depends on a free creative activity is also that which, independently and necessarily, posits itself in itself: the most subjective will be the most objective.

(Deleuze and Guattari 1994: 11)

Such an activity is liberating to the highest degree, since the object of the creative process (the concept or idea) is creative in itself. Therefore, it cannot be anticipated and restricted by censors or other professional semantic police. For the censor's list of forbidden ideas is continually "diagonalized" by new concepts that could never have been created before the proclamation of the censors' list of acceptable concepts itself (and therefore they are unbanable before the list of the banned is proclaimed).

The best classical presentation and summary of the relation between philosophy and liberation is perhaps in Plato's *Apology* where Plato has Socrates foreseeing that philosophizing would be his occupation in the afterlife (if there were to be one). For philosophizing is an infinite act that is an end in itself—just as singing is in Dante's *Paradisio*—and is exactly the kind of thing to do in the Elysian fields as well. Therefore, philosophy is liberating, the lovers of philosophy claim, since it is something of a divine action not dependent upon anything or anyone else. There might be other infinite, self-fulfilling and liberating activities (like playing saxophone with John Coltrane), but surely philosophizing is one of the primary ones.

PHILOSOPHY AS PROPONENT OF SLAVERY

The evidence provided by this trilogy however, immediately counters these immediate responses in defense of philosophy, namely, that it is an inherently liberating activity. The *actual* record of philosophy's lack of support for human liberation in general from ancient to modern times is shameful and scandalous. After all, none of the major philosophers from Plato to Berkeley argued for the abolition of slavery (the most obvious index of supporting human liberation). This record poses a deep and abiding dilemma for teachers of philosophy. Many of us know the anxiety that arises in us when we present Aristotle's *Politics, Book I* to a philosophy class and we deal with the hostile questioning of students who have easily punched a thousand holes through The Philosopher's "logic." Many of them rightly ask, "How could such a 'great' philosopher be so sloppy and arbitrary in his reasoning?" or "If this is a great philosopher, then how can philosophy be great?"

Such queries are not easily answered. True, we can find some exceptions in philosophy's scandalous historical record. For example, the Stoics were able to isolate an identical human essence in both emperor and slave while articulating a notion of human equality that abolitionists appealed to centuries later. But even they did not call for (or even deduce the value of) the abolition of actually existing slavery (Garnsey 1996: 128–152). Indeed, in his thorough survey of philosophical comments on slavery in ancient Greece and Rome and during early Christianity, Peter Garnsey cannot find a single *named* author advocating the abolition of slavery, although there are many critics of how the slave system was practiced (Garnsey 1996: 75–86). Aristotle does mention "many of those versed in law" as critics of slavery, but they remain unnamed and we have no extant passages from their writings. The best Garnsey can do for these critics that were made anonymous is to locate them intellectually:

> The intellectual origins of the critique lie ultimately in the activity of the sophists, which was centered in the second half of the fifth century and the early fourth and was marked by skeptical inquiry into traditional beliefs and practices. How far the critique was taken is a moot point, but Aristotle evidently thought that it was sufficiently dangerous to warrant a counter-attack.
>
> (Garnsey 1996: 76–77)

Early Christian philosophers beginning with Augustine were abolitionists neither of slavery nor of capital punishment. Augustine developed a refined ambivalent justification of slavery that was to have a deep impact in the future evasions of the Church on the issue of slavery. He granted that slavery was not natural: "[God] did not intend that His rational creature, who was made in His image, should have dominion over anything but the irrational creation—not man over man, but man over the beasts" (St. Augustine 1972: 693). But with entrance of sin into history, an immense qualification is introduced, slavery arose as a punishment for sinning. Consequently, one could simultaneously recognize its inherent injustice and accept wholeheartedly its institution!

So much for the liberating character of early Christian philosophy, but this failure of philosophy intensifies in the medieval period. For the Roman slave system (though not slavery *per se*) comes to an end in Western Europe by the eleventh century. This remarkable fact has been studied by a large cohort of historians and social thinkers from Marc Bloch to Pierre Dockès to Pierre Bonnassie, yet none of these researchers has come up with a medieval abolitionist who philosophically expressed the significance of the transition from slavery to serfdom as it was happening in front of their eyes (Bloch 1975; Dockès 1982; Bonnassie 1991). (It is only with the rise of organized heretical movements in the twelfth and thirteenth centuries that we find an intellectual support for the abolition of slavery.) This transition can only be traced through a rhizome composed of thousands of legal documents of the period, since no liberating philosophy could be found to provide a coherent strategy that would further it. On the contrary, the philosophies of the Church stood staunchly for the idea of slavery in the face of its actual disappearance! Thus, for example, in the thirteenth century (long after the demise of slave system in Western Europe), Thomas Aquinas' view of slavery gave an even more profound legitimation of slavery than Augustine's. For the latter saw slavery as the product of sin, while Aquinas argued that it was the result of reason: "possessions and slavery were not the product of nature, but were made by human reason for the advantage of human life" (Blackburn 1997: 89)!

This philosophical attachment to slavery continued into the transition to capitalism. The early bourgeois philosophers (so filled, we are told, with the desire for freedom) were not abolitionists either. Indeed, the "greats" were either active or passive supporters of slavery until the later eighteenth century. One of the first famous philosophers who wrote against slavery,

David Hume, did so only by substituting the chattel slavery ideology with a racist wage slave one. Indeed, even the great philosopher of liberation, Hegel, however aware he was of the Haitian Revolution (Buck-Morss 2000) at the time of writing *The Phenomenology of Spirit*, was a peculiarly obscurantist supporter of slavery. For example, in 1818, he could write in the *Encyclopedia of the Philosophical Sciences* with a straight philosophical face the following:

> The question has been asked, why slavery has vanished from modern Europe. One special circumstance after another has been adduced in explanation of this phenomenon. But the real ground why there are no more slaves in Christian Europe is only to be found in the very principle of Christianity itself, the religion of absolute freedom.
>
> (Hegel 1892: 293)

There are very few (if any) "great" philosophers who had been active abolitionists before African slavery's formal demise. Of course, philosophy's refusal to support *actual* human liberation did not end there, it continued after the end of the slave trade with its refusal to challenge imperialism, racism and sexism.

This history lesson, of course, poses a dilemma for any lover of philosophy: If philosophy is so liberating, why has it been such a thorough-going enemy of liberation?

END THE INFAMY! END PHILOSOPHY?

Given philosophy's questionable record with respect to slavery, the claim that philosophy has any special relation to human liberation should be the occasion for skepticism. Might philosophy indeed be like the "science" of torture, a form of knowledge only appropriate for a society hostile to human liberation or does philosophy (like work) have a value that transcends our "pre-history" of humanity? Is there something in the philosophical project that is worth continuing in the face of philosophy's historical shame? After all, it is no accident that philosophy has been, for most of its history, a supporter of slavery. It is historically demonstrable that most "great" philosophers have been members or employees of the ruling (*and* slave-owning) class of their day and they have created philosophies "born in oppression."

Although this was known by critics of philosophy long before Marx (should Diogenes—the one who claimed to have come to Athens to deface the currency—be given the prize for being the first?), we will attribute the discovery of the ideological character of philosophy, "Marx's Discovery" (Mah 1987).

Marx expressed this Discovery in many modalities and many locales in his voluminous work. One of the earliest versions (which was later recycled in the *Communist Manifesto*) is to be found in *The German Ideology*:

> The ideas of the ruling class are in every epoch the ruling ideas, i.e., the class which is the ruling material force of society, is at the same time its ruling intellectual force. The class which has the means of material production at its disposal, has control at the same time over the means of mental production, so that thereby, generally speaking, the ideas of those who lack the means of mental production are subject to it...
>
> (Marx and Engels 1970: 64)

After the Discovery was made—that is, the producers of concepts and ideas (philosophers) are those who "make the perfecting of the illusion of the class about itself their chief source of livelihood" (Marx and Engels 1970: 65)— the temptation to call for the abolition of the infamous "science" of slavery, philosophy itself, intensified. According to Marx's theory of ideology, philosophers could not keep themselves from defending slavery, for just as "during the time of the aristocracy was dominant the concepts of honour, loyalty, etc., were dominant, during the dominance of the bourgeoisie the concepts freedom, equality, etc.," so too the justifications of slavery we have mentioned above inevitably arose from the ruling classes' interest from the time of the Greek city states to the nineteenth-century European bourgeoisie the philosophers were continuous in advocating slavery regardless of the contradictions it spawned (Marx and Engels 1970: 65; Caffentzis 1989: 190–202). Marx's Discovery that the history of philosophy is a compendium of apologetic ideologies of the ruling classes of the past certainly tempted him to reject it as a viable field of thought. Indeed, the desire to end philosophy has been an important impulse in the thought of liberation since Marx's Discovery. As Marx first deduced the "progress" of philosophy (in a boisterous, youthful fashion), over time philosophical concepts became more universal because the new aspiring ruling class had to appeal to an ever more diverse set of allies. But whatever the level of claims, philosophy has been for the most part acting to obscure and invert the reality of oppression.

Why should anyone *not* want to end this infamy, this millennia-long cover up of acts of oppression, and mercifully "leave philosophy aside," especially given its innate well-tested tendency to obscure and pervert thought by its preferential option for the ruling, expropriating and oppressing class on the day? The subjects (especially women and descendants of slaves) who have been degraded and objectified by philosophers throughout history should be especially eager to execute this abolition.

PHILOSOPHY AS A STRATEGIC TOOL OF OPPRESSION

Marx's discovery of philosophy's "dirty secret" and his assessment of its history is problematic, however. Certainly much of the more recent work in the history of philosophy has begun to see philosophy as a "toolbox" of the ruling class, not just its smokescreen. That is, these ideas are not simply ideological justifications of already preconceived social and political practices beneficial to the ruling class, but they are used to invent and strategize about these very practices forged in the class struggle. From this perspective, Marx was quite wrong, as I demonstrated above, in claiming philosophy is ineffectual and epiphenomenal. The argument being that since philosophy is excited by fantasy objects instead of actual ones, it cannot be of use in transforming the "actual world," at best, philosophers could only "read" (and distort) a world eternally separated from it.

Contra Marx, there is a growing body of literature demonstrating that philosophers have contributed and continue to contribute greatly to "changing the world" by developing new concrete defenses for the maintenance of sexism, racism and classism. (A classic exemplar of this literature being Michel Foucault's analysis of Bentham's Panopticon in *Discipline and Punish* (Foucault 1979).

Silvia Federici has shown that the famous debate between Hobbes and Descartes concerning the nature of the body and the existence of the mind was also an important strategic discussion concerning the models of capitalist work discipline that were appropriate in the seventeenth century (Federici 2004).

As part of this effort, I have shown that the different philosophical tools developed by Locke, Berkeley and Hume were deployed to create concepts of money and strategies useful in dealing with the destabilizing challenges posed by quite different class conflicts in England, Ireland and Scotland. The genre that this work is a part of shows us that many philosophical ideas are not merely the fantasies and illusions created for apologetic purposes. On the contrary, they form part of the conceptual toolbox that is used by the ruling class for its own self-regulation and in developing strategies to triumph in the class struggle.

The discovery of the effectuality of philosophy immediately changes the demand for an end to philosophy. For if philosophy can be of use in developing strategies of oppression, can it not also become a source of strategies for liberation as well? Even though most philosophy is born of oppression, cannot there be an effective philosophy born of struggle?

APPROPRIATING PHILOSOPHY:
REFLECTING ON THE STRUGGLES

Since Marx's Discovery in the mid-nineteenth century, many have begun to attempt to create such "philosophies of struggle." For like the literature and architecture of the past, there is a wealth in philosophy that does not warrant its annihilation, although its poisonous passages inevitably mean that the process of appropriation must remain eternally incomplete (like the dumps of nuclear waste that will be radioactive for thousands of years!). The development of Feminist Philosophy and African-American Philosophy, for example, have been two fields where, instead of calling for the annihilation of philosophy, there have been attempts to re-appropriate its wealth to make it capable of forwarding human liberation. Is this the right decision concerning the philosophy of money? What part of the wealth of philosophy is not poisoned? What are the conditions of producing liberating philosophy today?

The key that reverses the dialectic can be found in Audre Lorde's incisive aphorism, "You can't take apart the master's house with the master's tools," but you need *some* tools to do the dismantling and then to go on to build a new house of liberation. Where are these tools to come from?

This is a difficult question to answer. Can it come from within the philosophy profession? Can the work of philosophy of liberation struggles be professionalized? This almost sounds like an oxymoron. After all, the increased participation of women and African Americans in philosophical institutions and networks in the USA can simply be an invitation to continue in "business as usual" mode with a slightly different gender and physiognomic composition. Indeed, the pre-eminent sociological student of philosophy, Randall Collins, argues that simply introducing more women into the profession would not change philosophical institutions: "it is predictable that as there are increasing numbers of women in the intellectual field with the overcoming of institutional discrimination, women will spread through the various positions which make up the dynamics of intellectual life" (Collins 1998: 78). In other words, as far as Collins is concerned, the entrance of women into the profession will have absolutely no impact on the networks of influence, investments of cultural capital and the struggle for professional dominance that have been going on in the machine of philosophical institutions for thousands of years. Collins would likely draw similar conclusions about African-American philosophers. Is he correct?

If this seamless absorption of feminist and African-American philosophers were to happen, inevitably it would mean the end of philosophy of oppression. For such a philosophy must arise from reflections on the struggles of the oppressed from *their perspective*. It requires the transformation of the materials of struggle into concepts that in turn can make these struggles more effective. But the success of such struggles would undoubtedly undermine the function—that is, the creation of concepts for the purpose of sustaining rule over recalcitrant subjects—of the institutional framework that has defined philosophy since ancient times. Hence, the dilemma of a philosophy of oppression: its professional success would lead to its demise, but its complete banishment from the institutions of philosophy (especially the universities) would also mean the abandonment of a tremendous intellectual wealth and reach. It is on the horns of this dilemma that the philosophers struggling against oppression must dance (or be impaled).

Notes

FOREWORD

1. Constantine George Caffentzis, *Clipped Coins, Abused Words & Civil Government: John Locke's Philosophy of Money* (New York: Autonomedia, 1989) was the first volume of the trilogy. The second was *Exciting the Industry of Mankind: George Berkeley's Philosophy of Money* (Dordrecht: Kluwer, 2000). *Clipped Coins* has also now been published in a new edition by Pluto Press.
2. David Hume, *The History of England*, Vol. 6, Chapter 60.
3. The Irish Fenians crossed Niagara Falls into Canada in 1866 and with further raids in 1870 and 1871, thus invading the royal realm.
4. George C. Caffentzis, "On the Scottish Origin of 'Civilization,'" in Silvia Federici (Ed.), *Enduring Western Civilization: The Construction of the Concept of Western Civilization and Its "Others"* (Westport, CT: Praeger, 1995), 13–36.
5. John Burrow, *A History of Histories: Epics, Chronicles, Romances and Inquiries from Herodotus and Thucydides to the Twentieth Century* (New York: Knopf, 2008), 313.
6. David Hume, *The History of Great Britain under the House of Stuart*, Vol. 1, 2nd edn (1759), 106 and 112.
7. Marx refers to Hume in contexts concerning the mutual variation among the factors the quantity of money, the value of the commodities in circulation, and the velocity of their exchange, in Volume 1 of *Capital* in one of the long footnotes in Chapter 3 on money, and again in *Theories of Surplus Value* (Vol. 1, 538) where he studies the relationship between the rate of interest and the rate of profit.
8. Patrick Colquhoun, *A Treatise on the Police of the Metropolis* (London, 1796), viii.
9. Quoted in Herbert Heaton, *The Yorkshire Woollen and Worsted Industries*, 2nd edn (Oxford: Clarendon Press, 1965), 351.
10. Possession and custody must be distinguished. The popular adage that "possession is nine-tenths of the law" refers to the number of royal writs defining private property.
11. Craig Becker, "Property in the Workplace: Labor, Capital, and Crime in the Eighteenth Century British Woollen and Worsted Industry," *Virginia Law Review* 69(8) (November 1983): 1487–1515.
12. Such a one was Thomas Lightoweller who, during the 1760s, taught coiners in the English Midlands as well as in Lancashire and Yorkshire.

13. John Styles, "'Our Traitorous Money Makers': The Yorkshire Coiners and the Law, 1760–83," in John Styles and John Brewer (Eds.), *An Ungovernable People: The English and their Law in the Seventeenth and Eighteenth Centuries* (London: Hutchinson, 1980), 180.

14. H. Ling Roth, *The Yorkshire Coiners, 1767–1783* (Halifax: King & Sons, 1906).

15. Not to be confused with Thomas Spence who struck and uttered coin of his own. See "Thomas Spence's Freedom Coins," in Camille Barbagallo et al. (Eds.), *Commoning: With George Caffentzis and Silvia Federici* (London: Pluto Press, 2019).

16. Fred Inglis (Ed.), *E.P. Thompson: Collected Poems* (Newcastle: Bloodaxe Books, 1999), 67; and J.M. Neeson, *Commoners: Common Right, Enclosure and Social Change in England, 1700–1820* (Cambridge: Cambridge University Press, 1993), 167–168 explains how rushes when soaked in fat provided a cheap substitute for candles.

17. David Graeber, *Debt: The First 5,000 Years* (New York: Melvillehouse, 2011), 361.

INTRODUCTION

1. See C. George Caffentzis, *Clipped Coins, Abused Words and Civil Government: John Locke's Philosophy of Money* (1989); *Exciting the Industry of Mankind: George Berkeley's Philosophy of Money* (2000); "Hume, Money, and Civilization; Or, Why Was Hume a Metallist?" (2001); "Civilizing the Highlands: Hume, Money, and the Annexing Act" (2005); and "Fiction or Counterfeit? David Hume's Interpretations of Paper and Metallic Money" (2008).

2. See Jacques Derrida, *Given Time: I. Counterfeit Money* (1992); and Mark Blaug et al., *The Quantity Theory of Money: From Locke to Keynes and Friedman* (1995). Though there is ample recognition of the achievements of Locke, Berkeley, and Hume in the realm of monetary theory and policy, it is by no means equally spread. The differential attention paid to Locke, Berkeley, and Hume in the history of economics literature can easily be judged by looking at some standard textbooks in the field. Consider Mark Blaug's advanced text, *Economic Theory in Retrospect* (1968). It has 21 index [page] references for Hume, 13 for Locke, and 3 for Berkeley. Henry William Spiegel's textbook, *The Growth of Economic Thought* (1983), which is more oriented to the humanities, shows a similar differential: 48 index references to Locke, 32 for Hume, and none for Berkeley. I discuss this differential in Caffentzis, *Exciting the Industry of Mankind*, 419n.

1. ON THE SCOTTISH ORIGINS OF CIVILIZATION

1. E. Frances White quotes Graham Connah (1987) on this point:

> The term "civilization" has been quietly abandoned by many writers, it is too vague a concept and too subjective to be useful. It also has unpleasant conno-

tations that are at best ethnocentric and at worst egocentric. It implies an "us" and "them" situation: we are "civilized," they are "primitive."

(White 1987)

2. There are two senses of "Civil Law" in English: one in contrast to Criminal Law and the other in contrast to Common Law. In the former sense, Civil Law regulates the conduct of exchange relations between private persons, while Criminal Law deals with conduct that implies liability to prosecution and punishment by the state. In the latter sense, Civil Law is a legal system based on Roman Law, whereas Common Law is based on the body of law developed in the English King's courts. Thus, there are two senses of legal "civilization," that is, the transformation of Criminal into Civil Law and the transformation of Common into Civil (or Roman) Law. In this essay, we deal exclusively with the second transformation. Civil Law is often called the court of Equity, cf. (Lord Kames 2014: 18–19).

3. The Scottish Enlightenment refers to a period roughly from the 1730s to the 1780s, and to a set of persons (from Hutcheson to Millar) that includes philosophers, engineers, chemists, lawyers, and other intellectuals working in the narrow strip between Glasgow and Edinburgh. These Scottish intellectuals organized the "hardware" (the steam engine) and the "software" (theories of human nature) appropriate for the original exemplar of industrial capitalism. A good sociological account of their circle can be found in Camic (1983).

4. A most unusual situation resulted from the Act of Union from the point of view of the "law of property, which nature herself has written upon the hearts of all mankind" (Edward Christian, quoted in Hay 1975: 19). The most basic property rights and their adjudication were determined by a border, as English Common Law was not truly sovereign north of Dumfries (Walker 1976).

5. The course of the Protestant Reformation in England was quite different from that of its Scottish version, a difference that had consequences for the tension between the Common and Civil Law. In England, Protestantism was driven by the Church of England, whose main interest was the destruction of the power of papal agents in England, and was therefore concerned with placing limits on Canon Law, which was derived from Roman models. In Scotland, the driving force was Calvinism, which demanded the generalizable Roman law.

6. The Pandects was the last major compilation of Roman law commissioned by Justinian in AD 530. It consists of fifty books, divided into laws, of selections from juridical writings from the republican period. It was meant to be the first complete legal code since pre-imperial times.

7. "Thanatocracy" is the term Peter Linebaugh has coined to describe the expanded use of capital punishment to regulate class conflict in eighteenth-century Britain (Linebaugh 1993).

8. Cesare Beccaria in 1764 published *On Crimes and Punishments*, where he not only criticized judicial torture but also argued for "a fixed code of laws, which must be observed to the letter," quite uncharacteristic of the Common Law.

9. For an account of the Gordon Riots emphasizing its class sentiments ("a groping desire to settle accounts with the rich, if only for a day, and to achieve some rough kind of social justice"), see Rude (1962: 289).

10. The elaborate division of agricultural labor that prevailed in the pre-Clearances Highlands is thus described by Smout:

> The arable was divided runrig, and the organization of the whole joint farm was a cooperative one between eight or a dozen tenants, who contributed something to the common plough and obeyed communal rules for the grazing. They were everywhere assisted in husbandry by a large class of sub-tenants ... normally these men held no more than a diminutive strip of arable and the right to graze a cow or a couple of goats on the pastures. They paid the tenant rent by working without wages upon his land for a certain time each week: the rest of the time they devoted to winning their own subsistence from the ground.
>
> (Smout 1972: 317)

11. The 1745 invasion was a major effort by the "crofters in the Highlands and the small craftsmen in the Lowlands" to overturn the increasing, encroaching pressure on their form of life emanating out of London, Edinburgh and Glasgow (Plumb 1950: 107).

12. Social science, Marxist and non-Marxist, has not transcended this schema, although refinements are always available. Nineteenth-century theorists of civilization integrated racial determinants; early twentieth-century variants included disquisitions on parallel stages of rationality and prelogicality, while even postmodernists like Michel Foucault, Jean-François Lyotard, and Jean Baudrillard depend on it for their ironies (Baudrillard 1983). Only by acknowledging that intellectual transmission is not simply a matter of diffusion from center to periphery can the stages metaphor be transcended.

2. CIVILIZING THE HIGHLANDS

1. Roger Emerson has independently developed a similar hypothesis for some time. His important contribution to our understanding of Hume's economic writings, which includes a defense of this reading of the *Political Discourses*, has been presented in a recent conference paper.

2. Corrections to the oversimplified identification of 'Forty-Fivers with Highlanders can be found in Pittock (1995b). He estimates that "only 43–6 per cent of the total troop strength [in Charles Edward's army in 1745] seem to have come from the Highlands" (Pittock 1995b: 60). The Jacobite Clans of the Highlands might be a myth, but some historians like Michael Lynch more radically point out that:

> The "Highlands" as such did not exist. For almost any purpose in Scottish history it is necessary to distinguish between Eastern, Central and Western

Highlands as well as between the mainland and the Western Isles. Allegience to the Jacobite cause varied significantly in the different parts of the Highlands.

(Lynch 1991: 369)

3. The importance of the Annexing Act for Scottish history and beyond has been recognized for some time now. Certainly the magisterial work on the Act is Annette Smith (1982). John Shaw (1983) puts the Commissioners in the context of the ruling elite of Scottish society. An important addition to the literature on the Annexing Act is Mackillop (2000), which argues that military recruitment was a "hidden variable" in understanding the purposes (and contradictions) of the Act. Mackillop writes:

> an important dimension of the annexed estates experiment lies not so much in the failure of its stated objectives as in the fact that it represents the earliest post-Culloden example of the significant contradictions and tensions that existed between agrarian improvement, military recruitment and subsequent estate resettlement.

(Mackillop 2000: 77)

Hume's concern to show that "nor need we fear, men, by losing their ferocity, will lose their martial spirit" is, in this light, not only a contribution to the militia/standing army debate, but it is also an intervention in the Annexing Act discussion (Hume 1955: 25). For if "civilising the Highlands" meant the end of military recruiting in the Highlands, then such a project might be aborted.

4. For a short introduction to these figures, see Stephen and Lee (1917).
5. These anxieties were actualized. It turned out, many of these estates were "disannexed" and their former owners' families received them back in 1784 when the Annexing Act was repealed (Smith 1982: 224). But the result was quite different from the aftermath of 1715, since no further Jacobite rebellion followed.
6. A number of commentators have identified the Annexing Act with the Scottish Enlightenment. For example, consider Annette Smith's eulogy for the Act:

> The most notable characteristic that may be attributed to members of the Board [of the Annexed Forfeited Estates], both individually and collectively, is their modernity in eighteenth-century terms. "Enlightenment Man" was forward-looking, far-sighted, excited by an interest in physical and mental experiment and change, and the commissioners and some of those who initiated the Annexing Act were typical of the best of their age.

(Smith 1982: 232)

Of course, such an identification depends upon what a commentator takes the typical positions of the Scottish Enlightenment to be. R.H. Campbell has a more nuanced view of the Annexing Act's relation to the Scottish Enlightenment, since he sees a preference for "free trade" as the "Enlightenment's legacy towards commercial policy" (Campbell 1982: 14). He argues that:

[mercantilist] characteristics were even more notable in the work of the Commissioners for those forfeited estates which were annexed to the Crown after the 1745 Rebellion, because in their case, while the political object of subjugating and integrating the Highlands received the approval of the Enlightenment, the economic policy of the Commissioners was one of active interventionism.

(Campbell 1982: 19)

But this identification of Enlightenment with a rejection of state intervention into the economy cannot be accurate, if we include Lords Kames as a card-carrying member of the Enlightenment, for he was one of the intellectual and bureaucratic leaders of the Commission. Although his famous ambiguous evaluation of the Annexing Act experiment, that is, the Commission's efforts were "no better than water spilt on the ground," might have given anti-interventionists much fodder. For an account of Kames' work on the Commission, see Ross (1972: 316–322).

7.   This document is to be found in the Minto Papers, National Library of Scotland, MS11035, item 22. From internal evidence, it appears that this Plan was drafted in the 1760s. The military recruitment aspect of the Annexed Estates Act that Mackillop emphasizes is quite evident in the Plan:

But from all the projects that may be set on foot for promoting industry and population, one evil is dreaded that ought to be prevented if possible, which is the extinction of the martial spirit among the Highlanders and rendering them efeminate like the Lowlanders...

8.   For a discussion of the contrast between the Highland clan elite's heritable title, oighreachd, and their heritable trusteeship, duthchas, see Macinnes (1996: 1–23). The slow abandonment of the duthchas and the capitalization of the oighreachd was a centuries-long process which the defeat of the 'Forty-Five simply accelerated. For example, Macinnes points out that not only were the English Whigs involved in colonial enrichment before and after the '45, some members of the Jacobite Highland clan elite were involved in the international British colonial project as:

planters, slave traders, colonial officials, military commanders and merchant adventurers. ... It is hardly surprising that the imperial classes who ruthlessly exploited the slave trade in the American South and the West Indies, where they regarded the naming of their slaves on a par with the naming of their livestock, should show limited sympathy in effecting the removal of their erstwhile clansmen.

(Macinnes 1996: 233)

For example, "The chiefs of Clan Cameron, one of the most committed Jacobite clans, had interests in American land, timber exportation, the Caribbean plantations and the Edinburgh money market" (Devine 1993: 26).

9. For the transformation of common law into civil (Roman) law, see Chapter 1, "On the Scottish Origin of Civilization." The distinction between Common and Civil (Roman) law should be distinguished from that between criminal and civil processes. The latter depends on the object of the offence: the state or the community versus the individual, while the former depends on their historical source and methodology: statutes derived from Roman Law versus legal customs preserved by precedent. Holdsworth gives the latter distinction a national character: "[We have] a contrast between the two rival ways of constructing a legal system—the logical and deductive Scottish method formed upon Roman models, and the empirical and inductive English method built up by decided cases on native lines" (Holdsworth 1938: 16). The legal meaning of "Civilization," therefore, has a different meaning in these contexts.

10. At this point, he claims that the "business" of the philosopher and the politician is the same (Hume 1955: 4). David Hume, *Writings on Economics*, edited by Eugene Rotwein (London: Nelson, 1955) (abbreviated as R).

11. On the crofting and clearance dénouement of the effort to civilize the Highlands, see Hunter (1976), Gray (1957), Lynch (1991), among others. As Malcolm Gray powerfully put the situation of the crofters in the Western Highlands after the '45: "The formative years—years of rising and passing hopes—had formed nothing but the enlarged image of an old society but a society that worked in economic conditions that were in some ways disastrously new" (Gray 1957: 73).

12. This is why the miser posed such a conundrum to the young Hume in the Treatise: if riches are "the power of acquiring the property of what pleases," the miser appears contradictory. For the miser "receives delight from his money; that is, from the power it affords him of procuring all the pleasures and conveniences of life." But since the miser systematically refuses to realize this power, is this really power? Hume attempts to sidestep this difficulty by imagining that what stops the miser for procuring his pleasures are "the more powerful motives of interest and danger" that block the miser's path to pleasure (Hume T: 204–205). The young Hume is not yet ready to separate the relation between riches and pleasure that Marx and Simmel see in the miser's abstract desire (Marx 1970: 125–137; Simmel 1978: 238–247). For them, the miser is the personified avant-garde of capital. Marx writes of him, "Our hoarder is a martyr to exchange value, a holy ascetic seated atop a metal column. He cares for wealth only in its social form, and accordingly hides it away from society" (Marx 1970: 134). But by 1752, however, Hume begins to see the autonomous power of capital—"business and serious occupation"—and grants that money-making can be an object of passion for itself. "And this is the reason why trade encreases frugality, and why, among merchants, there is the same overplus of misers above prodigals, as, among the possessors of land, there is the contrary" (Hume R: 53).

13. Carl Wennerlind has a useful critique of the view that Hume was a quantity theorist in (Wennerlind 2005).

14. From the oil-money analogy that begins Of Money to the water-trade analogy in On the Balance of Trade, Hume is definitely partial to fluids in his economic writings. But as Margaret Schabas has insightfully pointed out, Hume was also interested in electric fluids (as they were understood at the time). Electric analogies would provide Hume with an even more graphic illustration of the excitation of money (Schabas 2001).

15. The barometer–interest analogy is an additional expression of Hume's interest in fluids; the standard barometer of the eighteenth century used mercury as its measure of atmospheric pressure. By 1752, the barometer reading was a standard part of a weather report as, for example, printed in journals like the *Scots Magazine*.

3. HUME'S MONETARY EDUCATION IN BRISTOL

1. David Richardson (Ed.), *Bristol, Africa and the Eighteenth-Century Slave Trade*: Vol. 1 *The Years of Expansion 1698–1729*; Vol. 2 *The Years of Ascendency 1730–1745*; Vol. 3 *The Years of Decline 1746–1769*; and Vol. 4 *The Final Years, 1770–1807* (Bristol: Bristol Record Society, 1985, 1987, 1991 and 1996 respectively).

2. For an account of African slave-servants in Bristol, see Christine Eickelmann and David Small (2004) and Madge Dresser and Peter Fleming (2007: Chapter 7); and for Britain as a whole, see Peter Fryer (1984).

4. WHY WAS HUME A METALLIST?

1. According to Joseph A. Schumpeter, the term "metallism" has its roots in Knapp's *Die Staatliche Theorie des Geldes* (1905) (Schumpeter 1954: 288). It is somewhat cognate to the previous "bullionism" and later "commodity money theory."

2. Locke's definitions of mixed mode and substance ideas can be found in John Locke, *An Essay Concerning Human Understanding*, edited by Peter H. Nidditch (1975), 288 and 296 respectively. For a discussion of Locke's contrast between mixed mode and substance ideas and its relevance to the philosophy of money, see C. George Caffentzis, *Clipped Coins, Abused Words and Civil Government: John Locke's Philosophy of Money* (1989).

3. David Hume, *A Treatise of Human Nature*, edited by L.A. Selby-Bigge (2nd edition with text revised and variant readings by P.H. Nidditch) (1978). (Hereafter referred to as "N" with page numbers inserted parenthetically in the text.)

4. For the re-evaluation of Hume among the logical positivists, see Alfred Jules Ayer, *Language, Truth and Logic* (New York: Dover, 1952); and for the beginning of his transformation into a minor postmodern saint, see Gilles

Deleuze, *Empirisme et subjectivite: essai sur la nature humaine selon Hume*, 2nd edn (Paris: Presses universitaires de France, 1973).

5. A vast literature has developed since Kemp Smith's commentary. A recent summation of the field can be found in David Fate Norton (Ed.), *The Cambridge Companion to Hume* (Cambridge: Cambridge University Press, 1993), especially Robert J. Fogelin's "Hume's Scepticism."

6. I emphasize "Scots" because Hume considered himself more Scot than British, even though he is frequently termed the greatest of the British empiricists. For example, he writes "we" when referring to the Scots in this paean:

> Is it not strange that, at a time when we have lost our princes, our Parliaments, our independent Government, even the Presence of our chief Nobility, are unhappy, in our Accent & Pronunciation, speak a very corrupt Dialect of the Tongue which we make use of; is it not strange, I say, that, in these Circumstances, we shou'd really be the People most distinguish'd for Literature in Europe.
>
> (Hume 1932: 255)

His diatribes against the "barbarians on the Thames" are well known, cf. Duncan Forbes (1975: 189).

7. For an acute analysis of the forces that led to the Scottish intelligentsia's espousal of "free trade" in the context of a mercantilist empire, see Michael Fry (1999: 57).

8. For discussions of the imperial strategies of the Scottish Lowland elite, see Caffentzis (1995); Richards (1991): and Fry (1999).

9. In "The Scottish Origin of 'Civilization,'" Caffentzis (1995) argues that, in effect, Mansfield attempted to "civilize" English law by making it conform to the Civil Law systematics that the Scottish legal system incorporated from the Calvinist Institutes.

10. Richards (1991) has a very interesting account of the incorporation of Scottish personnel into the British state apparatus.

11. Almost all the commentary literature on Hume's economics recognizes that Hume mixed economic subjects with politics, as James Bonar wrote long ago in *Philosophy and Political Economy* (1923: 107). But there are no standard texts that pose the development problem of the Scottish Highlands as a major political economic problematic in Hume's circle's.

12. The novelistic narrative of the events is in Walter Scott's *Waverly*. William Ferguson points out that if another element of the Jacobite uprising had succeeded, namely, the landing in Scotland of 10,000 French troops under Marshal Saxe, the military story might well have ended differently indeed, see William Ferguson (1968: 147–148).

13. A classic, though dated discussion of Jacobitism can be found in Sir Charles Petrie's *The Jacobite Movement* (1959). A more recent text that deals with the

class complexity of Jacobitism in England is Paul Kleber Monod, *Jacobitism and the English People 1688–1788* (1989).

14. Although there is no doubt that the Jacobite risings had their center in the Highlands, there is now a growing historical literature distinguishing Highland society per se and Jacobite politics. Murray G.H. Pittock is an arch revisionist as shown in his *The Myth of the Jacobite Clans* (1995b), where he argues that there was certainly very strong Jacobite support outside the Highlands from 1689 on. This was often not seen in the 'Forty-Fiver perhaps because Charles Edward decided to make all his army (even the French support troops) wear Highland dress (Pittock 1995b: 55). Pittock also questions whether the Scotch merchants and tradesmen absolutely rejected the Jacobite uprisings, since many Episcopalians among them did come out in support of Charles Edward's "cause" (Pittock 1995b: 82).

15. One must be careful about essentializing the "Highland mode of life," for many elements of it like the kilt and the clan tartan were invented after the 'Forty-Fiver as Hugh Trevor-Roper famously pointed out in his article "The Invention of Tradition: The Highland Tradition of Scotland" (1983).

16. The Highlands before 1745 cannot be seen as a purely non-commercial society, however. It too was caught up in a generalized transition to capitalism and resistance to it before the Lowland "modernizers" took control of the process after the 'Forty-Fiver. As Allan I. Macinnes, another revisionist historian, puts it:

> Rather than accept historical Whiggish interpretations that Scottish Gaeldom was static socially and underdeveloped economically prior to the last Jacobite rising in 1745, emphasis is placed on the presumption of mobility and the bipartisan spirit of entrepreneurship underscoring the pre-Clearance Highlands. Absentee landlordism, indebtedness, rent-raising and the removal and relocation of clansmen were not products of the 'Forty-Five, but part of an ongoing process of commericialism and cultural assimilation that can be traced back to the early seventeenth century.
>
> (Macinnes 1996: x)

Lenman argues that the "financial straits of certain key local figures [in the Highlands]" was a condition for the 'Forty-Fiver while Walter Scott in Rob Roy makes one of the key elements of the book's plot an attempt to create a financial crisis involving the Highlands in order to instigate a Jacobite rising (Lenman 1984: 148).

17. For the demographic estimate, see Bruce Lenman (1981: 3).

18. A standard biography of David Hume is Ernest Campbell Mossner, *The Life of David Hume* (1954).

19. As Macinnes writes in *Clanship, Commerce and the House of Stuart*:

> The immediate aftermath of the 'Forty-Five was marked by systematic state terrorism, characterized by a genocidal intent that verged on ethnic cleansing … The clear intent of the Whig commanders by the time of Culloden was to

inflict a crushing defeat on Jacobite clans that would remembered for generations ... The first [phase] was the wholesale slaughter not only at Culloden
and in the days after the battle, but in succeeding weeks prior to the departure
of Cumberland at the outset of summer when he felt that Gaeldom had been
finally subjugated. The second was the selective terrorism directed against
Jacobite districts ... The third was the continuing and deliberate starvation of
Jacobite and neighbouring districts through the willful destruction of crops,
livestock and property with the stated intention to effect either clearance or
death.

(Macinnes 1996: 212)

20. For selections from the texts of the Disarming Act (1746) and the "Act for taking
away and abolishing the heritable jurisdiction in that part of Great Britain called
Scotland," see D.B. Horn and Mary Ransome (1957).

21. For a general discussion of these stages, see T.C. Smout, *A History of the Scottish
People 1560–1830* (1972). Macinnes writes of this period: "State-sponsored
terrorism was to give way to state-sponsored improvement" (Macinnes 1996).

22. Macinnes presents a more prickly picture of the operation:

In response to a plethora of civilising schemes from unctous ideologues and
unplaced opportunists, the Whig government had decided that 13 forfeited
estates of Jacobite chiefs and gentry were to be annexed inalienably to the
Crown in 1752. The Annexed Estates were thus created as corridors of
improvement that were to be models of planning and management from the
southern through the central Highlands with intersections in western and
northern districts. At the same time, resistance of clansmen to the forfei-
ture of their chiefs and leading gentry had been cowed by a final show trial
that led to the execution of James Stewart of the Glens for his supposed role
as accessory to the murder of Colin Campbell of Glenure—the government
factor immortalised as "the Red Fox."

(Macinnes 1996: 217)

23. For a list of the Commissioners, see Annette M. Smith (1982: 239–241). The
acquaintance Hume had with these commissioners was that they were either
correspondents, mentioned in his correspondence, or fellow members of the
Select Club or the Philosophical Society of Edinburgh. The "at least" is cautionary here. I believe that with more research many more of Commissioners can be
shown to be connected to Hume personally.

24. Of the thirty initial Commissioners appointed in 1755, ten were lawyers, the
largest occupational block; see Shaw (1983: 78).

25. For a discussion of Kames' activities on the Commission, see Ian Simpson Ross
(1972: 316–322).

26. The stages theory of savagery, barbarism and civilization developed by the
Scottish Enlightenment thinkers was greatly influenced by their juridical
training.

27. The essays "Of the Original Contract," "Of Passive Obedience" and "Of the Coalition of Parties" were added in subsequent editions of the *Essays*.

28. For Hume's experimental philosophy, see (N 4–6). An historian of the Annexing Act, Annette Smith, sees in the Board the prime project of "Enlightenment Man" in Scotland, who was "forward-looking, far-sighted, excited by an interest in physical and mental experiment and change, and the commissioners and some of those who initiated the Annexing Act were typical of the best of their age" (Annette Smith 1982: 232). It was, in effect, one of the first governing boards of a public "regional development" corporation.

29. Hume himself was not insensitive to the power of this form of life, once it was properly tamed, as his ambivalent role in the "Ossian affair" indicates; see Ernest Campbell Mossner (1967: 82–102).

30. For an interesting discussion of the nature and limits of Hume's Newtonianism as well as his familiarity with Newton's emphasis on forces, see Peter Jones (1982), especially 14.

31. One reason for this unity of the "public banks" was the competition they were facing from the "private" provincial banks in Glasgow and Aberdeen, according to Charles W. Munn (1981: 11–12).

32. Hume claims that the best form of recoinage would have a:

   penny's worth of silver taken from every shilling, the new shilling would probably purchase everything that could have been bought by the old; the prices of everything would thereby be *insensibly diminished* … In executing such a project, it would be better to make the new shilling pass for 24 halfpence, in order to *preserve the illusion, and make it be taken for the same.*
   (R 39, italics mine)

33. Of course, Munn is referring to the essays in *Political Discourses*, which were incorporated into *Essays, Moral, Political, etc.* in the following year.

34. But in the following paragraphs, Hume does point out that an increase in the money supply can have a positive effect on Industry and in the process can stimulate productivity in manufactures to such an extent that it might actually decrease the price of manufactured goods. Consequently, there cannot be any simple quantity theoretic relation between money supply and prices.

35. Many commentators on Hume's semantics do not note this tension between the ideational and conventional aspects of significance. They largely hold to the discussion in the First "idea/impression" Book of the *Treatise*. Pall Árdal seems to point in this direction, however, in his "Language and Significance in Hume's Treatise," he claims that "there is a difference between giving an account of the way in which we manage to think abstract thoughts although all ideas are of particulars, and the account to be given of the place of language in social life" (Árdal 1986: 783).

36. For Smith's views in the 1760s, see his *Lectures on Justice, Police, Revenue and Arms*, delivered in the University of Glasgow, reported by a student in 1763

(1956: 190–210). He compared the monetary system to a country's material infrastructure in the Lectures and argued that the least investment in the system with the same result is to the public good. "Hence the beneficial effects of the erection of banks and paper credit. It is easy to show that the erections of banks is of advantage to the commerce of a country" (1956: 191). He also criticized Hume's partiality to specie: "[Mr. Hume] seems, however, to have gone a little into the notion that public opulence consists in money [understood as specie]." Smith, in his chapter on money in the *Wealth of Nations*, continued favoring paper money, even though he deals explicitly with the 1764 banking crisis (Smith 1991: 264).

37. Neil Munro in *The History of the Royal Bank of Scotland, 1727–1927*, describes the "small note mania" of the 1750s in Scotland in the following way:

> To such an extent did the use of those trumpery paper promises by individuals of no substance extend, that the Scottish sense of humour found release in printing and distributing parodies of them as squibs. The so-called Wasp Note for "One Penny Sterling, or in the Option of the Directors, three Ballads six days after a Demand," elegantly printed in Glasgow, with an ornamental border of wasps, the motto "We Swarm," and the signature of "Daniel Mcfunn" is the best example of those satires.
>
> (Munro 1928: 122)

38. There was another dilemma Hume and his fellow Enlightenment intellectuals had to face: the generalization of highway robbery that largely had its roots in the financial mechanics of the cattle trade. Drovers returning from cattle trysts loaded with specie attracted highway robbers, and this situation set the stage for branch banking. As Peter Linebaugh pointed out in *The London Hanged: Crime and Civil Society in the Eighteenth Century*, there was a dialectical relation between the two kinds of expropriators, the bankers and the robbers:

> In Scotland, in the first half of the [eighteenth] century drovers dealt at the Crieff and Falkirk cattle trysts largely in gold and silver. After mid-century tents and sheds were erected where tellers from Edinburgh banks provided notes of credit. By the end of the century such banks had corresponding banks in London, if not in Smithfield [the main meat market in London] itself, so that drovers were no longer endangered by carrying large sums of rhino. Such financial safeguards increased the volume of trade and speed of realization.
>
> (Linebaugh 1992: 212)

39. I have been largely concerned with Hume's reflections on the forms of money and their differential impact on economic transformation in this chapter. I have not invoked Hume's discourse on the moral and political consequences of the extensive use of money and the expansion of commerce and (commercially oriented) industry. Money, for Hume, has a moral and political weight; it is not only a spur to industry and to the spread of luxury.

6. FICTION OR COUNTERFEIT?

1. Hume had a personal financial interest in national debt instruments and stocks, since he did not invest his substantial earnings in land. As E.C. Mossner writes:

   > While in London in 1761 he had invested in the public funds … Having long declaimed against the stocks, Hume was exposed to the many jokes of his friends. His rebuttal was that he had bought real stock and was not a jobber.
   > (Mossner 1954: 409–410)

2. Indeed, these passages have been the basis of the mistaken view that Hume was a "theoretical metallist," to use Schumpeter's phrase, see Wennerlind (2001) and Caffentzis (2001).

3. The full phrase in the first seven editions of the *Essays* is "Money having merely a fictitious value, arising from the agreement and convention of men," while in eighth and ninth editions it was replaced by the shorter, "Money having chiefly a fictitious value…" For a discussion of counterfeiting in this period, see Wennerlind (2002: 263–264).

4. The location of quotations from *A Treatise on Human Nature* will be abbreviated, for example, as (T 43), where the page number refers to the *Treatise*, edited by David Fate Norton and Mary J. Norton (Oxford: Oxford University Press, 2000). The locations of quotations from the Essays and Hume's correspondence on economic matters are abbreviated as (E 43), where the page number refers to David Hume's Essays Moral, Political and Literary, edited by Eugene Miller (Indianapolis, IN: Liberty Fund, 1987). The locations of quotations from *The History of England* are abbreviated as, for example, (HEiv 63), where the page number refers to the volume of the History indicated by the Roman numeral in the Harper and Brothers 1850 edition.

5. Some important articles in this research program include Schabas (1994 and 2001), Gatch (1996), Wennerlind (2001 and 2002) and Davis (2003).

6. Steven Shapin recruited Hume, along with Francis Hutcheson and Adam Smith, into the ranks of "Common Sense philosophers," who "agreed that social order was predicated upon trust in others' truthfulness" (Shapin 1994: 12). Shapin seems to have missed Hume's "pseudological" side, that is, for Hume, most of the "truths" basic to the social order are fictions.

7. There is a small literature on Hume's theory of fictions. Some early and more recent texts include Kemp Smith (1941: 133–137), Deleuze (1991 [1953]), Streminger (1980) and McRae (1980). They have little to say of the artificial fictions, however.

8. The gold coinage was also in peril by the 1770s. As Dyer and Gasper point out:

   > [It] had been ravaged by "the infamous and daring Practices of Coiners, Clippers, Seaters, &c." With newly-minted, full-weight coins being hoarded, melted down or exported, the domestic circulation had become a sink for the

worst coins; and there were fears that the country would soon be short of gold as it was of silver.

(Dyer and Gasper 1992: 440)

9. In an often puzzled over passage in the *Treatise*, Hume provides a counter-example to one of his most cherished principles: ideas are copies of impressions. He asks the reader to imagine a person who has never seen a particular shade of blue. He then asks us to imagine such a person confronted with a series of colored patches from dark to light blue that does not include the particular unseen shade of blue. Hume claims that such a person should be able, simply on the basis of the imagination, to "raise up to himself the idea of that particular shade, tho' it never been convey'd to him by his senses" (T 10). Cf. the following important articles on Hume's "shade of blue": Williams (1992), Fogelin (1984) and Losee (1992).

10. A number of important studies on this theme include: Thompson (1996), Nicholson (1994), Sherman (1996) and Ingrassia (1995).

11. This is not to say that coinage was passé in Britain, for, after all, during Hume's lifetime, most British foreign trade was transacted with gold and silver coinage. As Vilar points out:

Between 1733 and 1766, 65% of England's exports to Asia were in the form of silver bullion and, even more, of silver coin. The total value amounted to some L400 million sterling, as opposed to only L9 spent by France on such transactions.

(Vilar 1976: 285)

Indeed, it appeared that at least in foreign trade, Hume's pro-coinage views were vindicated at the end of his life (though without his tolerance of debasement). In 1774, the one of the most important steps in the development of the gold standard was taken by Lord Liverpool who ordered a full weight recoinage for gold coins and managed the passage of a law that:

Firstly ... limited silver currency: for sums about L50 payment in silver might be refused and payment in gold could be demanded; this reduced silver to the role of small cash coin; and secondly, the law laid down that once gold was recast at full weight, coins would be allowed to deteriorate by only 1 39/39 grains a guinea, a tiny proportion.

(Vilar 1976: 285)

Vilar sums up the monetary developments in England in the following words: "far from being in opposition to one another, the move towards gold coin as the universal standard, and the development of banking and credit, took place simultaneously" (Vilar 1976: 286).

12. Echoing Hume's observation concerning an absolute monarch's ability to repudiate of debt, Montesquieu notes a systematic opposition between absolute monarchs and banks, for "In a[n absolute monarchical] government of this

kind, none but the prince ever had, or can have, a treasure; and wherever there is one, it no sooner becomes great than it becomes the treasure of the prince" (Montesquieu 1966: 322).

13. Clyn Davies describes "The Great Debasement" in the following passage:

> The process of physical debasement from the original pure sterling silver standard reached 75 per cent silver by March 1542, 50 per cent by March 1545, 33 1/3 per cent by March 1546, and reached its nadir of 25 per cent under the young King Edward in 1551. The mainly copper-alloy coins were, in order to improve their acceptability, "blanched" from 1546 onwards, by applying a thin surface coating of purer silver, a subterfuge which quickly wore thin to show the red copper underneath—hence Henry VIII's well-earned nickname "old copper-nose."
>
> (Davies 1994: 199)

14. The sentence concerning the 1696 recoinage was included in the Errata of the first edition. Was this a sign of Hume's hesitancy?

CONCLUSION

1. Patrick Hyde Kelly and I in separate works—Kelly's *Locke on Money* (Locke 1991) and my *Clipped Coins, Abused Words and Civil Government: John Locke's Philosophy of Money* respectively—offered different versions of this twofold analysis of Locke's conception of money.

2. My discussion of Hume's support of metallic money and his critique of paper credit, as he called it, can be found in Caffentzis (2008: 146–167).

Bibliography

Allen, Graham (2011) *Intertexuality*. London: Routledge.

Ankarloo, Bengt and Henningsen, Gustav (Eds.) (1993) *Early Modern European Witchcraft: Centers and Peripheries*. Oxford: Clarendon Press.

Árdal, Pall S. (1986) "Language and Significance in Hume's Treatise." *The Canadian Journal of Philosophy* 16(4) (December): 779–784.

Armitage, David (2004) "John Locke, Carolina and The Two Treatises of Government." *Political Theory* 32(5) (October): 602–627.

St. Augustine (1972) *City of God*. London: Penguin Classics.

Ayer, Alfred Jules (1952) *Language, Truth and Logic*. New York: Dover.

Ayers, Michael (1984) "Berkeley and Hume: A Question of Influence." In Richard Rorty, J.B. Schneewind and Quentin Skinner (Eds.), *Philosophy In History: Essays in the Historiography of Philosophy*. Cambridge: Cambridge University Press, 303–327.

Bagehot, Walter (1965) *Collected Works*, Vols 1–8. Cambridge, MA: Harvard University Press.

Baier, Annette (1991) *A Progress of Sentiments: Reflections on Hume's Treatise*. Cambridge, MA: Harvard University Press.

Barstow, Anne Llewellyn (1994) *Witchcraze: A New History of the European Witch-Hunts*. San Francisco, CA: Pandora.

Baudrillard, Jean (1983) *Simulations*. New York: Semiotext(e).

Beccaria, Cesare (1764) *Dei delitti e delle pene [On Crimes and Punishments]*. Milan.

Berkeley, George (1957) *A Treatise Concerning the Principles of Human Knowledge*. Edited by Colin M. Turbayne. New York: The Liberal Arts Press.

Berkeley, George (1970) "The Querist." In Joseph Johnston (Ed.), *Bishop Berkeley's Querist in Historical Perspective*. Dundalk: Dundalgan Press, 124–204.

Bernard, Christopher (1995) "Hume and the Madness of Religion." In M.A. Stewart and John P. Wright (Eds.), *Hume and Hume's Connexions*. University Park, PA: Pennsylvania State University Press.

Berry, Christopher J. (1997) *Social Theory of the Scottish Enlightenment*. Edinburgh: Edinburgh University Press.

Biernacki, Richard (1995) *The Fabrication of Labor, Germany and Germany, 1640–1914*. Berkeley, CA: University of California Press.

Blackburn, Robin (1997) "The Old World Background to European Colonial Slavery." *The William and Mary Quarterly* 54(1): 65–102.

Blackstone, William (1892) *Commentaries on the Laws of England*. New York: Strouse and Co.

Blaug, Mark (1968) *Economic Theory in Retrospect*. Homewood, IL: Richard D. Irwin.

Blaug, Mark et al. (1995) *The Quantity Theory of Money: From Locke to Keynes and Friedman*. Aldershot: Edward Elgar Publishing.

Bloch, Ernst (1971) *On Karl Marx*. Chestnut Ridge, NY: Herder and Herder.

Bloch, Marc (1975) *Slavery and Serfdom in the Middle Ages: Selected Papers*. Translated by William R. Beer. Berkeley, CA: University of California Press.

Bonar, James (1923) *Philosophy and Political Economy*. London: George Allen and Unwin.

Bonnassie, Pierre (1991) *From Slavery to Feudalism in South-Western Europe*. Cambridge: Cambridge University Press.

Borsay, Peter (2002) "The Culture of Improvement." In Paul Langford (Ed.), *The Eighteenth Century, 1688–1815*. Oxford: Oxford University Press.

Boswell, James (1934) *Boswell's Life of Johnson*. Edited by George Birbeck Hill, revised and enlarged by C.F. Powell, Vol. 2. Oxford: Clarendon Press.

Brantlinger, Patrick (1996) *Fictions of State: Culture and Credit in Britain, 1694–1995*. Ithaca, NY: Cornell University Press.

Braunmuller, A.R. (Ed.) (1997) "Introduction." In William Shakespeare, *Macbeth*. Cambridge: Cambridge University Press.

Brewer, John (1980) "The Wilkites and the Law, 1763–74." In John Brewer and John Styles (Eds.), *An Ungovernable People: The English and Their Law in the Seventeenth and Eighteenth Centuries*. New Brunswick, NJ: Rutgers University Press.

Brewer, John (1988) *The Sinews of Power: War, Money and the English State, 1688–1783*. Cambridge, MA: Harvard University Press.

Bryson, Gladys (1968) *Man and Society: The Scottish Inquiry of the Eighteenth Century*. New York: Augustus M. Kelley.

Buck-Morss, Susan (2000) "Hegel and Haiti." *Critical Inquiry* 26(4) (Summer): 821–865.

Burke, Edmund (1961) *Reflections on the Revolution in France*. Garden City, NY: Doubleday.

Caffentzis, C. George (1989) *Clipped Coins, Abused Words, and Civil Government: John Locke's Philosophy of Money*. New York: Autonomedia.

Caffentzis, C. George (1995) "The Scottish Origin of 'Civilization.'" In Silvia Federici (Ed.), *Enduring Western Civilization: The Construction of the Concept of Western Civilization and Its "Others."* Westport, CT: Praeger Publishers.

Caffentzis, C. George (2000) *Exciting the Industry of Mankind: George Berkeley's Philosophy of Money*. Dordrecht: Kluwer.

Caffentzis, C. George (2001) "Hume, Money, and Civilization; or, Why was Hume a Metallist?" *Hume Studies* 27(2) (November): 301–335.

Caffentzis, C. George (2003) "Medical Metaphors and Monetary Strategies in the Political Economy of Locke and Berkeley." In Margaret Schabas and Neil de Marchi (Eds.) *Oeconomies in the Age of Newton*. History of Political Economy (Annual Supplement to Vol. 35). Durham, NC: Duke University Press.

Caffentzis, C. George (2005) "Civilizing the Highlands: Hume, Money and the Annexing Act." *Historical Reflections* 31(1) (Spring): 169–194.

Bibliography

Caffentzis, C. George (2008) "Fiction or Counterfeit? David Hume's Interpretations of Paper and Metallic Money." In Carl Wennerlind and Margaret Schabas (Eds.), *David Hume's Political Economy*. London: Routledge.

Camic, Charles (1983) *Experience and Enlightenment: Socialization for Cultural Change in Eighteenth-Century Scotland*. Chicago, IL: University of Chicago Press.

Campbell, John (1878) *The Lives of the Chief Justices of England*, Vol. III. New York: Cockcroft and Co.

Campbell, R.H. (1982) "The Enlightenment and the Economy." In R.H. Campbell and Andrew S. Skinner (Eds.), *The Origins and Nature of the Scottish Enlightenment*. Edinburgh: John Donald Publishers Ltd.

Cantillon, Richard (1964) *Essai sur la nature du commerce en general*, edited and translated by Henry Higgs. New York: Augustus M. Kelly.

Case, Karl E. and Fair, Ray C. (1999) *Principles of Economics*, 5th edn. Upper Saddle River, NJ: Prentice Hall.

Challis, C.E. (1992) *A New History of the Royal Mint*. Cambridge: Cambridge University Press.

Chisick, Harvey (1989) "David Hume and the Common People." In Peter Jones (Ed.), *The "Science of Man" in the Scottish Enlightenment: Hume, Reid, and Their Contemporaries*. Edinburgh: Edinburgh University Press.

Collins, Randall (1998) *The Sociology of Philosophies: A Global Theory of Intellectual Change*. Cambridge, MA: Harvard University Press.

Connah, Graham (1987) *African Civilization: Precolonial Cities and States in Tropical Africa, An Archeological Perspective*. Cambridge: Cambridge University Press.

Conroy, Graham P. (1969) "Did Hume Really Follow Berkeley." *Philosophy* 44(169) (July): 238–242.

Cullen, L.M. (1969) *Formation of the Irish Economy*. The Thomas Davis lectures. Cork: Mercier Press.

Cullen, L.M. (1972) *An Economic History of Ireland since 1660*. London: Batsford.

Davie, G.E. (1965) "Berkeley's Impact on Scottish Philosophers." *Philosophy* 40(153) (July): 222–234.

Davies, Clyn (1994) *A History of Money from Ancient Times to the Present Day*. Cardiff: University of Wales Press.

Davis, Gordon F. (2003) "Philosophical Psychology and Economic Psychology in David Hume and Adam Smith." *History of Political Economy* 35(2): 269–303.

Deleuze, Gilles (1973) *Empirisme et subjectivite: essai sur la nature humaine selon Hume*, 2nd edn. Paris: Presses universitaires de France.

Deleuze, Gilles (1991) *Empiricism and Subjectivity: An Essay on Hume's Theory of Human Nature*, translated and with an introduction by Constantin V. Boundas. New York: Columbia University Press [originally published in French in 1953].

Deleuze, Gilles and Guattari, Felix (1994) *What is Philosophy?* New York: Columbia University Press.

Derrida, Jacques (1994) *Given Time: I. Counterfeit Money*. Chicago, IL: University of Chicago Press.

Devine, T.M. (1993) *Clanship to Crofters' War: The Social Transformation of the Scottish Highlands*. Manchester: Manchester University Press.

Devine, T.M. (2000) *The Scottish Nation: A History 1700–2000*. New York: Viking.

Dockès, Pierre (1982) *Medieval Slavery and Liberation*. Translated by Arthur Goldhammer. Chicago, IL: University of Chicago Press.

Donn, Benjamin (1768) *The Young Shopkeepers, Stewards, and Factors Companion*. Bristol.

Dresser, Madge and Fleming, Peter (2007) *Bristol: Ethnic Minorities and the City, 1000–2001*. Bognor Regis: Phillimore Publishers.

Dyer, G.P. and Gaspar, P.P. (1992) "Reform, the New Technology and Tower Hill, 1700–1966." In C. E. Challis (Ed.), *A New History of the Royal Mint*. Cambridge: Cambridge University Press.

Eickelmann, Christine and Small, David (2004) *Pero: The Life of a Slave in Eighteenth-Century Bristol*. Bristol: Redcliffe Press.

Elias, Norbert (1978) *The Civilizing Process*. New York: Urizen.

Feavearyear, Sir Albert (1963) *The Pound Sterling: A History of English Money*, 2nd edn. Oxford: Clarendon Press.

Federici, Silvia (2004) *Caliban and the Witch: Women, the Body and Primitive Accumulation*. New York: Autonomedia.

Federici, Silvia (2013) "With Philosophy and Terror: Transforming Bodies into Labor Power." In Athanasios Marvakis, et al. (Eds.), *Doing Psychology under New Conditions*. Concord, ON: Captus University Press, 3–10.

Ferguson, Niall (2001) *The Cash Nexus: Money and Power in the Modern World, 1700–2000*. New York: Basic Books.

Ferguson, William (1968) *Scotland: 1689 to the Present*. New York: Praeger.

Finlay, Christopher J. (2007) *Hume's Social Philosophy: Human Nature and Commercial Sociability in* A Treatise of Human Nature. London: Continuum.

Fogelin, Robert (1984) "Hume and the Missing Shade of Blue." *Philosophy and Phenomenological Research* 45: 263–272.

Forbes, Duncan (1975) *Hume's Philosophical Politics*. Cambridge: Cambridge University Press.

Foucault, Michel (1979) *Discipline and Punish: The Birth of the Prison*. Translated by Alan Sheridan. New York: Random House.

Fry, Michael (1999) "A Commercial Empire: Scotland and British Expansion in the Eighteenth Century." In T.M. Devine and J.R. Young, *Eighteenth-Century Scotland: New Perspectives*. East Linton: Tuckwell Press.

Fryer, Peter (1984) *Staying Power: The History of Black People in Britain*. London: Pluto Press.

Garnsey, Peter (1996) *Ideas of Slavery from Aristotle to Augustine*. New York: Cambridge University Press.

Gatch, Loren (1996) "'To Redeem Paper with Money': David Hume's Philosophy of Money." *Hume Studies* 22(1): 168–191.

Gibbon, Edward (1952 [1776]) *The Decline and Fall of the Roman Empire*, Vol. I. Chicago, IL: Encyclopedia Britannica.

Gilboy, Elizabeth (1934) *Wages in Eighteenth Century England*. Cambridge, MA: Harvard University Press.

Gould, J.D. (1970) *The Great Debasement: Currency and the Economy in Mid-Tudor England*. Oxford: Clarendon Press.

Grafton, Anthony (1997) *The Footnote: A Curious History*. Cambridge, MA: Harvard University Press.

Gray, Malcolm (1957) *The Highland Economy 1750-1850*. Edinburgh: Oliver and Boyd.

Hall, Roland (1970) "Yes, Hume Did Use Berkeley." *Philosophy* 45(172) (April): 152-153.

Hamilton, Douglas (2005) *Scotland, the Caribbean and the Atlantic World, 1750-1820*. Manchester: Manchester University Press.

Harding, Alan (1966) *A Social History of English Law*. Harmondsworth: Penguin.

Hay, Douglas (1975) "Property, Authority and the Criminal Law." In Douglas Hay, Peter Linebaugh, John G. Rule, E.P. Thompson, and Cal Winslow (Eds.), *Albion's Fatal Tree: Crime and Society in Eighteenth-Century England*. New York: Pantheon Books.

Heckscher, Eli F. (1935) *Mercantilism*. London: Allen and Unwin.

Hegel, Georg W.F. (1892) *The Logic of Hegel*. Translated from the *Encyclopedia of the Philosophical Sciences*, by William Wallace. Oxford: Oxford University Press.

Heward, Edmund (1979) *Lord Mansfield*. Chichester: Barry Rose.

Holdsworth, Sir William (1926) *A History of English Law*, Vol. 8. Boston, MA: Little, Brown and Co.

Holdsworth, Sir William (1938) *A History of English Law*, Vol. 11. London: Methuen and Co.

Home, Henry [Lord Kames] (2014) *Principles of Equity*, edited by Michael Lobban. Indianapolis, IN: Liberty Fund.

Hont, Istvan (1983) "The 'Rich Country–Poor Country' Debate in Scottish Classical Political Economy." In Istvan Hont and Michael Ignatieff (Eds.), *Wealth and Virtue: The Shaping of Political Economy in the Scottish Enlightenment*. Cambridge: Cambridge University Press, 271-315.

Hont, Istvan (1993) "The Rhapsody of Public Debt: David Hume and the Voluntary State Bankruptcy." In Nicholas Phillipson and Quentin Skinner (Eds.), *Political Discourse in Early Modern Britain*. Cambridge: Cambridge University Press.

Horn, D.B. and Ransome, Mary (Eds.) (1957) *English Historical Documents 1714-1783*. New York: Oxford University Press.

Hughes, Pat, Root, Jane, and Heath, Christopher (1996) *The History and Development of Queen Square*. Bristol: Bristol City Council.

Hume, David (n.d.) *History of England*. Vol. 2. Philadelphia, PA: Claxton, Remson, and Haffelfinger.

Hume, David (1748) *A True Account of the Behaviour and Conduct of Archibald Stewart, Esq: Late Lord Provost of Edinburgh, in a Letter to a Friend.* London.

Hume, David (1767) *Essays and Treatises on Several Subjects*, Vol. 1. London: A. Millar.

Hume, David (1850) *The History of England from the Invasion of Julius Cæsar to the Abdication of James the Second, 1688*, 6 vols. New York: Harper & Brothers. [abbreviated as HE]

Hume, David (1932) *The Letters of David Hume, Vol. 1: 1727–1765.* Edited by J.Y.T. Grieg. Oxford: The Clarendon Press.

Hume, David (1955) *Writings on Economics.* Edited by Eugene Rotwein. Edinburgh: Thomas Nelson and Sons.

Hume, David (1978) *A Treatise of Human Nature*, 2nd edn with text revised and varient readings by P.H. Nidditch. Edited by L.A. Selby-Bigge. Oxford: Clarendon Press. [abbreviated as N]

Hume, David (1983) *An Enquiry Concerning the Principles of Morals.* Edited and with an Introduction by J.B. Schneewind. Cambridge: Hackett Publishing.

Hume, David (1987) *Essays Moral, Political, and Literary*, revised edition. Edited by Eugene F. Miller. Indianapolis, IN: Liberty Fund.

Hume, David (2000) *A Treatise of Human Nature.* Edited by David Fate Norton and Mary J. Norton. Oxford: Oxford University Press. [abbreviated as T]

Hunter, James (1976) *The Making of the Crofting Community.* Edinburgh: John Donald Publishers.

Hutchison, Terence (1988) *Before Adam Smith: The Emergence of Political Economy, 1662–1776.* Oxford: Basil Blackwell.

Ingrassia, Catherine (1995) "The Pleasure of Business and the Business of Pleasure: Gender, Credit, and the South Sea Bubble." In Carla H. Hay and Syndy M. Conger (Eds.) *Studies in Eighteenth Century Culture*, Vol. 24. Baltimore, MD: Johns Hopkins University Press.

Ison, Walter (1952) *The Georgian Buildings of Bristol.* London: Faber & Faber.

Johnson, Samuel (1971) *A Journey to the Western Islands of Scotland.* Edited by Mary Lascelles. New Haven, CT: Yale University Press.

Johnston, Joseph (1970) *Bishop Berkeley's Querist in Historical Perspective.* Dundalk: Dundalgan Press.

Jones, Peter (1928) *Hume's Sentiments: Their Ciceronian and French Context.* Edinburgh: Edinburgh University Press.

Jowitt, Earl (1959) *The Dictionary of English Law.* London: Sweet and Maxwell.

Junius (1812) *Junius, Including the Letters by the Same Author*, Vol. 2. London: F., C. and J. Rivington.

Junius (1978) *The Letters of Junius.* Edited by John Cannon. Oxford: Clarendon Press.

Lord Kames, Henry Home (2014 [1760]) *Principles of Equity.* Edited by Michael Lobban. Indianapolis, IN: Liberty Fund.

Kant, Immanuel (1922 [1781]) *The Critique of Pure Reason*. Translated by F. Max Muller. New York: The Macmillan Company.

Kemp Smith, Norman (1941) *The Philosophy of David Hume: A Critical Study of its Origins and Central Doctrine*. London: Macmillan and Co.

Kleber Monod, Paul (1989) *Jacobitism and the English People 1688–1788*. Cambridge: Cambridge University Press.

Kristeva, Julia (1980) *Desire in Language: A Semiotic Approach to Literature and Art*. Edited by Leon S. Roudiez. New York: Columbia University Press.

Kristeva, Julia (1986) *The Kristeva Reader*. Edited by Toril Moi. New York: Columbia University Press.

Larner, Christina (1981) *Enemies of God: The Witch-Hunt in Scotland*. Baltimore, MD: Johns Hopkins University Press.

Latimer, John (1970 [1893]) *The Annals of Bristol in the Eighteenth Century*. London: Butler and Tanner.

Lehmann, C. (1971) *Henry Home, Lord Kames, and the Scottish Enlightenment*. The Hague: Martinus Nijhof.

Leiberman, David (1983) "The Legal Needs of a Commercial Society: The Jurisprudence of Lord Kames." In Istvan Hont and Michael Ignatieff (Eds.), *Wealth and Virtue: The Shaping of Political Economy in the Scottish Enlightenment*. Cambridge: Cambridge University Press.

Lenman, Bruce (1977) *An Economic History of Modern Scotland: 1660–1976*. Hamden, CT: Archon Books.

Lenman, Bruce (1981) *Integration, Enlightenment, and Industrialization: Scotland 1746–1832*. London: Edward Arnold.

Lenman, Bruce (1984) *The Jacobite Clans of the Great Glen 1650–1784*. London: Methuen.

Levack, Brian (1987) *The Civil Lawyers in England 1603–1641: A Political Study*. Oxford: Clarendon Press.

Linebaugh, Peter (1985) "The Delivery of Newgate, 6 June 1780." *Midnight Notes* 8.

Linebaugh, Peter (1992) *The London Hanged: Crime and Civil Society in the Eighteenth Century*. New York: Cambridge University Press.

Locke, John (1959) *An Essay Concerning Human Understanding*. Collated and annotated by Alexander Campbell Fraser. New York: Dover.

Locke, John (1975) *An Essay Concerning Human Understanding*. Edited by Peter H. Nidditch. Oxford: Clarendon Press.

Locke, John (1980) *Second Treatise of Government*. Edited by C.B. MacPherson. Cambridge: Hackett Publishing.

Locke, John (1991) *Locke on Money*. Edited by Patrick Hyde Kelly, 2 vols. Oxford: Clarendon Press.

Locke, John (1997) "An Essay on the Poor Law [1697]." In *Locke: Political Essays*. Edited by Mark Goldie. Cambridge: Cambridge University Press, 182–200.

Lord Mansfield, Ashburton and Thurlow (1797) *A Treatise on the Study of the Law*. London: Harrison, Cluse and Co.

Losee, John (1992) "Hume's Demarcation Project." *Hume Studies* 18(1): 51–62.

Lynch, Michael (1991) *Scotland: A New History*. London: Century.

MacCormick, Neil (1982) "Law and Enlightenment." In R.H. Campbell and Andrew S. Skinner (Eds.), *The Origins and Nature of the Scottish Enlightenment*. Edinburgh: John Donald Publishers.

McGaughy, Taylor (2008) "'A Louse for a Portion'; Early- Eighteenth-Century English Attitudes Toward Scots, 1688–1725." PhD diss. Auburn University, Auburn, AL.

Macinnes, Allan I. (1996) *Clanship, Commerce and the House of Stuart, 1603–1788*. East Linton: Tuckwell Press.

Mackillop, Andrew (2000) *"More Fruitful than the Soil": Army, Empire and the Scottish Highlands, 1715–1815*. East Linton: Tuckwell Press.

McRae, Robert (1980) "The Import of Hume's Theory of Time." *Hume Studies* 6(2): 119–132.

Mah, Harold (1987) *The End of Philosophy, the Origin of "Ideology": Karl Marx and the Crisis of the Young Hegelians*. Berkeley, CA: University of California Press.

Manchester, Anthony Hugh (1966) "The Reformation of the Ecclesiastical Courts." *American Journal of Legal History* 10: 51–75.

Mann, F.A. (1982) *The Legal Aspect of Money*, 4th edn. Oxford: Clarendon Press.

Marcy, Peter T. (1966) *Eighteenth Century Views of Bristol and Bristolians*. Bristol: Bristol Historical Association.

Marx, Karl (1963a) *The Eighteenth Brumaire of Louis Napoleon*. New York: International Publishers.

Marx, Karl (1963b) *Theories of Surplus Value*. Translated by Emile Burns. Moscow: Progress Publishers.

Marx, Karl (1967) *Capital, Volume 1*. New York: International Publishers.

Marx, Karl (1970) *Contribution to a Critique of Political Economy*. Moscow: Progress Publishers.

Marx, Karl (1973) *Grundrisse: Foundation of the Critique of Political Economy*. London: Penguin Books.

Marx, Karl and Engels, Friedrich (1970) *The German Ideology*. London: Lawrence and Wishart.

Merryman, John Henry (1969) *The Civil Law Tradition*. Stanford, CA: Stanford University Press.

Millar, John (1803) *An Historical View of the English Government*, Vol. 2. London: J. Mawman.

Minchinton, W.E. (Ed.) (1957) *The Trade of Bristol in the Eighteenth Century*. Bristol: Bristol Record Society.

Mintz, Sidney W. (1985) *Sweetness and Power: The Place of Sugar in Modern History*. New York: Penguin.

Monroe, Arthur Eli (1966) *Monetary Theory Before Adam Smith*. New York: Augustus M. Kelly.

Montesquieu, Charles (1961) *The Persian Letters*. Edited, translated and introduced by J. Robert Loy. Cleveland, OH: World Publishing Co.

Montesquieu, Charles (1966) *The Spirit of the Laws*. Translated by Thomas Nugent. New York: Hafner Publishing Co.

Morgan, Kenneth (1992) *Bristol and the Atlantic Trade in the Eighteenth Century*. Cambridge: Cambridge University Press.

Morrisroe Jr., Michael (1973) "Did Hume Read Berkeley? A Conclusive Answer." *Philological Quarterly* 52(2) (April): 310–315.

Mossner, Ernest Campbell (1948) "Hume's Early Memoranda, 1729–1740: The Complete Text." *Journal of the History of Ideas* 9(4), Arthur O. Lovejoy at Seventy-Five: Reason at Work, (October): 492–518.

Mossner, Ernest Campbell (1954) *The Life of David Hume*. Oxford: Clarendon Press.

Mossner, Ernest Campbell (1959) "Did Hume Ever Read Berkeley? A Rejoinder to Professor Popkin." *The Journal of Philosophy* 56(25): 992–995.

Mossner, Ernest Campbell (Ed.) (1962) "New Hume Letters to Lord Elibank, 1748–1776." *Texas Studies in Literature and Language* 4(3) (Autumn): 431–460.

Mossner, Ernest Campbell (1967) *The Forgotten Hume*. New York: AMS Press.

Munn, Charles W. (1981) *The Scottish Provincial Banking Companies 1747–1864*. Edinburgh: John Donald Publishers.

Munro, Neil (1928) *The History of the Royal Bank of Scotland, 1727–1927*. Edinburgh: R.&R. Clark.

Murphy, Antoin E. (1997) *John Law: Economic Theorist and Policy-Maker*. Oxford: Clarendon Press.

Neal, Larry (1990) *The Rise of Financial Capitalism: International Capital Markets in the Age of Reason*. Cambridge: Cambridge University Press.

Nicholson, Colin (1994) *Writing and the Rise of Finance: Capital Satires of the Early Eighteenth Century*. Cambridge: Cambridge University Press.

Norton, David Fate (Ed.) (1993) *The Cambridge Companion to Hume*. Cambridge: Cambridge University Press.

Norton, David Fate and Norton, Mary J. (1996) *The David Hume Library*. Edinburgh: Edinburgh Bibliographical Society.

Norton, David Fate and Norton, Mary J. (Eds.) (2000) "Glossary." In *David Hume: A Treatise of Human Nature*. Oxford: Oxford University Press. [abbreviated as T]

Orr, Mary (2003) *Intertextuality: Debates and Contexts*. Cambridge: Polity.

Oxford English Dictionary, 2nd edn (1989) Edited by Darrell Raymond. Oxford: Oxford University Press.

Petrie, Charles (1959) *The Jacobite Movement*. London: Eyre and Spottiswood.

Pittock, Murray G.H. (1995a) "Jacobite Culture." In Robert C. Woosnam-Savage (Ed.), *1745: Charles Edward Stuart and the Jacobites*. Edinburgh: HMSO.

Pittock, Murray G.H. (1995b) *The Myth of the Jacobite Clans*. Edinburgh: Edinburgh University Press.

Plumb, J.H. (1950). England in the Eighteenth Century. Harmondsworth: Penguin.

Pocock, J.G.A. (1985) *Virtue, Commerce and History: Essays on Political Thought and History, Chiefly in the Eighteenth Century*. Cambridge: Cambridge University Press.

Popkin, Richard H. (1959) "Did Hume Ever Read Berkeley?" *The Journal of Philosophy* 56(12) (June): 535–545.

Popkin, Richard H. (1964) "So, Hume did Read Berkeley." *The Journal of Philosophy* 61(24) (December): 773–778.

Quaifee, G.R. (1987) *Godly Zeal and Furious Rage: The Witch in Early Modern Europe*. New York: St. Martin's Press.

Rashid, Salim (1990) "Adam Smith's Acknowledgments: Neo-Plagiarism and the Wealth of Nations." *The Journal of Libertarian Studies* 9(2) (Fall): 1–24.

Richards, Eric (1991) "Scotland and the Uses of the Atlantic Empire." In Bernard Bailyn and Philip D. Morgan (Eds.), *Strangers within the Realm: Cultural Margins of the First British Empire*. Chapel Hill, NC: University of North Carolina Press.

Richardson, David (Ed.) (1985) *Bristol, Africa and the Eighteenth-Century Slave Trade: Vol. 1 The Years of Expansion 1698–1729*. Bristol: Bristol Record Society.

Richardson, David (Ed.) (1987) *Bristol, Africa and the Eighteenth-Century Slave Trade: Vol. 2 The Years of Ascendency 1730–1745*. Bristol: Bristol Record Society.

Richardson, David (Ed.) (1991) *Bristol, Africa and the Eighteenth-Century Slave Trade: Vol. 3 The Years of Decline 1746–1769*. Bristol: Bristol Record Society.

Richardson, David (Ed.) (1996) *Bristol, Africa and the Eighteenth-Century Slave Trade: Vol. 4 The final Years, 1770–1807*. Bristol: Bristol Record Society.

Robertson, John (1985) *The Scottish Enlightenment and the Militia Issue*. Edinburgh: John Donald Publishers.

Ross, Ian Simpson (1972) *Lord Kames and the Scotland of His Day*. Oxford: Clarendon Press.

Rotman, Brian (1987) *Signifying Nothing: The Semiotics of Zero*. New York: St. Martin's Press.

Rude, George (1962) *Wilkes and Liberty: A Social Study of 1763 to 1774*. Oxford: Clarendon Press.

Savile, Richard (1996) *Bank of Scotland 1695–1995*. Edinburgh: Edinburgh University Press.

Schabas, Margaret (1994) "Market Contracts in the Age of Hume." In Neil de Marchi and Mary Morgan (Eds.), *Higgling: Transactors and Their Market in the History of Economics*, History of Political Economy, Annual Supplement to Vol. 26. Durham, NC: Duke University Press.

Schabas, Margaret (2001) "David Hume on Experimental Natural Philosophy, Money, and Fluids." *History of Political Economy* 33(3): 411–436.

Schabas, Margaret and Wennerlind, Carl (2011) "Hume on Money, Commerce, and the Science of Economics." *Journal of Economic Perspectives* 25(3) (Summer): 217–230.

Schumpeter, Joseph A. (1954) *History of Economic Analysis*. Edited from manuscript by Elizabeth Broody Schumpeter. New York: Oxford University Press.

Scots Magazine (1752a) "Abstracts of the Act for Annexing Certain Forfeited Estates to the Crown Unalienably." *Scots Magazine* (April): 161–166.

Scots Magazine (1752b) "Speeches in the Debate on the Bill for Annexing Certain Forfeited Estates to the Crown by A. Posthumius and C. Plinius." *Scots Magazine* (September): 417–427.

Scots Magazine (1752c) "Speeches in the Debate on the Bill for Annexing Certain Forfeited Estates to the Crown by M. Cato and Ca. Donatius." *Scots Magazine* (October): 465–472.

Scott, Walter (1986) *Waverly; or, 'Tis Sixty Years Since.* Edited by Claire Lamont. Oxford: Oxford University Press.

Shapin, Steven (1994) *A Social History of Truth: Civility and Science in Seventeenth-Century England.* Chicago, IL: The University of Chicago Press.

Shaw, John Stuart (1983) *The Management of Scottish Society 1707–1764: Power, Nobles, Lawyers, Edinburgh Agents and English Influences.* Edinburgh: John Donald Publishers.

Shell, Marc (1982) *Money, Language, and Thought: Literary and Philosophical Economies from the Medieval to the Modern Era.* Berkeley, CA: University of California Press.

Sherman, Sandra (1996) *Finance and Fictionality in the Early Eighteenth Century: Accounting for Defoe.* Cambridge: Cambridge University Press.

Simmel, Georg (1978) *The Philosophy of Money.* London: Routledge and Kegan Paul.

Smith, Adam (1937) *An Inquiry into the Nature and Causes of the Wealth of Nations.* Edited by Edwin Cannan. New York: Modern Library.

Smith, Adam (1956) *Lectures on Justice, Police, Revenue and Arms,* delivered in the University of Glasgow, reported by a student in 1763. Edited and introduced by Edwin Cannan. New York: Kelley and Millman.

Smith, Adam (1978) *Lectures on Jurisprudence.* Edited by R.L. Meek, D.D. Raphael and P.G. Stein. Oxford: Clarendon Press.

Smith, Adam (1991) *Wealth of Nations.* Amherst, NY: Prometheus Books.

Smith, Annette M. (1982) *Jacobite Estates of the Forty-Five.* Edinburgh: John Donald Publishers.

Smith, T.B. (1961) *British Justice: The Scottish Contribution.* London: Stevens and Sons.

Smout, T.C. (1972) *A History of the Scottish People: 1560–1830.* London: Fontana.

Spiegel, Henry William (1983) *The Growth of Economic Thought.* Durham, NC: Duke University Press.

Stephen, Leslie and Lee, Sidney (1917) *The Dictionary of National Biography.* Oxford: Oxford University Press.

Steuart, Sir James (1966) *An Inquiry into the Principles of Political Oeconomy,* Vol. 2. Edited by Andrew S. Skinner. Chicago, IL: The University of Chicago Press.

Streminger, G. (1980) "Hume's Theory of Imagination." *Hume Studies* 6(2): 91–118.

Taylor, Charles (1989) *Sources of the Self: The Making of the Modern Identity.* Cambridge, MA: Harvard University Press.

Thompson, James (1996) *Models of Value: Eighteenth-Century Political Economy and the Novel.* Durham, NC: Duke University Press.

Trevor-Roper, Hugh (1983) "The Invention of Tradition: The Highland Tradition of Scotland." In Eric Hobsbawn and Terence Ranger (Eds.), *The Invention of Tradition*. Cambridge: Cambridge University Press.

Vickers, Douglas (1959) *Studies in the Theory of Money, 1690–1776*. Philadelphia, PA: Chilton.

Vilar, Pierre (1976) *A History of Gold and Money, 1450–1920*. London: New Left Books.

Walker, David M. (1976) *The Scottish Legal System: An Introduction to the Study of Scots Law*. Edinburgh: W. Green and Son.

Webster, Noah (1828) *American Dictionary of the English Language*. New York: S. Converse.

Wennerlind, Carl (2001) "The Link Between David Hume's Treatise on Human Nature and His Ficudiary Theory of Money." *History of Political Economy* 33(1): 139–160.

Wennerlind, Carl (2002) "David Hume's Political Philosophy: A Theory of Commercial Modernization." *Hume Studies* 28(2): 247–270.

Wennerlind, Carl (2005) "David Hume's Monetary Theory Revisited: Was He Really a Quantity Theorist and an Inflationist?" *Journal of Political Economy* 113(1): 223–237.

Wennerlind, Carl and Schabas, Margaret (Eds.) (2008) *David Hume's Political Economy*. London: Routledge.

Whatley, Christopher A. (2000) *Scottish Society 1707–1830: Beyond Jacobitism, Towards Industrialization*. Manchester: Manchester University Press.

White, E. Frances. (1987) "Civilization Denied: Questions on Black Athena." *Radical America* 21(5) (Fall/Winter): 38–40.

Wiener, Philip P. (1959) "Did Hume Read Berkeley?" *The Journal of Philosophy* 56(12): 533–535.

Williams, William H. (1992) "Is Hume's Shade of Blue a Red Herring?" *Synthese* 92(1): 83–99.

Womack, Peter (1989) *Improvement and Romance: Constructing the Myth of the Highlands*. London: Macmillan.

Worton, Michael and Still, Judith (Eds.) (1990) *Intertextuality: Theories and Practices*. Manchester: Manchester University Press.

Youngson, A.J. (1973) *After the Forty-Five: The Economic Impact on the Scottish Highlands*. Edinburgh: Edinburgh University Press.

Index

ill refers to an illustration; *n* to a note; *t* to a table

Printed and bound by CPI Group (UK) Ltd, Croydon, CR0 4YY

23/04/2025

14661020-0004